The Empowered Student

Anthony A. Raptis

Successmakers Publishing
P. O. Box 913
Malibu, California 90265 USA
Phone 310 230-3664
Fax 310 573-0148

Email SmakerPub@aol.com

Second Edition

ISBN 0-9649018-9-7

Raul Gardea, *artistic contribution*
John Dearinger, *layout & design*
Dr. Gary Morgan, *editing*
Diana Osborne, *editing*

Acknowledgments

First, I want to acknowledge my students who have taught me the importance of
knowing what you want out of life. There are several individuals that I want to thank
for their contributions to this text. I want to thank Raul Gardea for his artistic
contribution, John Dearinger for his development of the layout and design, and Dr.
Gary Morgan for his editing and encouragement. I especially want to acknowledge the
major contribution made by my wife, Diana Osborne, whose influence is throughout
the text.

Preface

You have the power to direct and control your life. Your empowerment is in your hands. You can make the decisions which lead to your empowerment. Do you have the desire? Do you have the confidence? And do you have the skills? You need not wait to be empowered. You can begin now. You have taken the first step by using *The Empowered Student,* which is designed to help you fulfill your potential by offering a system of success, inventories, exercises, strategies, techniques, models, and triads as tools for self-empowerment.

While struggling to empower myself, I discovered many of the elements contained in *The Empowered Student.* As a teenager I lived in South Central Los Angeles where I saw many disempowered individuals. I include myself among those individuals. I began learning the value of self-confidence and personal drive, and the importance of acquiring and applying skills. I began to empower myself through my education at the community college where I learned about myself through the study of the social sciences. This growth process initiated my journey towards self-knowledge. I continued my personal evolution through the study of psychology and the psychotherapeutic process. This foundation led me back to the community college, where I taught personal growth and psychology courses and counseled students. I was able to combine my personal and academic experience to further the empowerment of students. As I worked with students, I began to observe that student problems and issues fell consistently into three categories: motivation, self-esteem, and skills. This observation led to my formulation of The Success Triad. The Success Triad became the framework that I used on a daily basis and became the foundation for *The Empowered Student.*

The primary purpose of *The Empowered Student* is to engage the student in the process of self-empowerment through the application of The Triadic System of Success. The Triadic System of Success consists of twelve triads comprised of the concepts and clusters of behaviors which most contribute to success. The Success Triad is the foundation of The Triadic System. You increase your performance by addressing issues of motivation, self-esteem, and skills. The Triadic System delineates the concepts and behaviors which most contribute to the development of motivation, self-esteem, and skills. For example, if you are seeking to increase self-esteem, The Self-Esteem Triad illustrates the importance of examining self-knowledge, self-responsibility and self-acceptance. If you are questioning issues of motivation, The Motivation Triad illustrates the importance of developing self-knowledge, knowing what you want, and goals. To promote student success, The Skills Triad emphasizes the importance of life and learning skills, study skills, and college survival skills.

The tools of *The Empowered Student* are both practical and conceptual. The triads are powerful conceptual tools for self-empowerment. *The Empowered Student* emphasizes the importance of self-awareness, self-knowledge, motivation, self-esteem, skills, identity, multiculturalism, and goal setting. Self-awareness is the foundation of self-knowledge. You cannot know yourself if you are not aware of the self you are to know. Our levels of self-awareness determine our levels of functioning. Self-awareness involves being "in touch" with your thoughts, feelings, and reactions. *The Empowered Student* contains techniques and strategies for developing self-awareness. Self-knowledge means we know where we are, where we come from, and where we are going. As we develop self-knowledge, we begin to empower ourselves; that is, we develop the ability to direct and take control of our lives. Self-Knowledge helps us become motivated, and motivation is the driving force behind our actions and is crucial to our success. Understanding, increasing and sustaining motivation is a major emphasis of *The Empowered Student*. Several categories and types of motivation are presented. Many motivational factors and types are identified, including "Have To/Want To" Motivation. Understanding these categories and types of motivation will help us understand our own sources of motivation.

A major theme of *The Empowered Student* is continuous attention to the dimensions of self- esteem. What is it? Do you have it. If not, how do you acquire it? How do you sustain it? By increasing self-worth, we increase self-esteem and self-confidence. An individual with an increased sense of self-esteem and self-confidence increases attempts at learning. Increased attempts at learning indicate persistence. Increased persistence results in higher levels of performance. Higher levels of performance create higher levels of academic success. Higher levels of academic success produce increased levels of self-esteem. This process is cyclic. This formulation clearly illustrates the importance of self-esteem in producing higher levels of academic performance.

Increasing self-esteem → increased self-confidence → increased attempts at learning → increased persistence → higher levels of performance → higher levels of academic success → increased self-esteem

Both learning skills and ways of applying those skills solidify our success. Learning effective decision making skills is empowering. Learning to study more effectively is empowering. Using conceptual tools such as The Triadic System of Success and The Success Triad is empowering. We become empowered by strengthening success-achieving behaviors. Learning to think critically empowers us. Thinking clearly about our racial and ethnic identities encourages self-knowledge. In a multicultural society, identity issues are very important because a clear sense of self is the basis of success.

The Empowered Student recognizes that we live in a complex society that is changing in very dramatic ways. *The Empowered Student* has a social dimension which is addressed through the concept of multiculturalism. Our society is a culture made of many cultures. The cultural background of an individual is a significant factor influencing educational attainment. Multiculturalism is the fabric of *The Empowered Student* which illustrates and incorporates many multicultural elements such as race and ethnicity, racial, ethnic and social awareness and attitudes, racism, victimization, labeling, and communicating across cultures.

Direction is a vital issue for students. Most students experience anxiety over where they are and where they are going. Students struggle to decide what to do with their lives. Setting goals is a primary method for establishing direction in life. Goal setting is a process which is evolutionary and continuous. The companion to *The Empowered Student*, *The Goal Setting Journal*, provides a systematic and comprehensive approach to the goal setting process and establishes a framework for life direction.

Models and methods for personal growth are presented in *The Empowered Student,* which contains a developmental model, The Journey toward Self-Knowledge and Success, and an interactive model of personal growth, The Self-Knowledge Cycle. Both of these models present a road map of the evolution of personal development. An additional personal growth model, the Johari Window, developed by Joseph Luft and Harry Ingham serves as a graphic model of human communication. The Johari Window illustrates the importance of covert factors in human experience. This model is used to understand awareness, motivation, communication, and attitudes.

You can empower yourself. You can take charge and control of your life. You can achieve your goals. You can learn to be more effective. You can change and become the person you want to become. You can become a more effective learner. You can motivate yourself and develop the confidence you need to get what you want out of life. You can achieve beyond your level of aspiration, and you can create rich and fulfilling possibilities for how to live your life. You can go beyond the familiar and make contact with new worlds. *The Empowered Student* provides methods, tools, strategies, models, and concepts by which you can achieve your personal success.

In order to achieve at an optimum level, you need to be fully committed to your growth and development. A commitment to the material and activities provided by *The Empowered Student* will facilitate your growth. A commitment to the journal process will help you set and achieve your goals. Active implementation of the strategies contained in *The Empowered Student* will help you make significant changes in your life. The Triadic System, an instrument for achieving success, will greatly enhance your success when applied to everyday life.

The Empowered Student, along with *The Goal Setting Journal,* is capable of picking you up from where you are and setting you down a different person. *The Empowered Student* is designed for those who want to take charge and control of their lives and their personal evolution. *The Empowered Student* contains the tools for anyone interested in self-fulfillment.

Table of Contents

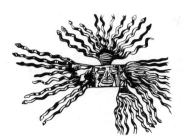

Introduction

Chapter 1 Success

Chapter 2 Empowerment

Chapter 3 Time Management

Chapter 4 Goal Setting

Chapter 5 Motivation

Chapter 6 Self-Esteem

Chapter 7 Self-Knowledge

Chapter 8 Multiculturalism

Chapter 9 Relationships

Chapter 10 Life Skills

Chapter 11 Learning Skills

Chapter 12 Study Skills

Chapter 13 College Survival Skills

Chapter 14 Careering

Introduction

Life is

birth
growth
development
problematic
ungraspable
meaningful
infinite
finite
light
love
pain
whole
material
spiritual
confusing
purposeful
connections
everchanging
inseparability
impermanence
relationship
simplicity
insecurity
suffering
harmony
struggle
conflict
change
stress
flux
living
beauty
process
learning
complexity
death

Life is...

Life is a challenge, a journey, and a quest. What is the nature of your life's journey? What does life mean to you? Do you celebrate life? Does your view of life generate excitement and joy about living? Do you expect life to be easy and without conflict? Life is difficult when we expect it to be what it is not. Desiring a life without any pain is wishing that life be something other than it is. Many expect life to be fair and are highly disappointed when it is not. Some believe life to be meaningful, purposeful, beautiful, and peaceful. Others perceive life to be difficult, unfair, unjust, and disempowering. How you define and perceive the nature of life determines how you experience life. Life's significance is a profound philosophical question.

Life is change. We resist change. We struggle against it. We have difficulty coping with it, and change is life. Life is insecurity, and we want it to be secure. Most of us are trying to acquire a state of security, and achievement is often a buffer against the insecurity of life. Life is reality, truth, existence and being. Life can be both finite and infinite. Life contains opposites and is paradoxical.

Broadening our view and perspectives on life enables us to live more in accord with it's nature. Questioning our view helps us understand the implications for living that our perspectives embrace. We cannot only seek to understand ourselves, but we can seek to understand the nature of life. If we are able to understand the nature of life, we can live in greater harmony and contentment with it. Many say that life is "what is." We struggle with "what is" and refuse to acknowledge "what is." If we see life as positive, enriching, loving, and safe, we respond accordingly. If we see it as negative, hostile, and unsafe, we also respond accordingly. Life is many different things to many different people. What is it to you?

Getting Started

All students go through a period of initial adjustment to college life, whether you live in a college dormitory or commute down the freeway to your local college. Entering college can be an overwhelming experience, especially when you are faced with long registration lines, closed classes, and high tuition. You may be away from home for the first time, in a new environment feeling all alone and alienated from your surroundings. Feeling as if you don't belong, you search for a friendly face. This initial impact may be complicated by culture shock. You may ask yourself, "Do I belong here? Everyone seems so different from me." You try to overcome your anxiety and fight the feeling of wanting to leave. Does this sound familiar? Your initial reactions and perceptions may be quite different as you say to yourself, "I'm finally away from home." Be assured that your initial reactions to the college environment are shared by many. Pause! Take a deep breath! Relax! It's going to be O.K.! College instructors/counselors find that what students need most when they enter college is encouragement, support, help, and reassurance. Feeling like you belong helps a great deal with your success in college. Most colleges have programs designed to help you succeed in college.

Readiness

Learning in the academic environment is hard work, and you must be ready to face that demand in order to succeed. To get the most from college, we must be "up to it." Does that imply a readiness? What does readiness mean? Readiness for college involves many factors, but most essential is a state of mind that includes a high level of motivation, positive self-esteem, and a broad range of skills.

The readiness to learn is frequently a response to pain. We learn that the easy way is really the hard way. We learn that nothing of value in life comes easy. We learn that we must endure present pain for future gain. We learn to postpone the immediate gratification of our impulses.

Personal change, growth, and academic learning require a state of readiness. Many of us may not be ready to undertake the tasks of life. We may not be ready to face the challenges and demands of living in a complex world which frequently offers little support. We may not be ready to commit ourselves to our education, work, and even our families.

Many of us may not have come to that juncture in our lives where we fully recognize that our past, family, and environment have had a powerful effect on us, and we are responsible and capable of choosing our own lives. This point of recognition signals a "readiness" to face the challenges and demands of growth.

Interest in Academics

If you are ready to face the challenges of learning, an active interest in academics will greatly enhance your chance for success. Many students lack interest in the subjects they are taking. This adversely affects motivation. But students with active interests in academics will find it easier to persist and succeed in academic activities. If you are "turned on," excited, or stimulated by ideas and intellectual discourse, the learning process is exciting. Ideas are fun, and if you are excited by ideas, you face a rewarding journey through the learning process. It is up to you to make the subjects that you pursue interesting. It is difficult to find the interesting aspects of a subject without involvement. Involvement generates interest. Interest sustains motivation. Boredom is an interference. You create your level of interest. If you find a subject uninteresting, then try to find at least one idea that you find interesting and see if you can build on that idea. Find other ways to generate interest. Active involvement in subject matter can generate interest. Be aware of your attention. Notice where your attention is focused. Staying focused on a subject is a problem for many students. Focused attention can stimulate learning. It may be frustrating when it's difficult to engage interest in difficult subjects. When you are poorly prepared for a subject or when you have limited knowledge of a subject, it may be difficult to generate interest. An attitude of excitement about learning is extremely important to cultivate. Learning is not always easy, but learning is almost always rewarding.

You are more likely to do poorly in subjects that bore you. Conversely, you are more likely to do well in subjects for which you have an interest. The more you can find personal relevance in a subject, the more likely it is to activate your interest. When you apply what you have learned, interest is activated.

Your general attitude towards life has a relationship to your ability to become interested in academic subjects. If you are excited about living and life, if many things turn you on, if you enjoy life, you have the attitude needed to become interested in learning. The sheer enjoyment of living attracts most students to the learning process.

The Empowered Student Assumes:

Students can be empowered.

The Triadic System is a comprehensive approach to student success.

The Success Triad provides a powerful basis for improving student academic performance.

Motivation is critical and requires frequent assessment to insure high levels of academic performance.

Self-esteem promotes academic performance.

Self-confidence enables the student to face academic challenges.

Skills contribute to the academic success of students.

Optimum performance is achieved when motivation, self-esteem, and skills are combined and developed.

Conscious control of academic performance promotes success.

Self-knowledge is the foundation of effective action.

Self-awareness is the initiator of the psychological evolution of the student.

Success-achieving behaviors can be encouraged and developed in all students.

Knowledge gained from *The Empowered Student* is transferable to all aspects of the student's life.

Psychological skills combined with practical skills promote academic success.

Psychological processes ultimately determine success.

Education promotes the personal and social development of students.

Environments may produce victims, and victims are capable of overcoming victimization.

Students come from different racial, ethnic, and social backgrounds, and this has a direct effect on their academic performance.

Multiculturalism is a social reality, and students need to learn to relate to people of many cultural backgrounds.

Identity issues have a direct influence on student academic performance.

Why Should You Read The Empowered Student?

- To gain personal insight about your abilities, values, and interests
- To build self-esteem
- To develop self-confidence
- To learn to communicate more effectively
- To learn to reduce stress
- To find out what is important to you
- To develop positive relationships
- To develop leadership skills
- To assess your strengths and weaknesses
- To provide for the future of your children
- To re-direct your life
- To re-enter college
- To overcome fear of failure
- To develop college success skills
- To become familiar with college environment
- To improve grade point average
- To know what resources are available to you
- To remember what you read
- To learn memory techniques
- To learn to concentrate better
- To set goals
- To develop time management skills
- To develop good study skills
- To develop test-taking and note-taking skills
- To learn what life is

Organization of The Empowered Student

 Chapter Inventory
The Chapter Inventory is designed to help evaluate beliefs about specific chapter topics. The inventory serves as preparation for the chapter by assessing your position relative to the chapter topic.

 **Chapter Triads**
Chapter Triads are designed to consolidate major chapter concepts into elements. The goal is to simplify and clarify the major ideas of the chapter. The triads are organizers of key concepts and processes. Triads are designed to be memorable and conceptual tools to facilitate growth through application.

 **Chapter Exercises**
Chapter Exercises are formulated to elicit responses which clarify and enhance understanding of the chapter topics. Many of the exercises help you analyze and evaluate your position. These evaluations help you determine where you are, and whether you should consider changes.

 **Chapter Activities**
Chapter Activities are designed to engage you in a process of gathering, tabulating, documenting, assessing, and applying information about you for your self-assessment.

 Chapter Strategies
Chapter Strategies are designed to overcome barriers and to develop behaviors which enhance effectiveness. Chapter Strategies are the how-to's of personal change regarding specific issues. They are consolidations of methods and procedures in overcoming barriers.

 **Chapter Conclusion**
The Chapter Conclusion is designed to help you think critically about the major concepts covered in the chapter. You are encouraged to think about the relevance, importance, and application of concepts contained in each chapter.

How to Use
The Empowered Student

Survey the **contents** of the entire book and get a feeling for the organization and content of the text. Notice what attracts your attention. Address your immediate needs. You may not want to read the text in a sequential manner.

Complete the chapter **inventories** which help you evaluate the major chapter concepts. As you complete each item of an inventory use your immediate reaction as a guide to your response. Be honest with your responses. Inventories are designed to help you assess your position relative to chapter concepts.

Internalize the chapter **triads** because they are instruments for personal change. The triad of a chapter should be the first thing you learn. Triads can guide your actions and decisions.

Complete chapter **exercises** and **activities** because they will amplify your understanding of the concepts and give you the opportunity to determine how the concepts apply to you. Exercises and activities give you an additional opportunity to assess yourself and consider change and growth.

Study, learn and **implement** chapter **strategies** because they are the tools and steps for personal change. Strategies are one of the most important features of *The Empowered Student* because they are guides for effective action.

Complete the chapter **conclusions** because they allow you to re-address the key concepts contained in the chapter. Chapter conclusions allow you to think critically about your learning.

Chapter 1

Success

Success

Take this self-inventory by rating yourself with the following scale:

5 = This statement is true <u>all</u> of the time.
4 = This statement is true <u>most</u> of the time.
3 = This statement is true <u>much</u> of the time.
2 = This statement is true <u>some</u> of the time.
1 = This statement is true <u>almost</u> none of the time.
0 = This statement is true <u>none</u> of the time.

_____ 1. People who are motivated succeed.

_____ 2. People who are confident succeed.

_____ 3. People who are skilled succeed.

_____ 4. I believe in my capacity to succeed.

_____ 5. I have a proper attitude for success.

_____ 6. I believe there are principles that govern success.

_____ 7. I have a personal philosophy for success.

_____ 8. I believe that others can offer me methods to succeed.

_____ 9. I know many individuals that I consider successful.

_____ 10. Success is a product of your will power to succeed.

Self-Esteem Skills

SUCCESS

Motivation

The common idea that success spoils people by making them vain, egotistic, and self-complacent is erroneous; on the contrary, it makes them, for the most part, humble, tolerant, and kind. Failure makes people cruel and bitter.

—W. Somerset Maugham

The Success Triad

The Success Triad is a conceptual model for student success. It illustrates the success factors of Motivation, Self-Esteem, and Skills and forms a comprehensive basis for student success. The Success Triad is a framework for thinking about issues and problems regarding student performance. It developed from a synthesis of thought abstracted from counseling and classroom experience. It became evident that motivation and self-esteem in combination with the development of appropriate skills were vital to student success. The Triad is a product of intense attention and careful listening to students presenting issues of academic performance and personal adjustment.

The Success Triad Hypothesis

The Success Triad assumes that increased levels of any success factor will improve academic performance and will increase the levels of the other success factors. Increased motivation will enhance levels of self-esteem and skills acquisition. Increased self-esteem will increase motivation and skills acquisition. Acquiring skills will increase motivation and self-esteem. Increased success factors substantially enhance academic performance. The Success Triad assumes that deficiencies in any one of the success factors, motivation, self-esteem, or skills, will adversely affect academic performance.

Factors of
The Success Triad

Motivation

Motivation is the most important success factor since almost all behavior is motivated. What you do is motivated. Our desire to succeed is governed by the depth and degree of our motivation. What we want and need give us an indication of our sources of motivation. Motivation is the driving force behind our actions. It is the purpose of our actions. Motivation is created by internal and external forces. Social motivators such as power, control and acceptance are powerful motivators. What are the sources of your motivation? We can motivate ourselves to do what we need to do in order to succeed.

Self-Esteem

Self-Esteem is an important success factor because it reflects our self-worth. Our accomplishments provide a valuable source of self-worth which in turn supports our self-esteem. Positive levels of self-esteem help us cope with difficult and disappointing situations. Belief in our abilities gives us the courage to approach and persist in new learning situations. When we perceive ourselves as able, we are more likely to approach new learning tasks with confidence. Positive self-esteem allows us to feel good about ourselves and our successes.

Skills

Skills acquisition promotes success and increases motivation and self-esteem. Skills support our survival, allow us to make a living and perform in a proficient and competent manner. Skills give us a sense of worth through our increased ability to do important operations and tasks. Skills build self-confidence and enhance motivation. Skills acquisition is essential in a complex world of high technology.

Success

Motivation

> Success is not the result of spontaneous combustion. You must set yourself on fire.
> —Reggie Leach

What is success to you? Are you on the road to success? How do you know that you're on the right road? The achievement of success has many roads.

Success is many things to many people. Some define success as the satisfactory completion of a goal. Others define it as gaining wealth and fame. Success is an individual determination and decision, although others can help clarify and direct our success. Sophocles said, "There is no success without hardship." And according to Robert Browning, "A minute's success pays the failure of years." *The Empowered Student* views success as the empowerment of individuals through the maximization of individual potential through self-realization.

The Empowered Student will help you succeed by identifying the keys to success through The Triadic System of Success. The Success Triad, the foundation of The Triadic System, identifies the success factors which are central to success. They include motivation, self-esteem, and skills. *The Empowered Student* will help you succeed by helping you get motivated, by increasing self-confidence, and by providing a range of skills which will help you manage your life, study more effectively, survive the college environment, and empower you for life. Success is achieved by engaging in a process of cognitive self-appraisal. By using The Triadic System, you determine how you set your worth and will explore, examine, discover, and evaluate your self-esteem. *The Empowered Student* will help you succeed by illustrating cognitive tools which include concepts, triads, and strategies. You will succeed by exploring, discovering, examining, and evaluating your self through empowering exercises and activities. You will learn to govern and direct your own success.

Determine what success means to you, and get started now. Use the powerful cognitive tools included in the text. Be aware, focused, and consistent in your effort to succeed. "The secret of success is constancy to purpose," according to Benjamin Disraeli.

The Triadic System

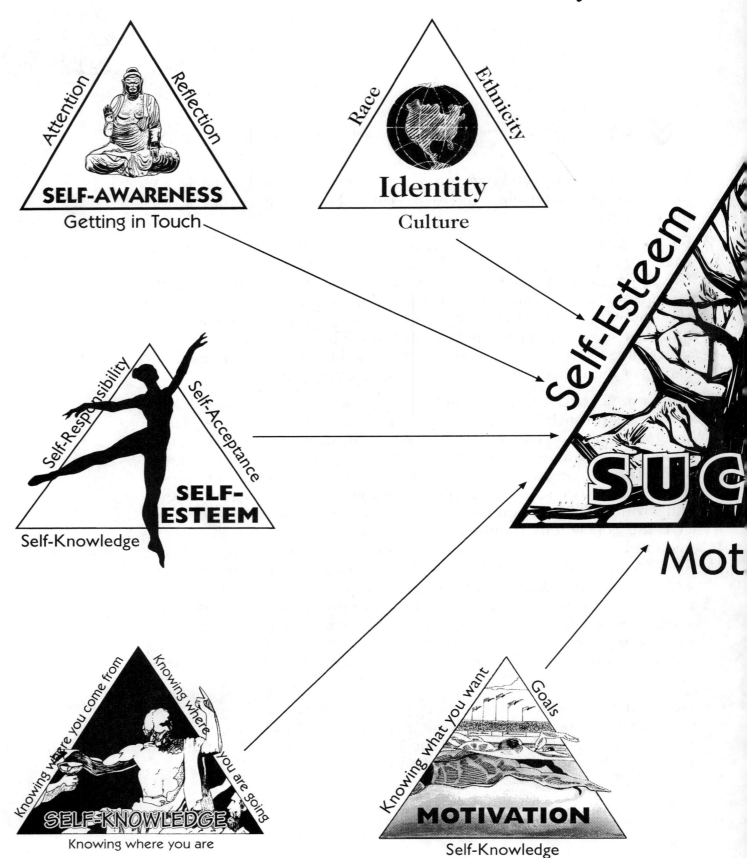

# of Success

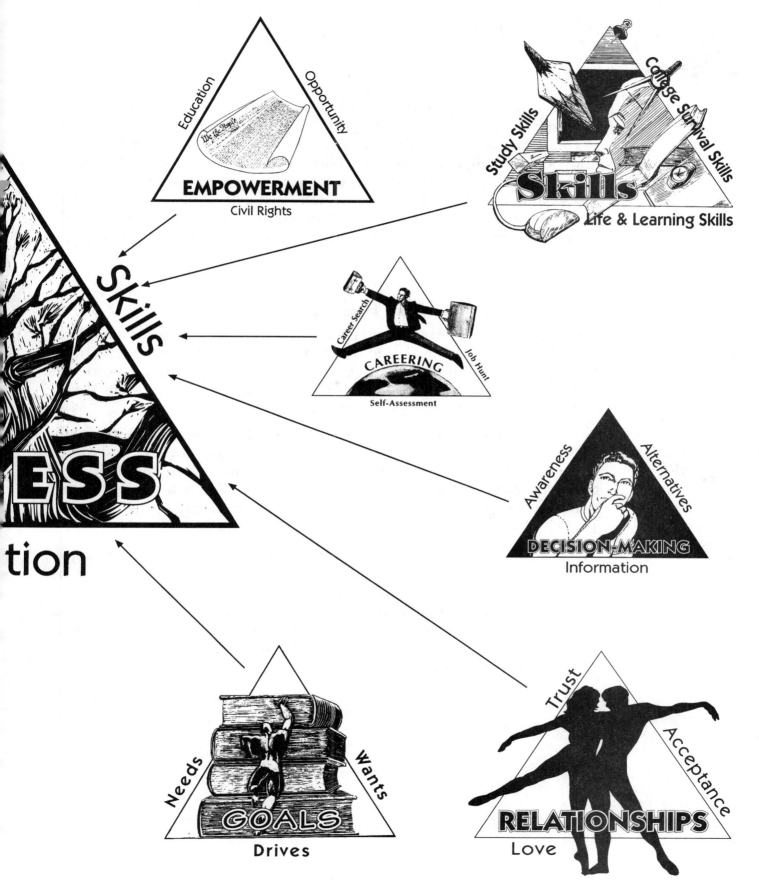

EMPOWERMENT
Education
Opportunity
Civil Rights

Skills
Study Skills
College Survival Skills
Life & Learning Skills

CAREERING
Career Search
Job Hunt
Self-Assessment

DECISION-MAKING
Awareness
Alternatives
Information

GOALS
Needs
Wants
Drives

RELATIONSHIPS
Trust
Acceptance
Love

Skills

ESS

tion

The Triadic System of Success

The Triadic System is an integrated and comprehensive system of success. It consists of twelve triads and thirty-six factors associated with success. The Success Triad is the foundation of the Triadic System. The auxiliary triads support the three factors of The Success Triad: Motivation, Self-Esteem, and Skills. The Triadic System is interactive and interdependent and is comprised of success-achieving behaviors and concepts. The system identifies the factors which most contribute to success. The Triadic System is a conceptual system and tool used for cognitive self-appraisal. It provides tools for maximizing processes which form the foundation of success.

The Triads and Factors

Triads are instruments for change. They are cognitive and behavioral tools, guides for evaluation and action, problem-solving models, theoretical systems, and road maps. Cognitive tools are extremely powerful, and people who succeed use powerful cognitive tools. Triads identify and clarify where you need to focus your energy in order to succeed.

Each triad consists of three factors. The most important factor is usually at the base of the triad. The factors of the triad are interactive and mutually dependent, and developing one factor will affect the other factors of the triad. Factors tell you what you need to do. You can assess success issues by addressing the factors of a triad. The majority of the factors of The Triadic System of Success are cognitive in nature.

The power of the triads lies in the economy and the wide range of applicability. For example, The Success Triad and its three factors can be applied to any human performance situation. We can examine any human performance situation in terms of motivation, self-esteem, and skills. We can examine the driving forces of our actions, our level of self-confidence expressed through self-esteem and the efficiency of performance executed through skill.

The Triads and Factors

The Empowerment Triad: Civil Rights, Education, and Opportunity, connects empowerment to these important factors. We learn that there is a social dimension to success and a free and just society is the basis of individual and collective success.

The Success Triad: Motivation, Self-Esteem, and Skills, forms a powerful basis for college and life success. Motivation is the driving force behind our efforts to succeed. Self-Esteem is associated with self-confidence and self-worth. Skills, based on knowledge, provide us with the tools to complete tasks effectively and efficiently.

The Motivation Triad: Self-Knowledge, Knowing what you want, and Goals, illustrates the importance of these factors in becoming motivated. Goals are the energizers of motivation. Self-Knowledge forms a powerful source of motivation, and knowing what you want is the basis for goal setting.

The Self-Esteem Triad: Self-Knowledge, Self-Responsibility, and Self-Acceptance, is the principal guide for developing and maintaining positive levels of self-esteem. Self-Knowledge is the foundation of positive levels of self-esteem. By taking self-responsibility and accepting ourselves, we establish our sense of self-worth.

The Skills Triad: Life and Learning Skills, Study Skills, and College Survival Skills, illustrates a broad spectrum of skills which promote life and college success. Skills enhance our level of performance and refine our problem-solving skills.

The Self-Knowledge Triad: Knowing where you are, Knowing where you come from, and Knowing where you are going, reveals the basis of self-knowledge. This Triad emphasizes that self-knowledge is the basis of life success.

The Self-Awareness Triad: Getting in touch, Attention, and Reflection, demonstrates the value of getting in touch with experience, attending to experience, and reflecting on experience. We learn that self-awareness is the basis of self-knowledge.

The Goals Triad: Drives, Needs, and Wants, helps us determine our direction. Knowing our sources of motivation and knowing what we want and need allows us to set our goals. The Goals Triad helps us understand our motivation and set our course.

The Decision-Making Triad: Information, Awareness, and Alternatives, provides a basic decision-making model for us. The Decision-Making Triad illustrates the importance of taking control of one's life through decision-making.

The Identity Triad: Culture, Race, and Ethnicity, enables us to question our identity. We learn that identity has a strong social component. We see that identity is an important success issue, and who we are is the basis of our success.

The Relationship Triad: Love, Trust and Acceptance, presents a concise model for assessing relationships. We can examine our relationships on the basis of love, trust, and acceptance. The Relationship Triad is a basic model for evaluating our relationships.

The Careering Triad: Self-Assessment, Career Search, and Job Hunt, delineates the major stages of the careering process. This Triad illustrates that career development usually starts with self-assessment continues with a career search and culminates in a job hunt.

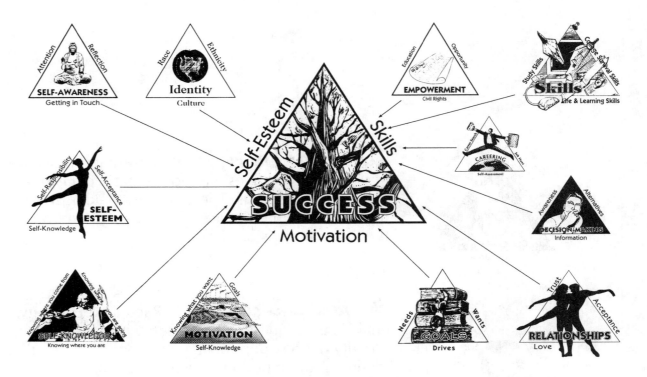

Application of The Triadic System of Success

The Triadic System is a way to conceptualize our success. It is applied by examining, clarifying, questioning, expanding, extrapolating, discussing, and implementing the factors and the triads within the system. The triads may be applied individually, collectively, partially, or as a whole. The Triadic System is comprised of concepts of success which are dynamic and interactive, and we can conceptualize our experience according to each of the triads.

The Triadic System may be used to identify and clarify how we can promote our success. For example, The Self-Esteem Triad emphasizes self-knowledge, self responsibility, and self acceptance as the essentials of positive self-esteem. We can address these factors in our daily experience by questioning the triads and responding to the factors. "How do I assess and develop my degree of self-knowledge, self-responsibility and self-acceptance?" We apply The Triadic System by questioning the triads and applying them to ourselves.

The Triadic System is a powerful cognitive tool that may be used to direct and guide our lives. Its application involves using and connecting the triads and factors to our experience. Success is seldom a product of chance but one that comes from applying concepts to our experience.

The Triadic System of Success

1. A system of success is important because _____
_____
_____

2. The Success Triad has helped me understand my success by _____
_____
_____

3. The Triadic System helps me understand _____
_____
_____

4. The Triadic System gives me confidence because _____
_____
_____

5. The triad which most applies to me is _____
_____
_____

6. The Triadic System of Success does several important things such as _____
_____
_____

7. I intend to apply the triads by _____
_____
_____

8. I believe I can apply The Triadic System of Success because _____
_____
_____

Elements of
A Strategy for Success

Everyone wants to succeed, and most people need a plan to succeed. No matter what kind of success you are looking for, there are common elements to a plan of success recognized by successful people. The elements include vision, passion, knowledge, attitude, affiliation, and power. A Strategy for Success is a plan containing the elements which promote success. **Vision** is a key element consisting of a conceptual plan for our life's direction. A vision is what you want to be. It's what you see for yourself. **Passion** is the driving force of our vision and reflects our motivation. Passion reflects our emotional strength and commitment to our vision. Successful people are passionate about their lives and the core activities which are a part of their vision. **Knowledge** is an element which includes both self-knowledge and general knowledge. Self-knowledge is the basis of life success, and general knowledge supports effective action. **Attitude** is another key element to life success. Attitudes may help or hinder our success; positive attitudes generate positive results. Our attitudes reflect our self-worth and beliefs about ourselves. Self-worth and self-esteem are important factors in choosing our affiliations. **Affiliations** are the range of people with whom we may contact or spend time. The people with whom we associate may significantly affect our success. **Power** permeates our lives, and personal power enables us to take control over our lives and accomplish our goals. Power is a product of motivation, self-esteem, and skill. Cultivating personal power through integrity, dependability, honesty, and responsibility will do much to further our success. A consciousness of the importance of power in all aspects of life promotes our success.

A success strategy helps eliminate doubt and confusion about what you should be doing and helps allay anxiety regarding success. Without a strategy, our efforts may be random and consume a great deal of energy and not be effective. A strategy for success helps you think systematically about your success, organizes your thoughts and actions, helps identify strengths and weaknesses, and allows you to learn from the experience of others.

A Strategy for Success

Vision   Create your life's vision by identifying your life's purpose.

Passion   Identify your passion. What drives you? What do you feel strongly about? How will you dedicate your time and life?

Knowledge   Develop self-knowledge. Become knowledgeable in your area of passion. Seek to learn.

Attitude   Generate positive attitudes. Negative attitudes produce failure. Develop a strong belief in self.

Affiliation   Choose your affiliates carefully. With whom do you spend your time? We tend to function at the level of our affiliations.

Power   Cultivate personal power through integrity, dependability, honesty, and responsibility.

Chapter Conclusion:
Critical Analysis and Application

Select a concept from this chapter which has the greatest relevance and importance to you. Explain the nature of the concept and why it is relevant and important to you. Critically analyze the concept by discussing its essential features. Determine how this concept can be applied to everyday life.

Select: _____

_____

_____

_____

_____

Explain: _____

_____

_____

_____

_____

Analyze: _____

_____

_____

_____

_____

Apply: _____

_____

_____

_____

_____

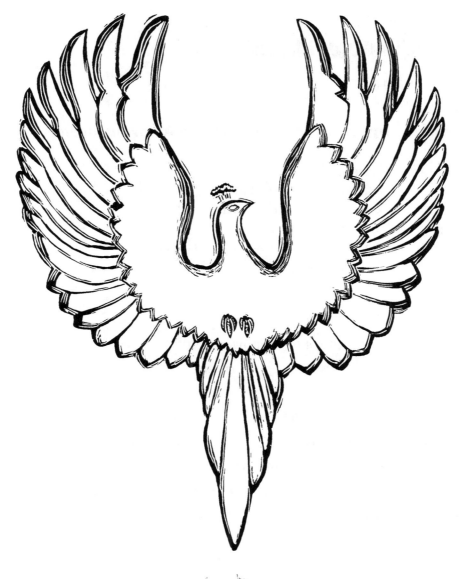

Chapter 2

Empowerment

Empowerment

Take this self-inventory by rating yourself with the following scale:

5 = This statement is true <u>all</u> of the time.
4 = This statement is true <u>most</u> of the time.
3 = This statement is true <u>much</u> of the time.
2 = This statement is true <u>some</u> of the time.
1 = This statement is true <u>almost</u> none of the time.
0 = This statement is true <u>none</u> of the time.

_____ 1. Education is the key to empowerment.

_____ 2. Civil Rights are the keys to empowerment.

_____ 3. Opportunity is the key to empowerment.

_____ 4. I feel empowered.

_____ 5. The environment disempowers the individual.

_____ 6. Money and resources are the key to empowerment.

_____ 7. I believe in my capacity to empower myself.

_____ 8. I believe that I am capable of empowering others.

_____ 9. Empowerment gives you the ability to do.

_____ 10. I believe that we have equal opportunity in our society.

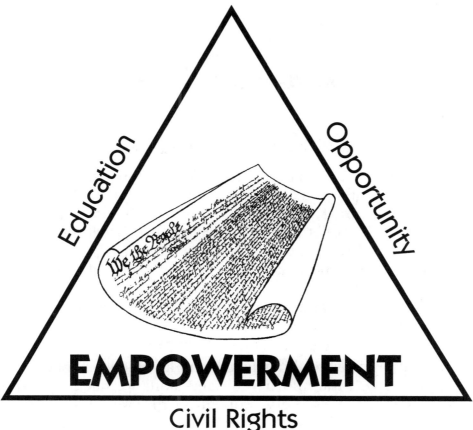

Education   Opportunity

EMPOWERMENT

Civil Rights

The more clear you are on what you want, the more power you will have.
—Anonymous

The Empowerment Triad

The Empowerment Triad consists of the following factors: Civil Rights, Education and Opportunity. No symbol seems to represent more to the American people regarding our civil rights than the Constitution of the United States. A society which offers protection in the form of civil rights, education, and opportunity does much to empower its citizens. Education is the key to empowerment because it provides the knowledge and skill needed to succeed in our society. Guaranteed civil rights and education do not guarantee empowerment if opportunity is lacking. It is essential that we not wait for others to empower us, but that we take the initiative to empower ourselves. We empower ourselves by taking complete responsibility for ourselves. A partnership in empowerment exists between the government and its citizens. We must work together to empower everyone in society.

Factors of The Empowerment Triad

Civil Rights

Civil rights are fundamental to a free and just society. Protection of civil rights strengthens a democracy, and denial of civil rights and discrimination against any particular group weakens a democracy and disempowers the individuals within it. Civil rights are guaranteed through legislative action and appropriate enforcement of these rights. The freedom of movement provided by a structure of civil rights allows all citizens to take advantage of the opportunities available in a society. Civil rights provide safety, security, and equality of treatment within a democratic society.

Education

Education provides knowledge, and knowledge is power. Education provides us with the information and skills we need to participate fully in our democratic society. Education provides for economic advantage through the information, knowledge, and skills which are needed in most careers. Education gives us the ability to think critically about our society and the nature of life. Education makes us more human and supports the pursuit of the truth through the study of the sciences and humanities. Through education, we can create a better future for ourselves, our family, and our community.

Opportunity

Opportunity empowers. Opportunity provides avenues for self-improvement and enrichment. Opportunity means equal access to education, employment, housing, and important social services. Opportunity allows us to use our knowledge and skill acquired through education. Opportunity can make the difference between success and failure. Through civil rights, education, and opportunity, we empower ourselves.

Empowerment

You can empower yourself. You can take charge and control of your life, and achieve your goals. You can learn to be more effective. You can change and become the person you want to become. You can become a more effective learner. You can get yourself motivated and develop the confidence you need to get what you want out of life. You can achieve beyond your level of aspiration, and you can create rich and fulfilling possibilities for how to live your life. You can go beyond the familiar and make contact with new worlds.

The Empowerment Philosophy

Empowerment is a positive philosophy which maintains the belief in the capacity of the individual to determine the course of his/her life. People are capable of taking charge and control of their lives by actively deciding who they are and who they are not. This approach to life includes the importance of self-determination, self-responsibility, and choice. This philosophy affirms the belief that individuals are able to solve their problems and overcome disempowering experiences. The central proposition of this way of life is the belief that the disempowered can become empowered.

Empowerment as a Social and Psychological Concept

Empowerment is a social and psychological concept through which individuals acquire power and gain access. We respond and act in a social environment, and the social context defines us as individuals. Empowerment is a way of opening doors for all people. The empowerment philosophy recognizes that success is not only a product of individual achievement but also occurs within a social context. Empowerment is an important concept for student success because it affirms that students can take charge and control of their learning and education. As a psychological concept, empowerment is a way of overcoming a sense of powerlessness and hopelessness. Power is personal and collective and to be empowered one must have both. Success is a psychosocial event. The pursuit of self-knowledge through self-realization is characteristic of the self-empowering process. The philosophy instills hope.

The Empowerment Triad

The Empowerment Triad illustrates the broader social context in which empowerment occurs. Protection of civil rights, accessing education, and the availability of opportunity are social aspects of empowerment. We empower ourselves through education. Success occurs within an environment of civil rights, education, and opportunity. The Empowerment Philosophy promotes equal social participation through equal opportunity. The ability to access quality education is important for empowerment.

Empowerment, Growth, and Change

Empowerment is the process of taking greater control over one's life through personal growth, education, and self-responsibility. It is moving from disempowerment to empowerment, from powerlessness to powerfulness, from lack of control to being in charge, from shame and humiliation to confidence and self-realization. Empowerment involves a choice to grow and change. We empower ourselves by growing and changing. We also empower ourselves by choosing to participate in a process which promotes growth and change. We grow by using the method of introspection. By "looking within," we explore our experience. We carefully examine our experience and seek to discover unknown aspects of our experience. We evaluate our experience with the intent to make decisions about who and what we are. We make decisions about what we have to change, what we need to attend to, and how we can gain greater control of our lives. We choose our identity. We can give into the pressures of others to label and see ourselves by their prescribed definitions or we can choose to define ourselves through our own analysis and choices.

The Empowered Individual

Taking Charge and Control

Empowered individuals take charge and control of their lives by actively deciding who they are and what they want. These individuals believe in their capacity to achieve their goals and maintain a hopeful attitude about their futures. Empowered individuals have and feel a sense of personal power. They derive this sense of power because they direct their own lives and don't see themselves as passive victims of their circumstances and conditions. Belief in their freedom to choose is fundamental to their way of life. Empowered individuals feel pain, loneliness and the whole spectrum of human feelings. They see these experiences as opportunities for growth and change. They are self-aware and recognize who they are and where they come from. They possess a strong sense of personal identity. These individuals are self-accepting and possess positive levels of self- esteem. Empowered individuals have a passion for living and seek answers to profound questions concerning life; they are compassionate and empathic and seek to understand the world of others. These individuals are integrated and whole and exhibit a quality of egolessness. They seek the transcendent aspects of life.

Growth and Change

Empowered individuals are committed to their growth and see change as fundamental to their life processes. Empowered individuals are highly motivated and focus on the resolution of problems. These individuals are confident and feel a profound sense of self-worth. They live in "the here and now." Empowered individuals are persistent and overcome disempowering experiences with a strong belief in their self-efficacy. These individuals are persistent and simply do not give up. Empowered individuals frequently want to serve others and make positive contributions to society. Empowered individuals empower others.

The Empowered Student

Motivated

Empowered students want to learn. They maintain a positive attitude. They are "turned on" to life with its problems, struggles, and challenges. They look deeply within themselves to find sources of motivation.

Confident

Empowered students are confident about their self-worth and abilities. They enjoy taking on new learning tasks and challenges. Their self-worth is based on who they are and not what they do. They possess a high level of self-esteem. Empowered students accept themselves and others.

Skilled

Empowered students have a broad range of skills. They recognize the need to acquire and develop skills, including study skills, life skills, and college survival skills.

Self-Determining

Empowered students are in control of their lives. They feel that they can control the direction of their lives, although many forces may obstruct their self-determination. Empowered students take charge of their responses to events, circumstances, and people. The power of the empowered student is in the individual's response to life's demands.

Responsible

Empowered students take responsibility for their thoughts, feelings, actions, and reactions. They keep their word and do what they say they are going to do. They take responsibility for their experience and for what they communicate. They take responsibility for their education.

Self-Aware

Empowered students are conscious of self. They are in touch with themselves and most aspects of their personal experience. Empowered students cultivate self-awareness.

Self-Actualizing

Empowered students are concerned about actualizing their potential and are committed to becoming all they are capable of becoming.

Goal-Directed

Empowered students set goals and seek constructive means to achieve them. They have clearly defined goals and are determined to reach them. Having direction is important to them.

Action-Oriented

Empowered students know that in order to bring about change and reach goals, they must have action plans and must be committed to act.

Active Learner

Empowered students use tools, strategies and techniques to facilitate learning. They are active learners. They are aware of how they learn best. Empowered students realize how important it is to know how to learn.

Decision-Maker

Empowered students consciously make decisions. They are capable decision makers. They define themselves through the decision making process. They realize that not to decide is to decide.

Problem Solver

Empowered students recognize that life involves facing and solving problems. They enjoy the challenge of solving problems. They learn problem solving strategies and techniques.

Persistent

Empowered students are tenacious in pursuing goals and acquiring learning. They realize that they must find ways to overcome obstacles and maintain a hopeful attitude. Empowered students do not yield in the face of obstacles.

Assertive

Empowered students know when and how to assert their point of view. They assert personal needs and preferences.

Ethical

Empowered students are concerned about personal integrity and credibility. They function from a foundation of well formulated values and are concerned about questions of right and wrong.

Non-Judgmental

Empowered students maintain a non-judgmental attitude towards self and others. This encourages acceptance of self and others. It also allows empowered students to hear ideas without prematurely rejecting them.

Appreciates Diversity

Empowered students appreciate the diverse society in which we live and look for ways to live in harmony with others. They confirm the positive aspects of the similarities and differences among people. Empowered students do not feel inferior or superior to anyone.

Multi-Lingual

Empowered students realize the power of language and seek to learn other languages to broaden personal perspectives.

Social Consciousness

Empowered students are conscious of themselves as social beings living in a social context. They seek to understand their world and their relationship to that world. They realize that their identity is largely a social construction. They are aware of the social problems that exist in our society. They are motivated to act for the common good of our society.

Global Perspective

Empowered students realize that we live in a global community, and events throughout the world have implications for all of us. They realize that we have a global economy and that we face stiff competition from abroad.

Empowered

Empowered students have personal power. They feel in charge and in control of their lives. They realize that to be empowered, they must empower themselves. They feel hopeful about the future and seek to empower others. They recognize that disempowering factors must be overcome.

The Empowered Student

1. List the characteristics you share with the empowered student.

Motivated, Responsible, Decision maker, persistent

2. Which of these characteristics is your greatest strength? Describe this characteristic in detail.

motivated, Responsible, Decision maker

3. Which of the characteristics you share with the empowered student needs further development? Explain and describe these characteristics, and how you would develop them.

Barriers to Academic Success

The purpose of this exercise is to help you understand the number and range of barriers that interfere with academic success. This text will help you address and resolve many of the issues which stem from these barriers. The following list of barriers to academic success has been compiled from the responses of students taking courses in college success. Check off the barriers which you believe impede your academic success.

Study and Learning Barriers

- ❏ Procrastination
- ❏ Motivation
- ❏ Homework overload
- ❏ General education
- ❏ Concentration
- ❏ Relevance of instruction
- ❏ Keeping focused
- ❏ Asking questions
- ❏ Listening to professor
- ❏ Preparation for college

- ❏ Making yourself study
- ❏ Memorization
- ❏ Getting started on projects
- ❏ Course requirements
- ❏ Professor expectations
- ❏ Subjects and concepts
- ❏ Teaching styles
- ❏ Learning disabilities
- ❏ Spelling
- ❏ Language problems

- ❏ Distractions
- ❏ Lack of student aids
- ❏ Controlling study time
- ❏ Attendance
- ❏ Boredom
- ❏ Lack of interest
- ❏ Sitting in class
- ❏ Place to study
- ❏ Comprehension
- ❏ Test anxiety
- ❏ Other_____

Personal and Physical Barriers

- ❏ Money
- ❏ Stress
- ❏ Turning off TV/radio
- ❏ Anger
- ❏ Self-esteem
- ❏ Impatience
- ❏ Health
- ❏ Sex
- ❏ Child care
- ❏ Fear
- ❏ Hunger
- ❏ Transportation

- ❏ Time
- ❏ Tension
- ❏ Work interference
- ❏ Talking on the phone
- ❏ Staying out late
- ❏ Daydreaming
- ❏ Lack of direction
- ❏ Self-discipline
- ❏ Depression
- ❏ Worry
- ❏ Drowsiness
- ❏ Drugs

- ❏ Lack of confidence
- ❏ Pressure
- ❏ Negative thoughts
- ❏ Feeling alienated
- ❏ Guilt about family
- ❏ Relationships
- ❏ Identity
- ❏ Getting up in the morning
- ❏ Values
- ❏ Pain
- ❏ Fatigue
- ❏ Alcohol
- ❏ Other_____

After you have completed the "barriers" questionnaire, list the barriers you have checked in each category.

If you have more barriers than space allows, use a separate sheet of paper.

Study and Learning	Scale 1-10
Total	

Personal and Physical	Scale 1-10
Total	

Average Score	

Average Score	

Rate:

Now that you have listed your barriers, rate each barrier on a scale of 1-10. A rating of 1 would indicate that this is not a very significant barrier whereas a rating of 10 would indicate great significance.

Calculate:

Calculate an average score for the barriers in each category. If your average score is above 5.0, it is advisable that you meet with your instructor or a college counselor to discuss your barriers. Any barrier which has a score of 7 or above should be discussed with your instructor or counselor.

Barriers

Identify one barrier from each list that you consider to be the most significant obstacle to your academic success. Describe and explain these barriers. How do you plan to overcome them? If you cannot generate solutions and/or alternatives to these barriers, where can you get help?

Barrier 1: Study and Learning

_____

_____

_____

_____

_____

_____

_____

_____

Barrier 2: Personal and Physical

_____

_____

_____

_____

_____

_____

_____

_____

_____

EMPOWERMENT

Education

Opportunity

Civil Rights

Expectations:
You Get What You Expect!

 If you truly expect to realize your dreams, abandon the need to be liked by all. Conforming to everyone else's expectations sacrifices your uniqueness and, therefore, your excellence.
— *Anonymous*

Expectations are anticipations and beliefs about the occurrence or outcome of life events and are usually associated with getting and receiving something from someone and/or a situation. Expectations are frequently connected to security, love, safety and esteem needs. Expectations significantly influence what will happen in a situation and directly affect the course of our actions and the actions of others. Expectations always operate and are not easily turned off or on. Some common expectations held by many include: expecting others to like us, expecting others to always be there for us, expecting life to be fair, expecting people to be nice, expecting to be happy, expecting catastrophes, and expecting others never to leave us. Expectations may come from our deepest fears and anxieties. Our deepest motives determine what we desire, need, and expect. Frequently, we are out of touch with our motives. Needs, desires and motives are the keys to understanding expectations.

Unfulfilled Expectations

When was the last time you were in a situation that didn't turn out the way you wanted? What kind of situation was it? Think back! Can you remember what you expected from the people and the situation? Did you expect certain things to happen? How did you feel when things didn't turn out the way you wanted? Were your expectations set before you entered the situation? What happens when expectations are not fulfilled?

Many of life's disappointments stem from unmet or unfulfilled expectations. The more we want and need from a person and/or situation, the more vulnerable we are to the possibility that our expectations will go unmet. Frequently, our expectations are kept a secret from others and even ourselves. This makes it difficult for others to meet your expectations when they are hidden or unexpressed. Communicating with others about what we want and expect from them creates an environment where mutual expectations can be discussed. Conflicts develop when what we expect is not consistent with the reality of our situation. The greater the discrepancy between what we expect and what actually happens, the greater the conflict. Since life is unpredictable and people are very complex, our expectations are frequently out of synch with reality. This is the basis for much of the pain of expectations. The number and quality

of our expectations are directly related to the level of our happiness. Unhappiness is the result of either unrealistic or unfulfilled expectations. If you desire happiness, you may have to change your expectations. In addition to unhappiness, other common reactions to unfulfilled expectations may be anger, disappointment, revenge, depression, and other emotional and behavioral reactions.

Living Up or Down to Expectations

Our success or failure in life is related to the level and quality of our expectations. We tend to live up to or down to expectations. Our expectations are related to our level of aspiration. Many of us expect and aspire to limited possibilities for ourselves whereas many of us expect and aspire to unlimited possibilities for ourselves. What were the major expectations your parents had for you? What did your teachers expect from you? What was expected from you in regard to your performance and achievement?

Awareness of Expectations

Many of the greatest difficulties in human relationships and other aspects of living arise from a lack of awareness of what we expect from others and from situations. Awareness of expectations is the basis for changing them. To be aware of our expectations necessitates an awareness of our innermost motives. Becoming aware and being honest about our expectations allows us to change our expectations. Our expectations are based on needs and therefore we should look closely at our needs if we want to change our expectations. Changing needs changes expectations. It is very difficult to live life without expectations. Letting go of unrealistic expectations means we can live freer and less conflict-burdened lives. Awareness of needs and motives is the starting point from which one can change expectations. Attaining freedom from unrealistic expectations lies in examining our needs and motives.

Expectations:
You Get What You Expect!

1. Think back on a situation in which your expectations were not met. Describe the situation in detail and include the events, people, place and time.

_____

_____

_____

_____

_____

_____

_____

_____

2. What were your expectations, and what did you want from the situation?

_____

_____

_____

_____

_____

3. How can you alter your expectations in similar situations in the future to avoid disappointment, resentment and anger?

_____

_____

_____

_____

_____

_____

4. What do you expect from this course?

_____
_____
_____
_____
_____
_____
_____
_____
_____
_____

5. What do you expect from your college experience?

_____
_____
_____
_____
_____
_____
_____
_____
_____
_____
_____
_____
_____

6. What do you expect from life?

_____
_____
_____
_____
_____
_____
_____
_____
_____
_____
_____
_____
_____

A Strategy for Self-Empowerment

1. **Commit** to the protection of civil rights, access to education, and opportunity for all.

2. **Get** motivated.

3. **Work** towards high levels of self-esteem.

4. **Learn** life and learning skills, study skills, and college survival skills.

5. **Read** for self-empowerment.

6. **Set** goals.

7. **Become** self-responsible, take charge and control of your life and become self-actualizing.

8. **Formulate,** articulate, and describe a vision for your life.

9. **Clarify** and understand your identity through self-knowledge.

Chapter Conclusion:
Critical Analysis and Application

Select a concept from this chapter which has the greatest relevance and importance to you. Explain the nature of the concept and why it is relevant and important to you. Critically analyze the concept by discussing its essential features. Determine how this concept can be applied to everyday life.

Select: _____

_____

_____

_____

_____

Explain: _____

_____

_____

_____

_____

Analyze: _____

_____

_____

_____

_____

Apply: _____

_____

_____

_____

_____

Chapter 3

Time Management

Time Management

Take this self-inventory by rating yourself with the following scale:

5 = This statement is true <u>all</u> of the time.
4 = This statement is true <u>most</u> of the time.
3 = This statement is true <u>much</u> of the time.
2 = This statement is true <u>some</u> of the time.
1 = This statement is true <u>almost</u> none of the time.
0 = This statement is true <u>none</u> of the time.

_____ 1. I am usually on time.

_____ 2. I am an effective time manager.

_____ 3. I maintain a weekly time schedule.

_____ 4. I never seem to have enough time.

_____ 5. I maintain weekly and monthly schedule planners.

_____ 6. A time schedule makes me feel restricted.

_____ 7. College students really don't need to manage their time.

_____ 8. Time management is a cultural thing.

_____ 9. I enjoy the structure provided by a good time schedule.

_____ 10. I feel like I'm wasting time.

_____ 11. Procrastination is my biggest time management problem.

_____ 12. I know how to set priorities.

_____ 13. There simply aren't sufficient hours in a day.

_____ 14. I keep my time commitments.

_____ 15. I use daily "to do" lists.

_____ 16. I maintain a study schedule.

_____ 17. I don't manage my time because I don't have goals.

_____ 18. I allow my friends to distract me from important activities on my time schedule.

Study Skills

College Survival Skills

Skills

Life & Learning Skills

➤ *Life is a maze in which we take the wrong turning before we have learnt to walk.*
—Cyril Connolly

The Skills Triad

Life skills significantly impact our success in life. They include decision-making, problem solving, time management, interpersonal communication, language, work content, and many others. Life skills are applied for our entire lifespan. Skills allow us to perform a broad spectrum of activities with efficiency and competence. Skills increase our capacity "to do." Skills are related to our overall level of performance. Skills increase our level of performance. The ability to apply what we learn increases our skill level. Beyond this, the future development of our society is based on high-tech skill development.

Factors of the Skills Triad

Life and Learning Skills

Life and learning skills lay the foundation for a productive and rewarding life. Managing our lives with skill enhances our effectiveness. Life skills help us cope and survive in home, school, and work environments. Life skills include a large category of skills from cooking meals to reading bus schedules, caring for children, communicating with others, managing our time, taking job interviews, making decisions, and performing various job related activities. Learning skills help us learn. We learn how we learn. Learning skills are a life skill because we learn for a lifetime.

Study Skills

Study skills include methods, procedures, and techniques which facilitate study and learning. Skillful and systematic approaches to study are usually more effective than random approaches to study and learning. Study skills make studying a habit, and we want study behavior to be habitual. Studying as a regular activity will enhance learning efficiency and effectiveness. Study skills help you learn more in less time. They also help you understand and remember what you are learning. Study skills build confidence and increase motivation because you know how to learn.

College Survival Skills

College survival skills are skills which help you succeed and survive in the college environment. They help you feel at ease and comfortable in the college setting. They help you understand the structure and operations of the college bureaucracy. You understand the system. College survival skills involve working with others to further your educational goals. You are able to cope with conflict and barriers which would impede your educational progress. College survival skills help you feel at home in the college environment.

52

Time Management

Time is what we want most, but what, alas, we use worst.
— William Penn

One of the best ways to get things done is to manage time effectively. The purpose of time management is to get things done in order to accomplish goals. Time management is concerned with managing the present in order to manage the future.

Managing your time has many benefits. The most important benefit is the necessity to examine your life. Are you achieving the things you want to accomplish? Are you getting what you want out of life? Are you meeting your commitments? Are you spending time doing the things that matter most? These questions relate to your level of happiness and satisfaction in life. Time management aims to make you more productive by showing you how to use time more effectively. Time management structures your life, and most of us function better when our lives are well structured. Time management allows you to know how you actually spend your time. As a consequence, you feel better about yourself because you know when you are being productive and when time is being wasted. Above all, you feel better about yourself because your life is organized, and because you have taken control of your life.

Time management demonstrates how much effort you are devoting to the present in order to achieve future goals. A time schedule should derive from your needs and values, but keep in mind that your present needs and values may not be consistent with your long range goals. Our time must be carefully balanced between present and future needs. If you are not experiencing success in reaching your goals, examine the way you use your time.

Time management is similar to a weight reduction program. Both require a high level of motivation, a present status assessment, monitoring, accurate and consistent record keeping, gradual change, and an assessment of progress. Time management requires a commitment because you will have to examine goals, priorities, values, make daily "to do" lists, review what you are doing and not doing, and you will have to make a real effort to change.

Many people believe time management requires sacrifice. The approach of this text is to encourage you to examine how you presently use your time. You are asked to monitor your time, construct a schedule, and assess what you actually do. Initially, a schedule is not based on what you think you should or must do, but on how you actually use your time. Using this approach, you can gradually change your time utilization.

Developing a Time Schedule

The Strategy for Developing A Time Schedule is a systematic method for developing and maintaining a time schedule. As in the previous strategy, you start by **assessing** your motivation to maintain a time schedule. A commitment to maintaining a time schedule will facilitate your time schedule development and utilization. **Monitoring** your time use is an important step in seeing how you actually spend your time and is an important preliminary step in the schedule developing process. Time monitoring gives you an overview of how you use your time and requires that you look closely at what you are doing. When you monitor your time, **record** how you spend 24 hours a day during a two week period. Monitoring your activities will give you valuable insight into how you use your time. The time monitor sheets consist of a 24 hour schedule divided into one hour increments. Each hour is divided by a center line that allows you to write in time use for the first and second half hour. Record your activities for each half hour. After you have monitored your time use for 14 days, review your time monitor sheets and evaluate them. Look at your activity totals at the bottom of each page. Calculate weekly totals and determine your major time users. You should be able to determine with some precision the amount of time you spend on each activity. At the end of the 14 day monitoring period, **construct** a tentative time schedule. **Begin** with committed times such as class, work, and travel times. Live with this schedule for a short period. Are you comfortable with this schedule? Are you getting things done? What insights have you derived from monitoring your time? Are you aware of how you use your time? As you live with this schedule **evaluate** your time utilization. Can you identify half hour increments that you consider wasted time? If you can identify wasted time, **change** unproductive time periods into productive time periods. If you are not successful at maintaining a time schedule, **re-evaluate** your motivation to maintain a time schedule. Maintaining a time schedule is helpful, not obligatory. If you feel compelled or coerced into maintaining a time schedule, you are less likely to keep a useful time schedule. A time schedule is not a promise to go far beyond the way you customarily use your time. The way you use your time is habitual. Most of us cannot easily change our habits. Therefore, plan to change your time utilization gradually.

A Strategy for Developing a Time Schedule

Step 1. **Assess** your motivation to maintain a time schedule.

Step 2. **Monitor** your time for two weeks. Monitor your time in half hour increments, 24 hours a day, seven days a week.

Step 3. **Record** what you actually do, not what you think you should do.

Step 4. **Construct** a tentative schedule based on your time monitoring.

Step 5. **Begin** with dedicated times such as class, work, and travel times.

Step 6. **Evaluate** your schedule, and identify half hour increments which you consider unproductive or wasted time.

Step 7. **Change** your time utilization gradually by converting unproductive periods into productive time periods.

Step 8. **Re-evaluate** your motivation to maintain your time schedule if you are not successful at maintaining a time schedule.

Daily Time Monitor

Day/Date: Monday

6:00 a.m.		I woke up — 6:30 a.m.
7:00 a.m. took a shower	wake up my children	7:30 a.m.
8:00 a.m. go to the school with my childrens		8:30 a.m.
9:00 a.m. take a breakfeast	go to my school	9:30 a.m.
10:00 a.m. start my classes		10:30 a.m.
11:00 a.m.		11:30 a.m.
12:00 p.m.		12:30 p.m.
1:00 p.m.	Return to my house	1:30 p.m.
2:00 p.m. Pick up my children	prepare food	2:30 p.m.
3:00 p.m. to eat with my children	wash the dishes	3:30 p.m.
4:00 p.m. help and review children homework		4:30 p.m.
5:00 p.m.		5:30 p.m.
6:00 p.m. Cleaning the kitchen		6:30 p.m.
7:00 p.m. watch tv		7:30 p.m.
8:00 p.m.		8:30 p.m.
9:00 p.m. Serve ceral to my kids	to Say "good night"	9:30 p.m.
10:00 p.m. to watch tv news	Do my homework	10:30 p.m.
11:00 p.m. Go to sleep		11:30 p.m.
12:00 a.m.		12:30 a.m.
1:00 a.m.		1:30 a.m.
2:00 a.m.		2:30 a.m.
3:00 a.m.		3:30 a.m.
4:00 a.m.		4:30 a.m.
5:00 a.m.		5:30 a.m.
6:00 a.m.		6:30 a.m.

Categories	Hours Spent
Work	0
Sleep	6 g
Eating	1
Grooming	30 mts
Class	4

Categories	Hours Spent
Study	2
Family	3
Commuting	1
Cooking	2
Exercise	

Categories	Hours Spent
Social	
TV	2
Errands mandados	
Housekeeping	3

Daily Time Monitor

Day/Date: Tuesday

6:00 a.m.	Wake up	6:30 a.m.
7:00 a.m. took a shower	wake up my kids	7:30 a.m.
8:00 a.m. go to the shool with my children		8:30 a.m.
9:00 a.m. take a breakfast	I went to the store	9:30 a.m.
10:00 a.m.	I went to the library	10:30 a.m.
11:00 a.m.		11:30 a.m.
12:00 p.m. I did my homework		12:30 p.m.
1:00 p.m.		1:30 p.m.
2:00 p.m. Pick up my chidren	prepare food	2:30 p.m.
3:00 p.m. eat with the kids	wash the dishes	3:30 p.m.
4:00 p.m. cleaning the kitchen		4:30 p.m.
5:00 p.m. help and review the homework of my kids		5:30 p.m.
6:00 p.m. Go to the school		6:30 p.m.
7:00 p.m.		7:30 p.m.
8:00 p.m.		8:30 p.m.
9:00 p.m.		9:30 p.m.
10:00 p.m. Pick up my chidren	go to sleep.	10:30 p.m.
11:00 p.m.		11:30 p.m.
12:00 a.m.		12:30 a.m.
1:00 a.m.		1:30 a.m.
2:00 a.m.		2:30 a.m.
3:00 a.m.		3:30 a.m.
4:00 a.m.		4:30 a.m.
5:00 a.m.		5:30 a.m.
6:00 a.m.		6:30 a.m.

Categories	Hours Spent
Work	
Sleep	
Eating	
Grooming	
Class	

Categories	Hours Spent
Study	
Family	
Commuting	
Cooking	
Exercise	

Categories	Hours Spent
Social	
TV	
Errands	
Housekeeping	

Empowering Activity 1

57

Daily Time Monitor

Day/Date:_____

6:00 a.m. _____	_____ 6:30 a.m.
7:00 a.m. _____	_____ 7:30 a.m.
8:00 a.m. _____	_____ 8:30 a.m.
9:00 a.m. _____	_____ 9:30 a.m.
10:00 a.m. _____	_____ 10:30 a.m.
11:00 a.m. _____	_____ 11:30 a.m.
12:00 p.m. _____	_____ 12:30 p.m.
1:00 p.m. _____	_____ 1:30 p.m.
2:00 p.m. _____	_____ 2:30 p.m.
3:00 p.m. _____	_____ 3:30 p.m.
4:00 p.m. _____	_____ 4:30 p.m.
5:00 p.m. _____	_____ 5:30 p.m.
6:00 p.m. _____	_____ 6:30 p.m.
7:00 p.m. _____	_____ 7:30 p.m.
8:00 p.m. _____	_____ 8:30 p.m.
9:00 p.m. _____	_____ 9:30 p.m.
10:00 p.m. _____	_____ 10:30 p.m.
11:00 p.m. _____	_____ 11:30 p.m.
12:00 a.m. _____	_____ 12:30 a.m.
1:00 a.m. _____	_____ 1:30 a.m.
2:00 a.m. _____	_____ 2:30 a.m.
3:00 a.m. _____	_____ 3:30 a.m.
4:00 a.m. _____	_____ 4:30 a.m.
5:00 a.m. _____	_____ 5:30 a.m.
6:00 a.m. _____	_____ 6:30 a.m.

Categories	Hours Spent
Work	
Sleep	
Eating	
Grooming	
Class	

Categories	Hours Spent
Study	
Family	
Commuting	
Cooking	
Exercise	

Categories	Hours Spent
Social	
TV	
Errands	
Housekeeping	

Empowering Activity 1

58

Daily Time Monitor

Day/Date:_____

6:00 a.m. _____	_____ 6:30 a.m.
7:00 a.m. _____	_____ 7:30 a.m.
8:00 a.m. _____	_____ 8:30 a.m.
9:00 a.m. _____	_____ 9:30 a.m.
10:00 a.m. _____	_____ 10:30 a.m.
11:00 a.m. _____	_____ 11:30 a.m.
12:00 p.m. _____	_____ 12:30 p.m.
1:00 p.m. _____	_____ 1:30 p.m.
2:00 p.m. _____	_____ 2:30 p.m.
3:00 p.m. _____	_____ 3:30 p.m.
4:00 p.m. _____	_____ 4:30 p.m.
5:00 p.m. _____	_____ 5:30 p.m.
6:00 p.m. _____	_____ 6:30 p.m.
7:00 p.m. _____	_____ 7:30 p.m.
8:00 p.m. _____	_____ 8:30 p.m.
9:00 p.m. _____	_____ 9:30 p.m.
10:00 p.m. _____	_____ 10:30 p.m.
11:00 p.m. _____	_____ 11:30 p.m.
12:00 a.m. _____	_____ 12:30 a.m.
1:00 a.m. _____	_____ 1:30 a.m.
2:00 a.m. _____	_____ 2:30 a.m.
3:00 a.m. _____	_____ 3:30 a.m.
4:00 a.m. _____	_____ 4:30 a.m.
5:00 a.m. _____	_____ 5:30 a.m.
6:00 a.m. _____	_____ 6:30 a.m.

Categories	Hours Spent		Categories	Hours Spent		Categories	Hours Spent
Work			Study			Social	
Sleep			Family			TV	
Eating			Commuting			Errands	
Grooming			Cooking			Housekeeping	
Class			Exercise				

Empowering Activity 1

59

Daily Time Monitor

Day/Date:_____

6:00 a.m. _____	6:30 a.m.
7:00 a.m. _____	7:30 a.m.
8:00 a.m. _____	8:30 a.m.
9:00 a.m. _____	9:30 a.m.
10:00 a.m. _____	10:30 a.m.
11:00 a.m. _____	11:30 a.m.
12:00 p.m. _____	12:30 p.m.
1:00 p.m. _____	1:30 p.m.
2:00 p.m. _____	2:30 p.m.
3:00 p.m. _____	3:30 p.m.
4:00 p.m. _____	4:30 p.m.
5:00 p.m. _____	5:30 p.m.
6:00 p.m. _____	6:30 p.m.
7:00 p.m. _____	7:30 p.m.
8:00 p.m. _____	8:30 p.m.
9:00 p.m. _____	9:30 p.m.
10:00 p.m. _____	10:30 p.m.
11:00 p.m. _____	11:30 p.m.
12:00 a.m. _____	12:30 a.m.
1:00 a.m. _____	1:30 a.m.
2:00 a.m. _____	2:30 a.m.
3:00 a.m. _____	3:30 a.m.
4:00 a.m. _____	4:30 a.m.
5:00 a.m. _____	5:30 a.m.
6:00 a.m. _____	6:30 a.m.

Empowering Activity 1

Categories	Hours Spent
Work	
Sleep	
Eating	
Grooming	
Class	

Categories	Hours Spent
Study	
Family	
Commuting	
Cooking	
Exercise	

Categories	Hours Spent
Social	
TV	
Errands	
Housekeeping	

Daily Time Monitor

Day/Date:_____

6:00 a.m. _____	_____ 6:30 a.m.
7:00 a.m. _____	_____ 7:30 a.m.
8:00 a.m. _____	_____ 8:30 a.m.
9:00 a.m. _____	_____ 9:30 a.m.
10:00 a.m. _____	_____ 10:30 a.m.
11:00 a.m. _____	_____ 11:30 a.m.
12:00 p.m. _____	_____ 12:30 p.m.
1:00 p.m. _____	_____ 1:30 p.m.
2:00 p.m. _____	_____ 2:30 p.m.
3:00 p.m. _____	_____ 3:30 p.m.
4:00 p.m. _____	_____ 4:30 p.m.
5:00 p.m. _____	_____ 5:30 p.m.
6:00 p.m. _____	_____ 6:30 p.m.
7:00 p.m. _____	_____ 7:30 p.m.
8:00 p.m. _____	_____ 8:30 p.m.
9:00 p.m. _____	_____ 9:30 p.m.
10:00 p.m. _____	_____ 10:30 p.m.
11:00 p.m. _____	_____ 11:30 p.m.
12:00 a.m. _____	_____ 12:30 a.m.
1:00 a.m. _____	_____ 1:30 a.m.
2:00 a.m. _____	_____ 2:30 a.m.
3:00 a.m. _____	_____ 3:30 a.m.
4:00 a.m. _____	_____ 4:30 a.m.
5:00 a.m. _____	_____ 5:30 a.m.
6:00 a.m. _____	_____ 6:30 a.m.

Empowering Activity 1

Categories	Hours Spent
Work	
Sleep	
Eating	
Grooming	
Class	

Categories	Hours Spent
Study	
Family	
Commuting	
Cooking	
Exercise	

Categories	Hours Spent
Social	
TV	
Errands	
Housekeeping	

Daily Time Monitor

Day/Date:_____

6:00 a.m. _____	6:30 a.m.
7:00 a.m. _____	7:30 a.m.
8:00 a.m. _____	8:30 a.m.
9:00 a.m. _____	9:30 a.m.
10:00 a.m. _____	10:30 a.m.
11:00 a.m. _____	11:30 a.m.
12:00 p.m. _____	12:30 p.m.
1:00 p.m. _____	1:30 p.m.
2:00 p.m. _____	2:30 p.m.
3:00 p.m. _____	3:30 p.m.
4:00 p.m. _____	4:30 p.m.
5:00 p.m. _____	5:30 p.m.
6:00 p.m. _____	6:30 p.m.
7:00 p.m. _____	7:30 p.m.
8:00 p.m. _____	8:30 p.m.
9:00 p.m. _____	9:30 p.m.
10:00 p.m. _____	10:30 p.m.
11:00 p.m. _____	11:30 p.m.
12:00 a.m. _____	12:30 a.m.
1:00 a.m. _____	1:30 a.m.
2:00 a.m. _____	2:30 a.m.
3:00 a.m. _____	3:30 a.m.
4:00 a.m. _____	4:30 a.m.
5:00 a.m. _____	5:30 a.m.
6:00 a.m. _____	6:30 a.m.

Categories	Hours Spent	Categories	Hours Spent	Categories	Hours Spent
Work		Study		Social	
Sleep		Family		TV	
Eating		Commuting		Errands	
Grooming		Cooking		Housekeeping	
Class		Exercise			

Daily Time Monitor

Day/Date: _____

6:00 a.m. _____	_____ 6:30 a.m.
7:00 a.m. _____	_____ 7:30 a.m.
8:00 a.m. _____	_____ 8:30 a.m.
9:00 a.m. _____	_____ 9:30 a.m.
10:00 a.m. _____	_____ 10:30 a.m.
11:00 a.m. _____	_____ 11:30 a.m.
12:00 p.m. _____	_____ 12:30 p.m.
1:00 p.m. _____	_____ 1:30 p.m.
2:00 p.m. _____	_____ 2:30 p.m.
3:00 p.m. _____	_____ 3:30 p.m.
4:00 p.m. _____	_____ 4:30 p.m.
5:00 p.m. _____	_____ 5:30 p.m.
6:00 p.m. _____	_____ 6:30 p.m.
7:00 p.m. _____	_____ 7:30 p.m.
8:00 p.m. _____	_____ 8:30 p.m.
9:00 p.m. _____	_____ 9:30 p.m.
10:00 p.m. _____	_____ 10:30 p.m.
11:00 p.m. _____	_____ 11:30 p.m.
12:00 a.m. _____	_____ 12:30 a.m.
1:00 a.m. _____	_____ 1:30 a.m.
2:00 a.m. _____	_____ 2:30 a.m.
3:00 a.m. _____	_____ 3:30 a.m.
4:00 a.m. _____	_____ 4:30 a.m.
5:00 a.m. _____	_____ 5:30 a.m.
6:00 a.m. _____	_____ 6:30 a.m.

Categories	Hours Spent		Categories	Hours Spent		Categories	Hours Spent
Work			Study			Social	
Sleep			Family			TV	
Eating			Commuting			Errands	
Grooming			Cooking			Housekeeping	
Class			Exercise				

Empowering Activity 1

63

Daily Time Monitor

Day/Date: _____

6:00 a.m. _____	_____ 6:30 a.m.
7:00 a.m. _____	_____ 7:30 a.m.
8:00 a.m. _____	_____ 8:30 a.m.
9:00 a.m. _____	_____ 9:30 a.m.
10:00 a.m. _____	_____ 10:30 a.m.
11:00 a.m. _____	_____ 11:30 a.m.
12:00 p.m. _____	_____ 12:30 p.m.
1:00 p.m. _____	_____ 1:30 p.m.
2:00 p.m. _____	_____ 2:30 p.m.
3:00 p.m. _____	_____ 3:30 p.m.
4:00 p.m. _____	_____ 4:30 p.m.
5:00 p.m. _____	_____ 5:30 p.m.
6:00 p.m. _____	_____ 6:30 p.m.
7:00 p.m. _____	_____ 7:30 p.m.
8:00 p.m. _____	_____ 8:30 p.m.
9:00 p.m. _____	_____ 9:30 p.m.
10:00 p.m. _____	_____ 10:30 p.m.
11:00 p.m. _____	_____ 11:30 p.m.
12:00 a.m. _____	_____ 12:30 a.m.
1:00 a.m. _____	_____ 1:30 a.m.
2:00 a.m. _____	_____ 2:30 a.m.
3:00 a.m. _____	_____ 3:30 a.m.
4:00 a.m. _____	_____ 4:30 a.m.
5:00 a.m. _____	_____ 5:30 a.m.
6:00 a.m. _____	_____ 6:30 a.m.

Categories	Hours Spent		Categories	Hours Spent		Categories	Hours Spent
Work			Study			Social	
Sleep			Family			TV	
Eating			Commuting			Errands	
Grooming			Cooking			Housekeeping	
Class			Exercise				

Empowering Activity 1

64

Daily Time Monitor

Day/Date:_____

6:00 a.m. _____	_____ 6:30 a.m.
7:00 a.m. _____	_____ 7:30 a.m.
8:00 a.m. _____	_____ 8:30 a.m.
9:00 a.m. _____	_____ 9:30 a.m.
10:00 a.m. _____	_____ 10:30 a.m.
11:00 a.m. _____	_____ 11:30 a.m.
12:00 p.m. _____	_____ 12:30 p.m.
1:00 p.m. _____	_____ 1:30 p.m.
2:00 p.m. _____	_____ 2:30 p.m.
3:00 p.m. _____	_____ 3:30 p.m.
4:00 p.m. _____	_____ 4:30 p.m.
5:00 p.m. _____	_____ 5:30 p.m.
6:00 p.m. _____	_____ 6:30 p.m.
7:00 p.m. _____	_____ 7:30 p.m.
8:00 p.m. _____	_____ 8:30 p.m.
9:00 p.m. _____	_____ 9:30 p.m.
10:00 p.m. _____	_____ 10:30 p.m.
11:00 p.m. _____	_____ 11:30 p.m.
12:00 a.m. _____	_____ 12:30 a.m.
1:00 a.m. _____	_____ 1:30 a.m.
2:00 a.m. _____	_____ 2:30 a.m.
3:00 a.m. _____	_____ 3:30 a.m.
4:00 a.m. _____	_____ 4:30 a.m.
5:00 a.m. _____	_____ 5:30 a.m.
6:00 a.m. _____	_____ 6:30 a.m.

Categories	Hours Spent
Work	
Sleep	
Eating	
Grooming	
Class	

Categories	Hours Spent
Study	
Family	
Commuting	
Cooking	
Exercise	

Categories	Hours Spent
Social	
TV	
Errands	
Housekeeping	

Empowering Activity 1

Daily Time Monitor

Day/Date:_____

6:00 a.m. _____	6:30 a.m.
7:00 a.m. _____	7:30 a.m.
8:00 a.m. _____	8:30 a.m.
9:00 a.m. _____	9:30 a.m.
10:00 a.m. _____	10:30 a.m.
11:00 a.m. _____	11:30 a.m.
12:00 p.m. _____	12:30 p.m.
1:00 p.m. _____	1:30 p.m.
2:00 p.m. _____	2:30 p.m.
3:00 p.m. _____	3:30 p.m.
4:00 p.m. _____	4:30 p.m.
5:00 p.m. _____	5:30 p.m.
6:00 p.m. _____	6:30 p.m.
7:00 p.m. _____	7:30 p.m.
8:00 p.m. _____	8:30 p.m.
9:00 p.m. _____	9:30 p.m.
10:00 p.m. _____	10:30 p.m.
11:00 p.m. _____	11:30 p.m.
12:00 a.m. _____	12:30 a.m.
1:00 a.m. _____	1:30 a.m.
2:00 a.m. _____	2:30 a.m.
3:00 a.m. _____	3:30 a.m.
4:00 a.m. _____	4:30 a.m.
5:00 a.m. _____	5:30 a.m.
6:00 a.m. _____	6:30 a.m.

Categories	Hours Spent	Categories	Hours Spent	Categories	Hours Spent
Work		Study		Social	
Sleep		Family		TV	
Eating		Commuting		Errands	
Grooming		Cooking		Housekeeping	
Class		Exercise			

Empowering Activity 1

66

Daily Time Monitor

Day/Date:_____

6:00 a.m. _____	_____ 6:30 a.m.
7:00 a.m. _____	_____ 7:30 a.m.
8:00 a.m. _____	_____ 8:30 a.m.
9:00 a.m. _____	_____ 9:30 a.m.
10:00 a.m. _____	_____ 10:30 a.m.
11:00 a.m. _____	_____ 11:30 a.m.
12:00 p.m. _____	_____ 12:30 p.m.
1:00 p.m. _____	_____ 1:30 p.m.
2:00 p.m. _____	_____ 2:30 p.m.
3:00 p.m. _____	_____ 3:30 p.m.
4:00 p.m. _____	_____ 4:30 p.m.
5:00 p.m. _____	_____ 5:30 p.m.
6:00 p.m. _____	_____ 6:30 p.m.
7:00 p.m. _____	_____ 7:30 p.m.
8:00 p.m. _____	_____ 8:30 p.m.
9:00 p.m. _____	_____ 9:30 p.m.
10:00 p.m. _____	_____ 10:30 p.m.
11:00 p.m. _____	_____ 11:30 p.m.
12:00 a.m. _____	_____ 12:30 a.m.
1:00 a.m. _____	_____ 1:30 a.m.
2:00 a.m. _____	_____ 2:30 a.m.
3:00 a.m. _____	_____ 3:30 a.m.
4:00 a.m. _____	_____ 4:30 a.m.
5:00 a.m. _____	_____ 5:30 a.m.
6:00 a.m. _____	_____ 6:30 a.m.

Categories	Hours Spent
Work	
Sleep	
Eating	
Grooming	
Class	

Categories	Hours Spent
Study	
Family	
Commuting	
Cooking	
Exercise	

Categories	Hours Spent
Social	
TV	
Errands	
Housekeeping	

Empowering Activity 1

Daily Time Monitor

Day/Date: _____

6:00 a.m. _____	_____ 6:30 a.m.
7:00 a.m. _____	_____ 7:30 a.m.
8:00 a.m. _____	_____ 8:30 a.m.
9:00 a.m. _____	_____ 9:30 a.m.
10:00 a.m. _____	_____ 10:30 a.m.
11:00 a.m. _____	_____ 11:30 a.m.
12:00 p.m. _____	_____ 12:30 p.m.
1:00 p.m. _____	_____ 1:30 p.m.
2:00 p.m. _____	_____ 2:30 p.m.
3:00 p.m. _____	_____ 3:30 p.m.
4:00 p.m. _____	_____ 4:30 p.m.
5:00 p.m. _____	_____ 5:30 p.m.
6:00 p.m. _____	_____ 6:30 p.m.
7:00 p.m. _____	_____ 7:30 p.m.
8:00 p.m. _____	_____ 8:30 p.m.
9:00 p.m. _____	_____ 9:30 p.m.
10:00 p.m. _____	_____ 10:30 p.m.
11:00 p.m. _____	_____ 11:30 p.m.
12:00 a.m. _____	_____ 12:30 a.m.
1:00 a.m. _____	_____ 1:30 a.m.
2:00 a.m. _____	_____ 2:30 a.m.
3:00 a.m. _____	_____ 3:30 a.m.
4:00 a.m. _____	_____ 4:30 a.m.
5:00 a.m. _____	_____ 5:30 a.m.
6:00 a.m. _____	_____ 6:30 a.m.

Categories	Hours Spent	Categories	Hours Spent	Categories	Hours Spent
Work		Study		Social	
Sleep		Family		TV	
Eating		Commuting		Errands	
Grooming		Cooking		Housekeeping	
Class		Exercise			

Empowering Activity 1

68

Daily Time Monitor

Day/Date:_____

6:00 a.m. _____	_____ 6:30 a.m.
7:00 a.m. _____	_____ 7:30 a.m.
8:00 a.m. _____	_____ 8:30 a.m.
9:00 a.m. _____	_____ 9:30 a.m.
10:00 a.m. _____	_____ 10:30 a.m.
11:00 a.m. _____	_____ 11:30 a.m.
12:00 p.m. _____	_____ 12:30 p.m.
1:00 p.m. _____	_____ 1:30 p.m.
2:00 p.m. _____	_____ 2:30 p.m.
3:00 p.m. _____	_____ 3:30 p.m.
4:00 p.m. _____	_____ 4:30 p.m.
5:00 p.m. _____	_____ 5:30 p.m.
6:00 p.m. _____	_____ 6:30 p.m.
7:00 p.m. _____	_____ 7:30 p.m.
8:00 p.m. _____	_____ 8:30 p.m.
9:00 p.m. _____	_____ 9:30 p.m.
10:00 p.m. _____	_____ 10:30 p.m.
11:00 p.m. _____	_____ 11:30 p.m.
12:00 a.m. _____	_____ 12:30 a.m.
1:00 a.m. _____	_____ 1:30 a.m.
2:00 a.m. _____	_____ 2:30 a.m.
3:00 a.m. _____	_____ 3:30 a.m.
4:00 a.m. _____	_____ 4:30 a.m.
5:00 a.m. _____	_____ 5:30 a.m.
6:00 a.m. _____	_____ 6:30 a.m.

Categories	Hours Spent	Categories	Hours Spent	Categories	Hours Spent
Work		Study		Social	
Sleep		Family		TV	
Eating		Commuting		Errands	
Grooming		Cooking		Housekeeping	
Class		Exercise			

Empowering Activity 1

69

Hourly Tabulation

Once you have completed the time monitors, you need to evaluate your time utilization in order to complete the Hourly Tabulation Sheet.

Calculate   Calculate daily totals for each activity listed at the bottom of the monitor page.

Enter   Enter the time use of each activity for each day of the monitoring period on the Hourly Evaluation Sheet.

Calculate   Calculate the 14 day time use total for each activity.

Add   Add total hours column to determine the total activity hours used in the 14 day period.

Complete   Complete the Time Use Evaluation.

Hourly Tabulation Sheet

Activity	Day 1	Day 2	Day 3	Day 4	Day 5	Day 6	Day 7	Day 8	Day 9	Day 10	Day 11	Day 12	Day 13	Day 14	Total Hours
Work															
Sleep															
Eating															
Grooming															
Class															
Study															
Family															
Commuting															
Cooking															
Exercise															
Social															
TV															
Errands															
House-keeping															
Other															

Total hours

Time Use Evaluation

1. Do you now have a greater awareness of how you use your time?

   Yes.

2. Which activities consume the most time?

   Doing my homework for English class and S.E.S

3. What do you consider wasted time?

   Watching tv

4. How would you change your time use?

   I would like change my time, reading in English, instead watch tv

5. Are you surprised at how you actually spend your time?

   Yes, because I always am looking the hour.

Weekly Time Schedule

	Monday	Tuesday	Wednesday	Thursday	Friday
6:00 a.m.					
7:00 a.m.					
8:00 a.m.					
9:00 a.m.					
10:00 a.m.					
11:00 a.m.					
12:00 p.m.					
1:00 p.m.					
2:00 p.m.					
3:00 p.m.					
4:00 p.m.					
5:00 p.m.					
6:00 p.m.					
7:00 p.m.					
8:00 p.m.					
9:00 p.m.					
10:00 p.m.					
11:00 p.m.					
12:00 a.m.					
1:00 a.m.					
2:00 a.m.					
3:00 a.m.					
4:00 a.m.					
5:00 a.m.					
6:00 a.m.					

Empowering Activity 2

	Saturday	Sunday
6:00 a.m.		
7:00 a.m.		
8:00 a.m.		
9:00 a.m.		
10:00 a.m.		
11:00 a.m.		
12:00 p.m.		
1:00 p.m.		
2:00 p.m.		
3:00 p.m.		
4:00 p.m.		
5:00 p.m.		
6:00 p.m.		
7:00 p.m.		
8:00 p.m.		
9:00 p.m.		
10:00 p.m.		
11:00 p.m.		
12:00 a.m.		
1:00 a.m.		
2:00 a.m.		
3:00 a.m.		
4:00 a.m.		
5:00 a.m.		
6:00 a.m.		

Important dates to remember

January	February	March
April	May	June
July	August	September
October	November	December

Introduction to
A Strategy for Managing Your Time

The primary reason to manage your time is to get things done in order to reach goals. The Strategy For Managing Time asks you to start by **assessing** your motivation to manage your time. You may be unwilling to do the activities required in the time management scheme unless you are experiencing significant conflict about your time utilization. Do you need to take control of your life and your time? The next step in this strategy is to **determine** your personal and educational goals. Goals are the "pulling" forces of time management and the motivators of effective time utilization. **Write** out your goals. The simple act of writing your goals increases your commitment to your goals by making them concrete and visual. **Clarify** your daily, weekly, and monthly goals by writing three separate lists. **Identify** the activities you will need to accomplish your daily, weekly, and monthly goals. **Make** lists of the activities you need to complete for your daily, weekly, and monthly goals. **Prioritize** your daily, weekly, and monthly activities by examining each of your lists and establishing a rank order. **Identify** time periods you will use to complete the activities that lead to your goals. **Return** to your "to do" list and check-off activities and tasks completed. This strategy provides a basic framework for time management and emphasizes the importance of assessing motivation, setting goals, identifying and completing activities which lead to goal attainment and to effective time utilization.

A Strategy for Managing Your Time

Step 1. **Assess** your motivation to manage your time.

Step 2. **Determine** your personal and educational goals.

Step 3. **Write** down your goals.

Step 4. **Clarify** your daily, weekly, and monthly goals.

Step 5. **Identify** activities needed to accomplish your daily, weekly, and monthly goals.

Step 6. **Make** a "to do" list for your daily, weekly, and monthly goals.

Step 7. **Prioritize** your daily, weekly, and monthly activities.

Step 8. **Identify** time periods on your time schedule that you will use to accomplish these activities.

Step 9. **Return** to your "to do" list and check-off activities and tasks completed.

Introduction to Daily To Do List

To keep yourself organized and to insure that you are working on your priorities, maintain a daily To Do list. List the activities that need to be completed and rank each activity. This can be done very quickly. It is important to review your daily To Do list at the end of the day and check-off the activities that have been completed. Be sure to save your daily To Do lists. At the end of the week, you may want to compare your accumulated To Do lists with your set priorities. You may want to ask yourself, "Am I completing my priority activities? Are my activities clearly creating movement towards my goals?" If you are not getting your important activities completed, what is preventing you from completing these activities?

DAILY TO DO LIST - *Example*

Activity	Rank	Check-Off
Study	1	✓
Review time schedule	2	✓
Save money	3	
Wash clothes	9	
Go to market	8	✓
Cook dinner	10	✓
Classes	6	✓
Exercise	12	
T.V.	14	
Clean house	11	
Work	7	
Call doctor	5	✓
Go to book store	13	
Feed dogs	4	✓

DAILY TO DO LIST

Activity	Rank	Check-Off

Setting Priorities

Priorities are ideas, values, beliefs, activities, and objects to which we have assigned significance. Setting priorities involves examining goals, establishing time schedules, connecting activities with goals, ranking and rating activities, and establishing a time frame for the completion of activities. When we set priorities, we declare that certain activities have greater significance for us than other activities. Setting priorities requires careful and deliberate thought about what matters to us. Setting priorities compels us to examine and clarify our values.

Activities Reveal Priorities

The range of our activities reveals our priorities in life. Priorities may include family and relationships, religion, work, entertainment, athletics, hobbies, money, health and fitness, travel, and other selected activities.

Setting Priorities

Setting priorities helps determine what to do in the short run to insure that you will accomplish what you want in the long run. Setting priorities answers the question, "What should I do and when?" Setting priorities helps us determine what we should be doing in the here and now. We can ask ourselves, "How should I be spending my 'here and now' to address my priorities?" In dealing with priorities we are continuously assessing what is significant and important to us.

Priorities are about determining what we want to do in life. Since we cannot do all the things we want to do, we need to determine the degree of significance of activities. Priorities reflect what we want out of life. Priorities establish a greater degree of focusing and expediency in reaching goals. We have priorities because we set goals. Priorities are similar to objectives because they lead to the attainment of goals. Priorities are reducible to activities. In setting priorities, we need to determine which activities are most important and which activities will further the attainment of our goals.

Listmaking

Listmaking is the primary tool for setting priorities. You will need to make a list of your goals and the things that are most important to you. You will also need to make a To Do list. How will the activities on your To Do list promote your goals, and the things that are most important to you? Next you will need to review your To Do list and determine the urgency of each activity on your list. After examining the importance of each activity, review your time schedule. When will these activities be accomplished and when will these activities be completed? How will these activities further the attainment of your goals?

Priorities should be set monthly, at minimum. Setting monthly priorities is more complicated than doing a daily To Do list. Review the strategy for setting priorities. After reviewing the example, complete the Setting Priorities work sheet.

A Strategy for Setting Priorities

Step 1.   **Set** goals.

Step 2.   **Establish** a list of "To Do" activities related to goals.

Step 3.   **Connect** the activities with set goals.

Step 4.   **Rate** each activity on a scale of 1 to 10, 10 being the most important.

Step 5.   **Rank** the list of activities.

Step 6.   **Re-set** lists of activities based on ranking and set due dates.

Step 7.   **Re-set** lists of activites based on due dates.

Step 8.   **Check** off completed activities.

Setting Priorities: Example

Goals

Step 1.
    a. Earn a B.A. in Psychology

    b. Make the Dean's List

    c. Travel to Europe this summer

    d. Increase income

    e. Increase study time

STEP 2 - Goal Related Activities   STEP 3   STEP 4   STEP 5

To Do	Goal Connection	Rating	Ranking
Study 3 hours daily	a, b, e	10	1
Ask for raise	d	9	3
Research psychology requirements	a	6	8
Gather travel information	c	7	7
Meet with study group	a, b, e	9	4
Begin assignments	a, b, e	8	5
Look for another job	d	5	9
Research psychology program	a	4	10
Review time schedule	e	10	2
Save money	c, d	8	6

Empowering Activity 3

STEP 6

Rank	Activity	Due
1	Study 3 hours daily	Daily
2	Review time schedule	Daily
3	Ask for a raise	9/2/94
4	Meet with study group	Thursday 5-7 pm
5	Begin assignments	9/1/94
6	Save money	Daily
7	Gather travel Information	10/14/94
8	Research psychololgy requirements	9/7/94
9	Look for another job	9/12/94
10	Research psychololgy programs	10/10/94

STEP 7   STEP 8

Rank	Activity	Due	✓
1	Study 3 hours daily	Daily	✓
2	Review time schedule	Daily	✓
6	Save money	Daily	
4	Meet with study group	Thursday 5-7 pm	
5	Begin assignments	9/1	
3	Ask for a raise	9/2	
8	Research psychololgy requirements	9/7	
9	Look for another job	9/12	
7	Gather travel information	10/4	
10	Research psychololgy programs	10/10	

Setting Priorities

Goals

Step 1.
   a. _____

   b. _____

   c. _____

   d. _____

   e. _____

STEP 2 - Goal Related Activities   STEP 3   STEP 4   STEP 5

To Do	Goal Connection	Rating	Ranking

Empowering Activity 3

STEP 6

Rank	Activity	Due

STEP 7   STEP 8

Rank	Activity	Due	✓

Empowering Activity 3

Procrastination

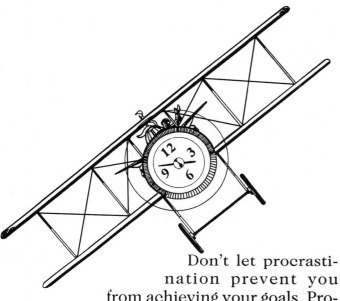

Don't let procrastination prevent you from achieving your goals. Procrastination is a common student problem.

Most of us procrastinate at some time in our lives. We procrastinate to avoid doing those things which we perceive as unpleasant. The more we perceive an activity as unpleasant, the more likely we are to procrastinate. We postpone, put off, delay doing things we "must" do for many reasons. The things we "should" or "must" do are frequently things we do not want to do. Getting ourselves to do what we "should" or "must" do may create a great deal of stress. Procrastination usually involves a choice of how to spend your time. You are in a situation where you decide whether to spend your time doing something pleasurable or something less pleasurable. Procrastination can be a superficial problem or a deeply rooted problem. Unfortunately, many of us seem unable to see the future benefit of present effort.

There are many causes of procrastination, both apparent and nonapparent. The apparent reasons can be relatively easy to identify. For example, some people may not enjoy solving complicated mathematical equations. Since they do not enjoy this activity they may choose to avoid or procrastinate doing homework which requires the solving of math problems. Although apparent reasons for procrastination may be obvious, this does not mean that these causes are easy to overcome. The nonapparent causes of procrastination may be very difficult to access. Procrastination is self-defeating, so why would any of us set out to defeat ourselves? The reasons may be nonapparent. The following causes of procrastination may be apparent or nonapparent. They include some of the following: low self-esteem and perfectionism, low frustration tolerance, hostility, fear of success, fear of failure, self-defeat, and a lack of role models.

When we procrastinate, we even worry about procrastinating. Worrying may be very unpleasant. The painfulness of worrying is often more painful than doing the task. Do it now! Stop worrying! Worrying is the price we pay for procrastination.

Causes of Procrastination

Low Self-Esteem

Low levels of self-esteem contribute to a broad range of human problems. When we don't feel good about ourselves, we generally don't exercise our best effort. It's easier to procrastinate when we are down on ourselves. Self-downing can cause depression, anger, and resentment which all interfere with our performance. Feeling good about ourselves contributes and facilitates doing things we consider important. Many of us seem to lack the capacity to stay with unpleasant tasks, especially when they are frustrating. We want things to be easy, and when they're not we seem unable to tolerate the frustration brought about by doing difficult tasks. Hostility is frequently a by-product of low self-esteem. We procrastinate because we feel hostile towards others and ourselves.

Perfectionism

Low self-esteem can produce procrastination in the form of unrealistic demands and expectations. When undertaking an assignment some students expect to do a perfect job. Perfection in academic endeavors is seriously problematic because perfection is impossible to achieve, thus intensifying feelings of low self-esteem. When you fail to achieve perfection on required tasks, you may procrastinate undertaking those tasks on future occasions.

Low Frustration Tolerance

Rushing to complete an assignment without sufficient planning, organizing, and thought may be examples of low frustration tolerance. Many academic activities are tedious and require patient and persistent effort. Many learning situations result in frustration, and we may procrastinate to avoid facing that frustration.

Hostility

Many students become hostile and angry with themselves and others, including their instructors, when they fail to do work expected of them. Hostility causes resentment and defiance; therefore, we may refuse or postpone doing important tasks.

Fear of Success

Individuals fear success for many reasons. A principal reason is that they feel undeserving of success. Somehow they are not entitled to the rewards of success. Success may go contrary to what they have been taught all of their lives.

Fear of Failure

Procrastination may be a justification or an excuse for failure. If you never give it your best effort, you do not have to own up to what you consider to be substandard performance. The quality of your work diminishes when you procrastinate because you don't give yourself sufficient time to do your best job. You may be setting yourself up for failure.

Self-Defeat

Many people are self-defeating. Self-defeat has its roots in our past. Many of the reasons for defeating ourselves are unknown to us. Refer to the Johari Window for illustrations of unknown motives.

Models

Models are living examples of individuals we can emulate. For many of us our parents are our primary models. Many individuals do not have both parents who can provide them with valuable modeling experiences. These people may not have learned skills which make them more resistant to procrastination. Others can teach us valuable lessons regarding the importance of getting the job done now!

Overcoming Procrastination

Nothing is so fatiguing as the eternal hanging on of an uncompleted task..
—William James

The following strategy has been formulated to help you overcome procrastination. For many, procrastination is a deeply entrenched problem. Your level of motivation or desire to overcome this problem will significantly influence the success of your efforts. Understanding the root cause of your procrastination will also significantly influence your ability to overcome this problem.

Assess

Anytime we undertake changing behavior, our attitudes will greatly affect whether we will succeed in our efforts. We may have a wonderful plan to change an undesirable behavior, but without a deep internal desire to make changes, change will be very difficult. The desire to change frequently derives from deep dissatisfactions and painful experiences. When procrastination becomes very disruptive to your life, you may be ready to change. Some individuals find it difficult to complete their term papers on time. Failure to complete term papers on time may cause considerable discomfort. A person may quickly learn that delaying completion of terms papers is too disruptive not to complete them on time. Thus, the first step in overcoming procrastination is to assess your motivation to change that disruptive behavior.

Admit

As most people will agree, admitting that you have a problem is a preliminary step to overcoming the problem. Failure to recognize that you have a problem makes it virtually impossible to solve the problem.

Analyze

Analyze the causes of your procrastination problem. There are apparent and nonapparent reasons for procrastination. The greater the procrastination problem, the more likely that nonapparent reasons are behind the problem. Review the causes for procrastination and give them careful consideration.

Monitor

In problem-solving, it is important to know the size of the problem before you attempt to fix it. You determine the size of a problem by monitoring and measuring the problem. You can count the number of times you procrastinate doing important tasks on a daily, weekly, and monthly basis. Choose a system to count the number of times you procrastinate doing important tasks on a daily basis. Monitor this behavior for about two weeks. Determine the frequency of your procrastination.

Realize

Think about the short and long range consequences of postponing important activities. Be conscious of those consequences. Realizing the consequences of postponing important activities may deter procrastination. Knowing the consequences of your behavior helps you keep on target.

Remind

Remind yourself of the long-term benefits of accomplishing important tasks. Reminding ourselves of the long-term benefits of completing important tasks encourages us to complete the tasks. The more often we complete those tasks, the better we feel about ourselves.

Know

Know what you are going to accomplish specifically and what the benefits will be. Knowing the task helps with completing the task. Specificity helps us know the task. Specificity makes the task concrete and tangible.

Plan

Plan for gradual change. Do not expect to overcome the problem with procrastination overnight. Overcoming procrastination is a constant struggle and challenge. Look for opportunities not to procrastinate. Without a plan, procrastination is nearly impossible to overcome.

Procrastination

1. On a scale of 0 to 10, low to high, how would you rate the level of your procrastination problem?

    Low 0   1   2   3   4   5   6   7   8   9   10   High

2. What are some apparent reasons for your procrastination?

    _____
    _____
    _____
    _____
    _____
    _____

3. Are you motivated to overcome the problem with procrastination and why?

    _____
    _____
    _____
    _____
    _____
    _____
    _____

4. What will you do to overcome your problem with procrastination?

    _____
    _____
    _____
    _____
    _____

A Strategy for Overcoming Procrastination

Step 1. **Assess** your motivation to overcome procrastination.

Step 2. **Admit** the problem you have with procrastination.

Step 3. **Analyze** the causes of your procrastination.

Step 4. **Monitor** the frequency of your procrastination.

Step 5. **Realize** the short and long range consequences of postponing important activities.

Step 6. **Remind** yourself of the long-term benefits of accomplishing the activities.

Step 7. **Know** what you are going to accomplish specifically and what the benefits will be.

Step 8. **Plan** for gradual change. Do not expect to overcome the problem with procrastination overnight.

Chapter Conclusion:
Critical Analysis and Application

Select a concept from this chapter which has the greatest relevance and importance to you. Explain the nature of the concept and why it is relevant and important to you. Critically analyze the concept by discussing its essential features. Determine how this concept can be applied to everyday life.

Select:_____

_____

_____

_____

_____

Explain:_____

_____

_____

_____

_____

Analyze:_____

_____

_____

_____

_____

Apply:_____

_____

_____

_____

_____

Chapter 4

Goal Setting

Goals

Take this self-inventory by rating yourself with the following scale:

5 = This statement is true <u>all</u> of the time.
4 = This statement is true <u>most</u> of the time.
3 = This statement is true <u>much</u> of the time.
2 = This statement is true <u>some</u> of the time.
1 = This statement is true <u>almost</u> none of the time.
0 = This statement is true <u>none</u> of the time.

_____ 1. I set goals.

_____ 2. I have clear educational goals.

_____ 3. I have a dream and a vision for my life.

_____ 4. I have written goals.

_____ 5. I feel hopeful about achieving my goals.

_____ 6. I see a connection between what I am doing in school and what I will be doing in the future.

_____ 7. I can see the long term benefits of present efforts.

_____ 8. I understand the goal setting process.

_____ 9. I'm in college to prepare for a career.

_____ 10. I have short, medium and long term goals.

Needs

Wants

GOALS

Drives

All rising to great places is by a winding stair.
—Francis Bacon

The Goals Triad

The Goals Triad consists of three factors which include Drives, Needs and Wants. We set our course in life through careful consideration of these factors. Drives are usually of a physical nature, such as thirst, hunger, and sex. Drives are powerful sources of motivation. Wants are what we desire and are also powerful sources of motivation. Needs such as food, clothing, and shelter are fundamental to our survival. Needs are physical, social, and psychological in nature as indicated by security, esteem, and belonging. Fulfilling our needs is a powerful source of motivation. Drives, needs, and wants are both physical and psychological sources of motivation. Frequently, we do not know what drives us, what we want, and what we need. It is our task to determine how we are driven, what we want, and what we need in order to set our goals.

Factors of The Goals Triad

Drives

Drives are internal states which direct our actions. They are usually considered physical in nature, but are frequently described as psychological. Drives may function as survival mechanisms. Individuals may be seen as driven by forces within their psyches or minds. We may not be conscious of the forces which direct our actions. Some individuals are driven to gain approval from others, and they may or may not be aware of this driving force within them. At times we may need help to understand our motivation. There are methods to help us become more aware of the driving forces within us.

Needs

Needs such as belonging, esteem, love, connection, power, and prestige may be significant motivational forces in our lives. Social needs govern much of our behavior. Needs are both physical and social in nature and frequently emanate from drives. Understanding needs is a very important part of understanding motivation. Awareness of needs can help us find productive ways to satisfy them. Needs play an important role in goal setting because we are attempting to satisfy our needs through the attainment of our goals.

Wants

Wants are the things we desire that go beyond drives and needs. Wants may be related to preferences. Wants are less fundamental to our survival although they may be powerful sources of motivation. Wants direct our actions, and wants may be activated by basic drives and needs. Wants and needs frequently overlap, and what we want may be seen as a need. Wants are important guides for how to live our lives because the satisfaction of wants produces contentment and may contribute to our state of happiness.

Goal Setting

 There is perhaps nothing worse than reaching the top of the ladder and discovering that you're on the wrong wall.

— Joseph Campbell

Goals give purpose and meaning to life. Goals establish direction by helping us set our course. The pursuit of goals can be a source of joy and excitement. The process of working toward goals enriches our lives and fills the emptiness that many of us experience. Goals help eliminate confusion and doubt about what we should be doing with our lives. An aimless and wandering life can generate much unhappiness and disillusionment.

Goals as Organizers

Goals are the organizers of our lives. By setting goals we design our lives. Consciously setting goals can be a difficult endeavor. Ideally, the goals we set come through careful consideration of what we want. When goals come from others, and we do not clearly own our goals, we are headed for difficulty. Many of us lack a clear idea of what we want out of life. Discovering what we want emanates from a process of achieving self-knowledge. Self-knowledge is the foundation of goal setting. Clarity about what we want out of life and the goals we have set frequently put us in conflict with others because they may not want for us what we want for ourselves. Thinking for ourselves is an important part of goal setting.

Risking Failure and Rejection

Reaching for our goals frequently involves the possibility of failure. If we are to achieve our goals, we may also have to risk rejection. An important aspect of goal attainment is persistence in the face of failure. Believing in ourselves and understanding that many things are achievable over time if we persist serves to strengthen our confidence. If we do not risk failure and rejection, we may settle for the familiar and comfortable. We must go beyond self-imposed limitations to achieve. Goal setting involves reaching beyond our perceived limitations. In setting goals, we stretch and reach beyond the familiar. Much is possible if we are willing to risk.

Discovery of Wants

As we begin to discover what we want from life, we can begin to formulate goals based on those things. Formulating goals involves writing and stating goals. After we have written and stated our goals, we need to devise plans to achieve our goals. A goal setting plan needs to be stated in specific steps for us to reach our goals.

Goals and Objectives

A goal requires specific steps leading to a desired outcome. The steps taken to achieve that outcome are called objectives. Objectives are the work, the activities, the stages we go through to achieve our goals. The more specific and concrete the objectives, the easier it is to evaluate the progress toward the completion of goals. A system of evaluating progress toward goals is desirable because it gives us information we may need to redirect our efforts, and it lets us know whether we are on course.

Attaining Goals

A very important aspect of goal setting is developing the knowledge of what it takes to attain goals. Once we have established our goals, we need to develop a strategy for attaining them. The college library is a good source of information to develop strategies on how to "get there." However, the most important source of knowledge for getting there is other people. By talking with others who have attained goals similar to our own, we are able to profit from their experience. Developing a comprehensive network of individuals who can help us reach our goals is indispensable. Increasing our knowledge of the world around us is also vital to goal attainment. For example, success in business is connected to our knowledge of the global economy. Knowledge of how organizations and institutions function provides us with knowledge of how to "get there." Seeking professional assistance such as counseling is also a helpful alternative.

Attitudes about Goal Setting

People have different attitudes about goal setting. Some can be overly serious and obsessive about goals. Others can refuse to do the difficult tasks of goal setting and therefore do not set goals at all. Yet others can be so extreme in dedicating their lives to achieving goals that they fail to live in the present. It is important to achieve a balanced attitude about goal setting in which you neither obsess over goals nor neglect the goal setting process. By setting goals, we empower ourselves because we are taking responsibility for the direction of our lives. Goals help us take charge and control of our life direction.

The Importance of Goals

Goals are very important because they define our direction. Goals impact our attitudes about life. Goals create opportunity. Goals define and re-define who we are because of self-image changes. They give us a sense of accomplishment, and they help us identify what is important in life. Goals provide the structure by which we live our lives. They increase our survivability by giving our lives meaning and purpose and by giving us something to look forward to in our future.

Everyday Obstacles to Goal Setting

Numerous obstacles impede the goal setting process. Some are part of everyday life. For example, routine, disorganization, time, money, and energy are everyday obstacles to the attainment of goals. Our daily routine is a major obstruction to the enhancement of self-awareness and the enhancement of motivation. Routine becomes all we know. It may be an enclosed pattern of activity which prevents us from changing. Routine obstructs change. Disorganization prevents a systematic approach to our life direction. Disorganization is defeating and frequently overwhelming. Goals are the organizers of our lives; disorganization is contrary to setting goals. Time quickly becomes full of obligation with the result of not leaving time for anything else. We can easily believe that we don't have the time to do what we want. Changing how we use our time is difficult, and changing time use means we are ready to change our lives. Many of our goals require money to support and accomplish. Lack of money may be a real obstacle to the achievement of goals. Both time and energy are finite resources. It takes energy to pursue an academic program while working full-time at a career. Many of us suffer from a depletion of energy, and this lack of energy could prevent the attainment of goals. Other obstacles reflect our mental disposition. Some of these barriers are based on deficiencies which prevent effective action. A lack of self-awareness, motivation, self-confidence, support, and positive relationships inhibit effective planning and goal setting. Lack of awareness of needs, wants, and preferences greatly obstructs the identification and setting of goals. A lack of motivation is the biggest obstacle to the achievement of goals.

Support from Others

Although we may be very self-reliant in our quest to achieve goals, support from others usually plays a vital role in goal attainment. We face many obstacles in achieving goals, and weathering the stresses and strains of accomplishment without support from others may be overwhelming. Communication with others provides the emotional and mental support we need to fulfill goals.

Fear

Most of us experience some type of fear that obstructs our attainment of goals. Fear has many forms. Some common and frequently debilitating fears include fear of success, failure, rejection, intimacy and inadequacy. Fears may be extremely difficult to overcome. Examining and exploring our fears may help us release ourselves from the grip of fear. The pursuit of goals involves periods of uncertainty, doubt, and fear. Persistence in the face of these obstacles will help us succeed. Giving up the effort to achieve goals results in defeat and a sense of failure. At times we need to redirect our efforts. We may have to change goals, but we don't have to give up goals entirely.

Self-Doubt

Many of us have doubts about our capacity to achieve our goals. That self-doubt may be indicative of a lack of self-confidence. We may fail to make a committed effort to achieve because we have given up before we have started. Self-doubt is a big obstacle to goal setting. Until we know what our capacities are and until we have experimented sufficiently with various alternatives, we may not be ready to make a firm commitment to a set of goals. Feeling confident about our capacity to achieve our goals facilitates goal setting.

Relationships

Relationships frequently restrict our range of activity. The people we are closest to frequently are those who hold us back. They may not want for us what we want for ourselves. Positive relationships promote growth of the participants. Restrictive relationships inhibit growth and prevent the attainment of goals. The many obstacles to goal setting may seem overwhelming; but our capacity to circumvent these obstacles is also powerful and abundant.

The Goal Setting Process

You don't need to accept life the way it comes to you. Instead, you can use the power of goal-setting to design your life so it comes to you the way you would like to get it.

—*Anonymous*

The Goal Setting Process is a continuous, dynamic, evolutionary, exploratory, unfolding activity involving self-examination, self-discovery, and self-evaluation in order to heighten awareness and understanding of self to identify needs, wants, preferences, desires, and wishes for the purpose of setting goals. The Goal Setting Process is a process involving continuous adjustment to changing needs, wants, and preferences. What we want, need and prefer today may not be what we want, need and prefer six months from now. Therefore, we constantly engage in a process of self-evaluation and self-examination to determine our direction and goals.

Stages of The Goal Setting Process

1. Self-Knowledge
2. Knowing what you want
3. Making decisions & taking responsibility
4. Reaching and stretching
5. Risking failure and rejection
6. Formulating goals and objectives
7. Knowledge of how to get there
8. Believing in yourself

The Goal Setting Process consists of the following stages, phases, activities, insights, and understandings: self-knowledge, knowing what you want, making decisions and taking responsibility, reaching and stretching, risking failure and rejection, formulating goals and objectives, knowledge of how to get there, and believing in yourself. Self-knowledge is the foundation of any complex human activity. Through self-knowledge we discover what we want, make effective decisions, and take responsibility for our actions. Increased self-knowledge gives us the courage to reach and stretch beyond the familiar. Risking failure and rejection becomes less threatening when we know ourselves. If we do not reach and stretch and risk failure and rejection, we limit our range of activities and, therefore, our goals. Expanded self-knowledge facilitates discovering what we want and consequently allows us to formulate goals and objectives. Once we have determined our goals, we need to develop knowledge of how to get there. Getting there involves an extensive range of problem solving activities frequently requiring the assistance from others. A profound sense of self-knowledge establishes a strong belief in one's worth and ability to succeed. Believing in ourselves greatly enhances goal attainment.

Elements of The Goal Setting Process

The Goal Setting Process is a compilation of twelve elements covering an extensive range of areas relating to goal setting. The incorporation of these elements in the journal system makes it a comprehensive approach to goal setting. The elements include a careful exploration and evaluation of self and family. Who we are and where we come from greatly influence decisions regarding direction. Another element, dreams reveal important information about our wishes. And our vision forms a foundation for our meaning and purpose in life. Education is an element that will significantly influence the nature and scope of our goals. Our personality characteristics have a tremendous impact on goal selection and attainment. The identification of goal achieving behaviors promotes goal attainment. Work experience may provide important information in setting career goals. We need information in order to make effective decisions and set goals. The writing of goals and objectives furthers our commitment to the attainment of our goals. Setting priorities helps us determine what is important and organizes our activities. Time management facilitates goal attainment by providing a structure for effective time utilization. A Strategy for Achieving Goals provides us with clearly defined steps leading to goal attainment. The exploration and evaluation of these twelve elements provide a comprehensive system for goal setting.

Elements of The Goal Setting Process

1. Self
2. Family
3. Dreams and Vision
4. Education
5. Personality
6. Goal Achieving Behaviors
7. Work
8. Information
9. Writing Goals and Objectives
10. Priorities
11. Time Management
12. Strategy for Achieving Goals

Setting Your Goals

Write your goals for the current school term. Include school, family, career, and personal. Write additional long term goals for the next five years. Finally, what are your life goals?

What are your goals for this semester?

School ___ To get the better puntuation on this semester and get my G.E.D. Diploma.

Family ___ To spend more time with them and enjoy them as much a I can.

Career ___ To get my degree of Sience Secretarial.

Personal ___ To get a computer.

What are your goals for the year?

School _To study very hard to get the best grades that I had never had._

Family _To enjoy them as much as I can._

Career _To improve my grades._

Personal _To take the ~~destion~~ desition of marry._

What are your goals for the next five years?

School

Family

Career

Personal

What are your life goals?

School _____

_____

_____

_____

_____

_____

Family _____

_____

_____

_____

_____

_____

Career _____

_____

_____

_____

_____

_____

Personal _____

_____

_____

_____

_____

_____

Other _____

_____

_____

A Strategy for Achieving Your Goals

Step 1.   **Commit** yourself to setting goals.

Step 2.   **Write** your goals and objectives.

Step 3.   **Post** several copies of your goals and objectives.

Step 4.   **Read** your goals and objectives weekly.

Step 5.   **Practice** visualizing yourself completing your goals.

Step 6.   **Tell** others about your goals.

Step 7.   **Reward** yourself for completion of activities and objectives leading to your goals.

Step 8.   **Develop** self-confidence and a belief in your capacity to achieve your goals.

Chapter Conclusion:
Critical Analysis and Application

Select a concept from this chapter which has the greatest relevance and importance to you. Explain the nature of the concept and why it is relevant and important to you. Critically analyze the concept by discussing its essential features. Determine how this concept can be applied to everyday life.

Select: _____

_____

_____

_____

_____

Explain: _____

_____

_____

_____

_____

Analyze: _____

_____

_____

_____

Apply: _____

_____

_____

_____

Chapter 5

Motivation

Motivation

Take this self-inventory by rating yourself with the following scale:

5 = This statement is true <u>all</u> of the time.
4 = This statement is true <u>most</u> of the time.
3 = This statement is true <u>much</u> of the time.
2 = This statement is true <u>some</u> of the time.
1 = This statement is true <u>almost</u> none of the time.
0 = This statement is true <u>none</u> of the time.

_____ 1. I know who I am.

_____ 2. I know what I want.

_____ 3. I have goals.

_____ 4. I am motivated to do the things I need to do.

_____ 5. I use techniques to get myself motivated.

_____ 6. I am motivated to complete the activities assigned in my coursework.

_____ 7. I have a very positive outlook and attitude toward life.

_____ 8. I have no difficulty getting myself started in the morning.

_____ 9. I enjoy the challenge of an academic workload.

_____ 10. I am interested in all of my subjects.

_____ 11. I persist in the face of a difficult project.

_____ 12. I do not hold myself back when I know what I want.

_____ 13. I am pursuing what I want.

_____ 14. I am accomplishing my goals.

_____ 15. I feel energized.

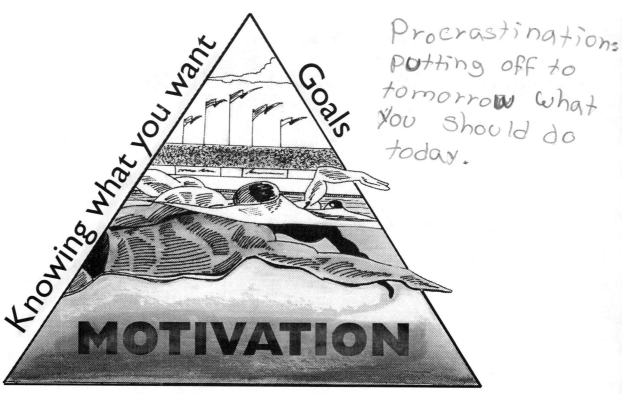

don't

Procrastination: putting off to tomorrow what you should do today.

Goals

Knowing what you want

MOTIVATION

Self-Knowledge *(Wishdom)*

> *No matter how smart or talented you are, no matter how many opportunities you have, if you are not motivated, you will probably not accomplish much, which means you won't have many choices in life. No accomplishments, no choices.*
>
> —David Campbell

The Motivation Triad

The Motivation Triad consists of Self-Knowledge, Knowing what you want, and Goals. Self-knowledge is the foundation of human growth. Without self-knowledge, our energies are diffused. Confusion and self-doubt permeate the life of an individual who lacks self-knowledge. It is the powerhouse of motivation. Anyone with an extensive degree of self-knowledge is motivated to act positively and on their own behalf.

The clearer and the deeper our knowledge of ourselves, the better the position we are in to know what we want. Knowing what we want gives our actions purpose. Knowing what we want gives us joy, pleasure, and happiness in the process of fulfilling our wants. A sure formula for unhappiness is to not do what you want to do in life. Specificity and concreteness in defining our wants helps us translate our wants into goals.

Goals energize motivation. The desire we have to achieve our goals generates motivation. The greater our commitment to achieving our goals, the more sustainable our motivation. Goals give meaning and purpose to life. They help define our actions. The achievement and attainment of goals gives us the fulfillment we seek. Life is an endless process of setting and achieving goals.

Factors of The Motivation Triad

Self-Knowledge

Self-knowledge is being aware of your thoughts, feelings, and reactions. It is knowing where you are, knowing where you come from, and knowing where you are going. Self-knowledge is knowing the purpose of your behavior, and is fundamental to positive action. Awareness and knowledge of motives help you understand your motivation, and knowing the sources of your motivation facilitate changing motivation. People who know themselves have a vision for their lives, and a vision for life may be a powerful source of motivation. Self-knowledge is the primary source of motivation because people who know themselves know what they want and set goals.

Knowing What You Want

Knowing what you want is essential to motivation. It gives you a sense of purpose and builds confidence. Knowing what you want may be hidden from view, and discovering what you want may involve a comprehensive process of self-evaluation. Doing what you want in life is a prescription for happiness, contentment, and satisfaction.

Goals

Goals are the energizers of motivation, and are formulations of what we want. People who know themselves have goals and know what they want. Reminding ourselves of the goals we have set will help sustain motivation. It is important to visualize your goals and believe in your ability to achieve your goals. The more accurately goals reflect what you want, the more powerful your motivation.

Motivation

How exciting are your dreams? Most people don't aim too high and miss, they aim too low and hit.
—Anonymous

We tend to label ourselves "lazy" when we are not doing what we "must" or "should" do. You should do your homework, but you can't always get yourself motivated to do it. Is this laziness? Are you uninterested? Or are you possibly in over your head? How do you create motivation? Virtually everyone wants to do something. We do not appear to lack motivation when we are doing what we want to do. When faced with situations that we perceive as unpleasant, we pursue something more desirable. Distractions are plentiful, and there is always something else that we would rather be doing.

Motivation is generally thought to be an internal state which drives the individual to act. It usually emanates from a state of tension. This state produces a need or drive, and action may be initiated. This tension disrupts the homeostatic balance which the individual wants to preserve. Many of the initiators of action are both internal and external. Usually, we try to achieve balance, safety, and security. Many of our psychological and physiological states produce needs that compel us to act.

Complexity of Motivation

Issues of motivation permeate all aspects of human performance. Motivation is a complex and difficult process to understand. As human beings, it is difficult to be definitive about our own motivation. Yet this concept is commonly used and we somehow assume that we understand what we mean when we refer to motivation. Our motivations are so complex that we may not be fully aware of them. We are frequently driven by forces of which we are not conscious. These are the forces behind our actions; understanding these forces helps us understand our motivation. How many times have you asked yourself, "Why am I doing this?" You act in certain ways, and you don't know why you do, even when the behavior has negative consequences.

Growth and Deficiency Motivation

Innumerable sources of motivation combine to form complex motivational patterns. These fall into two major categories: "growth" and "deficiency" motivation. Many of us are motivated to act based on a deficiency because we are lacking psychological and physical support. Deficiency motivation is compensatory. We are compensating for something missing in our lives. Deficiency motivation is not a source of negative

motivation. In deficiency motivation, activities are not engaged in for their own sake. They compensate for something else. Growth motivation emanates from the desire to grow. Growth motivation is driven by the need to grow and change. In growth motivation, activities are engaged in for their own sake. Growth factors are powerful sources of motivation.

The growth motivational factors include self-actualization, excitement for learning, self-knowledge, competence, and challenge. The deficiency motivational factors include: insecurity, approval, unhappiness, pain/pleasure, materialism, sense of struggle, success of others, failure of others, proving oneself, anxiety, wanting to fill the void, the desire to be independent, overcoming inferiority, the desire to help others, dissatisfaction, rewards, self-improvement, recognition, love, and identity.

Understanding Our Motivation

Questioning our sources of motivation helps us to understand our motivation. The list of motivational factors that follows includes both growth and deficiency sources of motivation. Deficiency motivation occurs more frequently on this list, although you should keep in mind that deficiency does not mean negative sources of motivation. Many sources of motivation are compensatory in nature. Other sources of motivation attempt to reduce tension and return the body to a state of balance through the fulfillment of needs and drives. The desire to maximize pleasure and minimize pain greatly affects human behavior. Overcoming obstacles activates motivation. Motivation is so complex that it cannot be completely reduced to a list of factors, yet many students have found this approach very useful. Most of us are motivated by factors of which we are not conscious. Obviously, we may have great difficulty in understanding our motivation.

Increasing and Sustaining Motivation

To optimize our performance, it is imperative that we increase motivation. Frequently, motivation means that we must get ourselves to do the things we don't want to do because we realize that these tasks lead to our ultimate success. Many students have difficulty with studying, yet study behavior is the basis for academic success. A major issue is encapsulated in the questions, "How can I get myself to do all the work I must do when I don't feel like doing it?"

Many of us are confused about what we want out of life, school, and relationships. When we don't know what we want out of life, we lose motivation. Setting goals, identifying what you want, and understanding your needs can do much to increase motivation. Much of what we do is governed by a desire to fulfill a need. Exploring and examining our needs can help us gain greater self-understanding which may lead to increased motivation.

Examining and understanding our needs and wants increases our motivation. Examining our motivation can help us maintain and strengthen our motivation. If we can figure out what we are driven by, we may learn to increase our motivation or re-direct our motivation.

A clear sense of who we are and what we want are the prerequisites of sustained motivation. Clarity about ourselves (who and what we are) may be difficult to achieve. Yet learning, which contributes to our self-understanding, creates a powerful motivation.

Knowing what you want · Goals
MOTIVATION
Self-Knowledge

Types of Motivation

Intrinsic Motivation

Intrinsic motivation is the performance of activities for the rewards contained within the structure of the activity. As any good non-professional athlete would agree, the pleasure derived from playing the game is greater than the result of winning the game. (Many professional athletes play for the extrinsic rewards, such as high salaries.) The feel of hitting a perfect backhand crosscourt drive in tennis is exhilarating. In other words, while it's fun to win, it's how you play the game that really counts. You can hit many good shots in tennis and still lose the match, but for dedicated tennis players, how they play the total game makes the difference in winning.

The intrinsic motivation of acquiring an education is not the culmination of an earned degree, but the process of getting to the end result. The learning experiences which incorporate value, pleasure, meaning, competency, insights, and understanding constitute the intrinsic sources of motivation.

Extrinsic Motivation

Extrinsic motivation is the drive to perform activities for a desired result. The activity may not be meaningful or pleasurable, but one is constantly aiming for the result. Studying only to achieve high marks is a type of extrinsic motivation. The tennis player who plays only to win is motivated only by extrinsic factors. The strength of the results determines our persistence in activities which are motivated by extrinsic factors. If we are motivated to achieve by extrinsic factors and fail to achieve the results we desire, the strength of our engagement in this activity will diminish.

General Motivation

Your general level of motivation is determined by your attitude and willingness to be actively involved in a broad range of activities. General levels of motivation reflect your state of being. Your general level of motivation is associated with your willingness to learn, grow, and change.

Situation-Specific Motivation

In situation-specific motivation, the characteristics of the situation significantly impact on your willingness to respond. The situation elicits your behavior. You may be willing to do things in given situations that you would not customarily do. Your situational level of motivation might indicate a willingness to read English literature in a classroom, for example, but not alone at your desk at home.

Task-Specific Motivation

The characteristics of a particular task and your perception of that task determine your motivational level as you approach the task. What you find appealing, others may not find appealing. Thus, your perception of a task determines your level of motivation in regard to that task.

Growth Motivation

Growth motivation is strongly associated with the concept of self-actualization. Self-actualization is a humanistic concept which presupposes that there is an inherent tendency in persons to become all that they are capable of becoming. Even in adverse situations and conditions, including negative relationships and during periods of turmoil, this tendency still pushes the individual toward growth. This inherent tendency pushes us toward learning, growing, and changing. We are sometimes motivated to act because of the need to be self-actualizing. When we act from the need to actualize ourselves, we are acting from a very positive force. It is this form of self-expression that leads to a sense of self-fulfillment and becomes a major source of motivation.

Factors of Growth Motivation

1. Self-Actualization

An inherent tendency exists in all of us to fulfill our potential and become all we are capable of becoming. Even in the most adverse situations, this tendency seeks expression. We always seek to move in the direction of growth and good health. The self-actualized person moves in the direction of autonomy by living a life focused on the here and now.

2. Excitement for Learning

The joy and excitement for learning is motivating. We tend to pursue and persist in activities which give us joy, excitement, and fulfillment. The acquisition of knowledge motivates many people.

3. Self-Knowledge

Knowledge of self is the basis for effective action. Increased self-knowledge creates motivation. Therefore, the ability to relate academic learning to self-knowledge becomes a powerful motivator.

4. Competence

The desire to master skills and to acquire knowledge to cultivate a sense of competence is motivating. Most of us enjoy a sense of feeling competent. Most of us want to do something well and we devote time and energy to develop that competence. When we do something competently, we feel good about ourselves.

5. Challenge

Many individuals enjoy a challenge. The thrill of overcoming obstacles can be exhilarating. Challenge keeps life interesting, provides meaning, and sustains enjoyment. Challenge frequently tests our strength and endurance. Our triumphs bring great satisfaction.

Deficiency Motivation

Many of us operate from a position of deficiency to energize ourselves into action. Some of us may respond either to great pain in our lives or to a crisis which causes us to redirect our lives. Pain is a powerful motivator and the avoidance of pain is also a powerful motivator. A great deal of human motivation derives from a desire to overcome obstacles. Fear plays an important role in motivation. Many of us are motivated by fear. Specifically, we worry about what the future holds for us. The exact source of motivation varies from individual to individual, but we are all governed by internal or external stimuli which drive us to act. Our attitudes and actions reflect our level of motivation.

Factors of Deficiency Motivation

1. Insecurity

The fear of insecurity can motivate. Insecurity drives the individual to seek security. For instance, most students see college as a key to a secure future. Psychological insecurities, such as fear, may also be substantial obstacles to motivation. Like many of the motivational factors on this list, insecurity can enhance or diminish motivation.

2. Approval

Approval from others is a strong motivational factor. We want and seek approval from others, especially from significant others. We may not be conscious of how strongly we are motivated to acquire the approval of others. Disapproval can destroy motivation.

3. Unhappiness

Some students are unhappy for many different reasons, and this forms the basis for them wanting to change their lives. They see college as the best environment in which to do this.

4. Pain/Pleasure

Pain drives many to grow and learn. Most of us want to reduce pain in our lives, and we see academic success as a means to reduce pain. Most of us pursue pleasure. Most of us want to maximize pleasure and minimize pain.

5. Materialism

Most of us also want the material rewards of our society and are willing to work hard to get them. We strongly value getting and having things. We tend to see material possession as the reward of our hard work.

6. Sense of Struggle

The struggle to overcome is the basis of motivation for many students. Students are faced with innumerable sources of conflict which create turmoil and confusion in their lives. However, excessive conflict can destroy the motivation to achieve academically.

7. Success of Others

We see others enjoying their success and we want to do the same thing. Seeing successful people motivates. Most of us want to be valued and respected by successful people. We are a very success-oriented culture, and that success is frequently measured by achievement.

8. Failure of Others

The failure of others motivates us to avoid similar disappointments. When witnessing the failure of others, we tend not to want to see ourselves in the same position. Seeing others fail is disturbing and causes us to reflect upon our own failures and deficiencies.

9. Proving Oneself

Some of us feel a strong need to prove ourself to others. We want to prove that we are capable of accomplishing our goals. Being "put down" by others is sometimes the source of wanting to prove to others our capabilities.

10. Anxiety

The desire to reduce or eliminate anxiety is a force which drives most individuals to act. Anxiety is a very uncomfortable experience, so we desire to control it through constructive and sometimes destructive means. We defend against anxiety, so that even achievement may be a response to anxiety.

11. Wanting to Fill the Void

Many of us are filled with the sense of the void. Our lives can be empty and hollow. Most of us want to fill that sense of void. A lack of self-knowledge frequently creates a void in our lives.

12. The Desire to Be Independent

Many students are caught between the dependent and independent continua of relationships. The desire to overcome dependency is a strong motivation. Most students seek to be in charge and in control of their own lives.

13. Overcoming Inferiority

Many students have a deep sense of inferiority. Feelings of inferiority are very painful. Most of us seek to overcome these painful feelings. Also, most of us who have feelings of inferiority have been misguided into this belief.

14. The Desire to Help Others

Many students see themselves as wanting to help others. They want to help people and contribute to the community. Most students are sensitive to the broad range of problems which exist in our society.

15. Dissatisfaction

All of us have numerous dissatisfactions in our lives. We seek satisfaction from our relationships and our activities. Our dissatisfactions reflect the conflicts and obstacles in our lives.

16. Rewards

Rewards come in many forms and they have a powerful effect on behavior. Most students are clearly in college for anticipated rewards. The learning process has many intrinsic rewards such as learning new skills, solving problems, and acquiring new ideas. Many of us are also motivated by extrinsic rewards such as money, approval, material objects, and prestige.

17. Self-Improvement

Many of us see ourselves as a project to be improved upon. The desire to be self- improving can be very positive, but it also has many pitfalls. Most of us cannot let go of the need to improve ourselves. We always seem determined to find a shortcoming that needs to be improved.

18. Recognition

For many of us, a life without recognition is meaningless. We want to be recognized. We feel validated and know that we exist when we are recognized. The desire to be recognized can be deeply rooted.

19. Love

All of us want to love and be loved. Love is a powerful creative force. We tend to seek certainty that others love us. We are willing to do many things to acquire the certainty of love. We feel empty and hollow when we are not loved. Many of us do our best when we feel loved.

20. Identity

Having a strong sense of who we are is motivating. Many re-entry students feel a loss of identity because of previous life roles. Many students of color feel a loss of self due to a lack of cultural and historical knowledge.

21. Fear

Most of us experience a broad range of fear, and these fears become a source of motivation. Fear is both painful and disruptive. We seek through our actions to diminish and eliminate fear. Fear underlies much of what we do.

22. Power

Many individuals feel powerless and, as a consequence, pursue power. Issues concerning power permeate their social lives. Power issues operate in all social situations. Many individuals seek personal power and power over others.

Motivational Factors Inventory

Determine the strength of each of the following motivational factors. Using the scale of 1-10, low to high, rate the strength of your motivation for each factor.

1. Self-Actualization ....Low   1 2 3 4 5 6 7 8 9 10   High

2. Excitement for Learning .... Low   1 2 3 4 5 6 7 8 9 10   High

3. Self-Knowledge ....Low   1 2 3 4 5 6 7 8 9 10   High

4. Competence ....Low   1 2 3 4 5 6 7 8 9 10   High

5. Challenge ....Low   1 2 3 4 5 6 7 8 9 10   High

6. Insecurity ....Low   1 2 3 4 5 6 7 8 9 10   High

7. Approval ....Low   1 2 3 4 5 6 7 8 9 10   High

8. Unhappiness ....Low   1 2 3 4 5 6 7 8 9 10   High

9. Pain/Pleasure .... Low   1 2 3 4 5 6 7 8 9 10   High

10. Materialism ....Low   1 2 3 4 5 6 7 8 9 10   High

11. Sense of Struggle ....Low   1 2 3 4 5 6 7 8 9 10   High

12. Success of Others ....Low   1   2   3   4   5   6   7   8   9   10   High

13. Failure of Others ....Low   1   2   3   4   5   6   7   8   9   10   High

14. Proving Oneself ....Low   1   2   3   4   5   6   7   8   9   10   High

15. Anxiety ....Low   1   2   3   4   5   6   7   8   9   10   High

16. Wanting to Fill the Void .... Low   1   2   3   4   5   6   7   8   9   10   High

17. The Desire to be Independent ....Low   1   2   3   4   5   6   7   8   9   10   High

18. Overcoming Inferiority ....Low   1   2   3   4   5   6   7   8   9   10   High

19. The Desire to Help Others .... Low   1   2   3   4   5   6   7   8   9   10   High

20. Dissatisfaction ....Low   1   2   3   4   5   6   7   8   9   10   High

21. Rewards .... Low   1   2   3   4   5   6   7   8   9   10   High

22. Self-Improvement ....Low   1   2   3   4   5   6   7   8   9   10   High

23. Recognition ....Low   1   2   3   4   5   6   7   8   9   10   High

24. Love..Low   1   2   3   4   5   6   7   8   9   10   High

25. Identity...Low   1   2   3   4   5   6   7   8   9   10   High

26. Fear ....Low   1   2   3   4   5   6   7   8   9   10   High

27. Power ....Low   1   2   3   4   5   6   7   8   9   10   High

Graphing Your Motivational Profile

After you have rated the motivational factors, graph the strength of each by filling in the appropriate space after the motivational factor.

	LOW 1	2	3	4	5	6	7	8	9	High 10
1. Self-Actualization										
2. Excitement of Learning										
3. Self-Knowledge										
4. Competence										
5. Challenges										
6. Insecurity										
7. Approval										
8. Unhappiness										
9. Pain/Pleasure										
10. Materialism										
11. Sense of Struggle										
12. Success of Others										
13. Failure of Others										
14. Proving Oneself										
15. Anxiety										
16. Wanting to Fill the Void										
17. The Desire to be Independent										
18. Overcoming Inferiority										
19. The Desire to Help Others										
20. Dissatisfaction										
21. Rewards										
22. Self-Improvement										
23. Recognition										
24. Love										
25. Identity										
26. Fear										
27. Power										

Evaluating Your Motivational Profile

1. Review your motivational profile. Identify the factors which are your greatest sources of motivation. List the factors with the highest ratings.

_____

_____

_____

_____

2. Explain why these motivational factors are significant to you.

_____

_____

_____

_____

3. List the motivational factors with the lowest ratings.

_____

_____

_____

_____

4. Explain why these motivational factors are less significant to you.

_____

_____

_____

_____

5. Review your motivational profile. What does the profile reveal to you? Are you more aware of what motivates you? Which factors work in combination to motivate you?

_____

_____

_____

_____

Have-To / Want-To Motivation

In life there are many things that we "want to" do and there are many things that we "have to" do. Usually the things that we "have to" do are not the things we enjoy doing. When we "have to" do something, we tend to feel forced or compelled to complete that activity. Most of us tend to resist doing something we are forced to do even if that force is driven from within. If we read and study the texts required in our courses, and we often read them because we "have to" and not because we "want to," we will resist learning the content of the texts. If we study only to do well on an exam and not because we enjoy the information and ideas that we are learning, our motivation may be diminished. At times we may feel compelled to study when we don't want to study and we may also do well on exams and in the course, but this sense of coercion greatly diminishes the enjoyment of learning. Many students return to college after several years of interruption to find that they are much better students because now they "want to" learn. Motivation is greatly enhanced when we do not feel forced or compelled to act.

Increasing Want-To Motivation

Motivation is increased when our actions are consistent with our desires. Motivation is impeded by obligation, force or any form of coercion. Enhancing motivation requires that we increase Want-To Motivation. Tuning into our feelings is an important guide to Want-To Motivation. When our actions are consistent with our feelings, we increase the strength of Want-To Motivation.

1. List the activities in your life that you feel you **have** to do.

_____

_____

_____

_____

2. List the activities in your life that you feel you **want** to do.

_____

_____

_____

_____

3. How often do you feel obligated or forced to do things you do not want to do?

___0-5 times a day

___6-10 times a day

___11-15 times a day

___15+ times a day

4. How can you increase the frequency of things you want to do in the course of a day?

_____

_____

_____

Assessing Your Academic Motivation

Motivation is a complex and dynamic internal state governed by desires, needs, wants, and incentives. We approach, sustain, and complete academic activities with varying degrees of desire. Our motivation varies according to the specific tasks and situations presented to us.

Assess your general level of academic motivation by listing the types of academic tasks and activities you enjoy and do not enjoy.

1. List the academic tasks and activities you enjoy.

_____   _____

_____   _____

_____   _____

2. List the academic tasks and activities you do not enjoy.

_____   _____

_____   _____

_____   _____

3. On a scale of 1 to 10, how would you rate your level of academic motivation?

   Low   1   2   3   4   5   6   7   8   9   10   High

Why?

_____

_____

_____

_____

_____

_____

The Johari Window

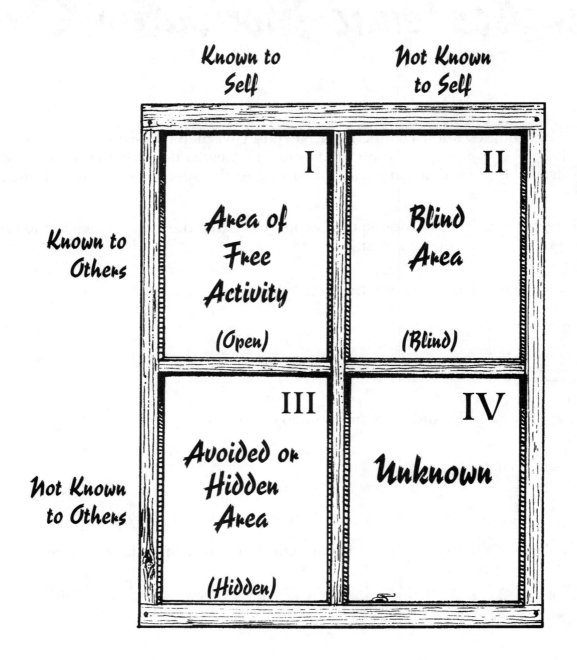

Known to Self

Not Known to Self

Known to Others

Not Known to Others

I

Area of Free Activity

(Open)

II

Blind Area

(Blind)

III

Avoided or Hidden Area

(Hidden)

IV

Unknown

A Graphic Model of Awareness, Attitudes, Communication, and Motivation

The Johari Window

The Johari Window is a model of personal awareness. It is used to conceptualize human awareness, attitudes, communication, and motivation. This graphic model illustrates the complexity of human interaction through a common object found in our experience. A window consisting of four panes illustrates types of awareness, self-perceptions, perceptions by others, and the importance of unknown factors in determining behavior. The primary goal of the Johari Window is to help you increase openness in relationships, improve communication, and increase self-awareness in interaction with others.

Each of the window panes is called a quadrant. Quadrant I refers to the area of free activity which contains factors known to self and known to others. Quadrant. II, the blind area, contains factors perceived by others of which you are unaware. Quadrant III, the avoided or hidden area, represents things you know but do not reveal to others. For example, we may have a clear knowledge of our inadequacies but conceal them from others. Finally, Quadrant IV represents the area of unknown activity. Neither you nor others are aware of certain behaviors or motives. The existence of unknown factors may be assumed because, eventually, some of these unknown factors become known. In many instances, we discover that we were unaware of our true and honest motives.

Many principles of change affect the Johari Window and the size of its quadrants. One principle states that a change in any one quadrant will affect all the other quadrants. Another principle states that energy is depleted by hiding, denying, and concealing motives and intentions which are involved in interactions. Threats affect the size of the Johari Window quadrants by decreasing openness and awareness, whereas mutual trust tends to increase awareness. Forced awareness or exposure is undesirable and usually ineffective. Interpersonal learning means a change has taken place, Quadrant I has grown larger, and one or more of the other quadrants has therefore become smaller. The more Quadrant I is increased, the more openness exists and the more the influence of covert factors is diminished.

The source of this material is a NTL publication, Human Relations Training News, 1961, 5(1), 6-7
The concept of the Johari Window is the work of Joseph Luft and Harry Ingham.
Additional information can be found in Of Human Interaction by Joseph Luft, Palo Alto, CA, National Press Books, 1969.

 *The following observations have been generated from experimenting with the Johari Window:*

Observation 1
Human interation is significantly affected by unknown factors.

Observation 2
You may not have access to those unknown factors that govern your behavior.

Observation 3
Feedback from others is critical for increasing awareness.

Observation 4
Your blind area may cause much difficulty for you and others.

Observation 5
Unknown factors are frequently the source of conflict in interpersonal relationships.

Observation 6
Your knowledge and awareness of yourself and others through interaction is always incomplete. There is always something going on that you don't know or are unaware of.

Observation 7
You can stop avoiding and hiding.

Observation 8
Constricted awareness causes conflict.

Observation 9
Expanded awareness contributes to harmony. The more aware you are, the greater the potential for harmony to exist.

Observation 10
There is much resistance and defense to increase awareness.

Observation 11
Surface unknowns may be quickly accessible.

Observation 12
Nothing magnifies a problem more than not being aware of its existence.

The Johari Window

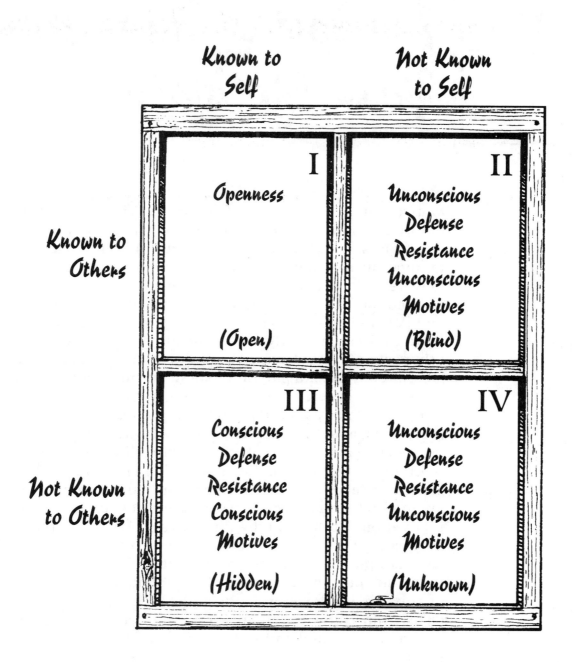

Known to
Self

Not Known
to Self

Known to
Others

Not Known
to Others

I
Openness

(Open)

II
Unconscious
Defense
Resistance
Unconscious
Motives

(Blind)

III
Conscious
Defense
Resistance
Conscious
Motives

(Hidden)

IV
Unconscious
Defense
Resistance
Unconscious
Motives

(Unknown)

A Graphic Model of Motivation

Using the Johari Window to Understand Your Motivation

Motivation is very complex. The Johari Window illustrates that our motivation is influenced by unknown factors which are hidden from self and others. (Quadrant IV) Being unaware of our motivation has major implications for self-understanding. We may never have complete knowledge of our motivation. Motives are frequently avoided, hidden, and unknown. (Quadrant II, III, and IV) Yet if we are to understand ourselves, knowledge of our motives is essential. By communicating openly and freely with others about our motives, communication and understanding is facilitated. In seeking to understand our motivation, it is useful to talk with others about what motivates us. Revealing motives that we normally hide from others may help us understand our motivation at a deeper level. Others who see us from a different perspective may see the motives we are blind to. If we can listen to others without defending and resisting, we might be able to learn more about our motivation through our interactions. There are methods and procedures which can help us access unknown motivation. Methods of dream analysis and psychotherapy can help us in understanding and uncovering unknown motivations. An example of an unknown motivation is the fear of success that some people experience. The individual may not be aware of this driving force without assistance. The Johari Window clearly illustrates that many of our motives are unknown from our view. The implication for understanding motivation is the need to be alert to unconscious motivation.

A Strategy for Increasing Motivation

Step 1. **Identify** and understand needs and wants.

Step 2. **Set** goals based on your needs and wants.

Step 3. **Identify** barriers which prevent fulfillment of needs and wants.

Step 4. **Develop** strategies to overcome barriers that prevent the fulfillment of needs and wants.

Step 5. **Develop** a powerful emotional connection to the achievement of your goals.

Step 6. **Build** self-confidence.

Step 7. **Create** a vision for your life.

Chapter Conclusion:
Critical Analysis and Application

Select a concept from this chapter which has the greatest relevance and importance to you. Explain the nature of the concept and why it is relevant and important to you. Critically analyze the concept by discussing its essential features. Determine how this concept can be applied to everyday life.

Select: _____

_____

_____

_____

_____

Explain: _____

_____

_____

_____

_____

Analyze: _____

_____

_____

_____

_____

Apply: _____

_____

_____

_____

_____

Chapter 6

Self-Esteem

Self-Esteem

Take this self-inventory by rating yourself with the following scale:

5 = This statement is true <u>all</u> of the time.

4 = This statement is true <u>most</u> of the time.

3 = This statement is true <u>much</u> of the time.

2 = This statement is true <u>some</u> of the time.

1 = This statement is true <u>almost</u> none of the time.

0 = This statement is true <u>none</u> of the time.

_____ 1. I feel good about myself.

_____ 2. I am clear about who I am.

_____ 3. I am aware of how I feel.

_____ 4. I am a confident person.

_____ 5. I assume 100% responsibility for myself.

_____ 6. I have a strong need to achieve.

_____ 7. It is my own decision to be in college.

_____ 8. I have few self doubts.

_____ 9. I fear failure.

_____ 10. I fear success.

_____ 11. I feel academically competent.

_____ 12. I enjoy speaking in class.

_____ 13. I do not feel inferior to other students.

_____ 14. I am shy.

_____ 15. I feel attractive to the opposite sex.

_____ 16. I like my body image.

_____ 17. I avoid drugs.

_____ 18. I seldom doubt my self-worth.

_____ 19. I feel safe and secure in most situations.

_____ 20. I am proud of myself and my accomplishments.

_____ 21. I have high self-esteem when I'm in a love relationship.

Self-Responsibility

Self-Acceptance

SELF-ESTEEM

Self-Knowledge

So much is a man worth as he esteems himself.
—*Rabelais*

The Self-Esteem Triad

The Self-Esteem Triad contains the critical ingredients which support and sustain self-esteem. It consists of Self-Knowledge, Self-Responsibility, and Self-Acceptance.

The first principle factor which contributes to self-esteem is self-knowledge. Self-knowledge is the foundation for high self-esteem. When individuals find themselves immersed in multiple conflicts, self-esteem is diminished. Without self-knowledge it is difficult to resolve conflicts. Without the resolution of conflicts, it is difficult to maintain positive self-esteem. High self-esteem requires manageable levels of conflict.

The second principle factor which contributes to self-esteem is self-responsibility. Assuming responsibility greatly enhances the individual's capacity to solve problems and reduce and eliminate conflict. This capacity significantly contributes to positive self-esteem. When the individual takes one hundred percent responsibility for his/her experience, a tremendous amount of control over one's life is generated.

The third principle factor contributing to self-esteem is self-acceptance. High levels of self-acceptance sustain positive levels of self-esteem. Self-esteem fluctuates greatly during the course of a day if it is not anchored to a strong sense of self-acceptance. Self-acceptance derives from self-knowledge and when we assume responsibility for that self-knowledge, self acceptance is promoted. Self-acceptance may also mean accepting the unacceptable in ourselves.

Factors of The Self-Esteem Triad

Self-Knowledge

Self-knowledge is the basis of effective action. Self-knowledge involves the harmonious integration of thoughts, feelings, and actions. Self-knowledge is the foundation of knowing what we want and forms the basis for setting goals. The process of coming to know self is the most human of all activities because only humans reflect on who they are, where they come from and where they are going. The development of self-knowledge is the basis of meaningful and positive action.

There are specific steps that we can take which can contribute to the development of self-knowledge. The most immediate action that we can take is to cultivate self-awareness. Without expanding self-awareness our self-knowledge will always be limited. Self-knowledge implies knowing ourselves at different levels, at different depths, experiences, and dimensions. We may have a superficial knowledge of self or we may have a profound knowledge of self. In-depth knowledge of self involves knowing our true, honest, authentic, and real selves.

Deciding to know ourselves at a deeper level initiates a journey toward self-discovery. Although others cannot show us how we can come to know ourselves, they can provide landmarks which indicate whether we are on course.

 Perhaps the most valuable result of all education is the ability to make yourself do the thing you have to do, when it ought to be done, whether you like it or not; it is the first lesson that ought to be learned; and however early a man's training begins, it is probably the last lesson that he learns thoroughly.

— Thomas Huxley

Self-Responsibility

I am totally responsible for my experience. I am responsible for what I say and do. I *own* what I say, and I am accountable for what I do. I am not responsible for your experience, although I am aware that I can affect your experience. You are not responsible for my experience, although what you do affects my experience. I am in a relationship with you; I am responsible for my problems; you are responsible for your problems. I own my problems; you own your problems. We may choose to help each other solve our mutual problems. But I can't help you solve your problems by owning your problems. Through dialogue, we may be able to help each other in our solution of problems.

Self-Acceptance

Self-acceptance is a constellation of positive self-attitudes which nurture and support our sense of value and purpose. Self-acceptance is an attitude of comfort, security and ease about who and what we are. Self-acceptance is an approval of what we feel and think about ourselves.

Self-acceptance is a harmonious integration of thoughts and feelings about ourselves. The most vital aspect of self-acceptance is compassion. Compassion for ourselves allows us to accept the things about ourselves that we do not like. Compassion allows us to be human.

Much of our capacity to love and accept ourselves has its basis in the family. Many individuals do not feel that they were truly loved and accepted by their families. As a consequence, they grow up feeling unworthy and not deserving of love and acceptance. This feeling of unworthiness may persist throughout a person's life. Families that communicate love and acceptance to all members promote a sense of worthiness that may contribute to self-love and acceptance.

People do not love and accept themselves for many reasons. Self-love and acceptance are attitudes which are the result of learning. Many of us are well instructed in self-hatred. The lessons of self-hatred and rejection are multiple and varied. The lessons are the negative responses we receive from others that make us feel unworthy. Social life provides us with many opportunities to hate ourselves. We continuously process our life experience, and the conclusions and interpretations we make become an essential part of how we view ourselves. We can view ourselves as worthy of love and acceptance or unworthy of love and acceptance. Without a sense of worth, life is a burden and something to get through without much fulfillment and enjoyment. Cultivating our sense of self-worth and acceptance is something we must do consciously and continuously. To be surrounded by people who love and support you is fortunate. This love and support contributes to a sense of self-worth and acceptance.

Self-Worth

Self-worth is determined by the appraisals we make of ourselves and the appraisals others make of us. In assessing our self-worth, it is important to determine the extent to which we rely on others to determine our sense of self-worth. A strong reliance on others always leaves us vulnerable. The frequency and quality of experiences which make us feel worthwhile protect us against threats to our self-worth. It is important to be vigilant in regard to the ways we devalue ourselves and in the ways we are devalued by others. The exploration of issues pertinent to how self-worth is maintained and enhanced furthers our understanding of this internal process. All of us protect ourselves against threats to our self-worth. The centrality of self-worth in determining levels of self-esteem requires a close examination in order to understand how we can increase our self-esteem.

Sources of Self-Worth

Individuals maintain and enhance their sense of self-worth in numerous ways. Many feel worthwhile because they adhere to their values and standards. Others look to their accomplishments and talents. Some individuals derive their sense of self-worth from the way they respond to and manage challenges. Many of us feel worthwhile because of the feedback we receive from friends and family. Many individuals recognize the importance of good relationships in determining a sense of self-worth. Loving and being loved is perhaps the most significant way we maintain self-worth. When others need us, we feel worthwhile. When we love others, we also feel worthwhile.

Self-Esteem

> It is a great mistake to fancy oneself greater than one is, and to value oneself at less than one is worth.
>
> — Goethe

Many problems of a personal nature which we encounter invariably embody issues of self-esteem. More than any other factor, self-worth is related to our self-esteem. Worthiness issues come up in our daily experiences and interactions with others. Frequently our sense of self-worth is confronted or challenged. Some of us may need to evaluate how we feel and how we derive our sense of value on a continual basis. For many, it does not take much to activate feelings of doubt, confusion, and self-hate when interacting with others.

Being in Charge

Real self-esteem is built on a foundation of truthfulness about who and what we are. A central issue in achieving and maintaining positive levels of self-esteem focuses on the principle of being in control of one's life. Being in charge of our lives through active decision-making and assuming responsibility for our lives is essential for high levels of self-esteem.

Thinking and Self-Esteem

To a large extent, how we think determines how we feel, and how we think and feel determine how we act. A careful examination of our self-concept can do much to increase our level of self-esteem. How we think about ourselves determines whether we see ourselves as worthy or unworthy. Learning to accept ourselves is the principal process by which we maintain adequate levels of self-esteem. The process for increasing self-esteem includes increasing self-awareness, self-knowledge, self-understanding, and self-acceptance.

Realistic Self-Respect

Self-esteem is realistic self-respect derived from favorable self-impressions and positive impressions from others which contribute to our sense of self-worth. Many people lack self-esteem when confronted with diffi-

cult and unpredictable circumstances, events, conditions, experiences, and people. A lack of self-esteem stems from a conscious or unconscious decision not to value oneself.

Causes of Low Self-Esteem

Most causes of low self-esteem generally fall into three major areas: negative past experiences, living in an environment that does not support positive self-esteem, and habitual ways of thinking which do not foster self-worth. Early family experiences may lay the foundation for a life-long struggle with issues of self-esteem. Parents may inadvertently instill a sense of worthlessness in their children by the way they talk to them, treat them, and the expectations they have for them. Unfortunately, people often trap themselves in situations and conditions reminiscent of childhood which sustain their sense of worthlessness. It is easy to view ourselves negatively when everything around us conveys messages of low self-worth. All the people and situations whom we contact and encounter in our daily routine, whether on the job, at home, or in our personal lives may hinder or support our sense of self-worth. It is also difficult to change our habitual ways of thinking. Getting a handle on negative self-perceptions associated with negative thinking requires diligent effort.

Self-esteem supports our emotional and psychological well-being. The maintenance of self-esteem is crucial for a happy and fulfilling life. One should never underestimate the importance of self-esteem.

How to Nurture Self-Esteem

The California Task Force on Self-Esteem has identified the following factors which nurture self-esteem:

1. Accepting Ourselves

Self-acceptance derives from an honest look at and appraisal of ourselves. Self-acceptance requires an examination of everything we have been taught about ourselves, and the conclusions we have drawn from those experiences regarding our acceptability. Self-acceptance is the result of deep self-understanding. Seeing ourselves as human with all the faults and frailties that most of us have can help us become more self-accepting. Our humanness can be an additional basis for accepting ourselves.

2. Setting Realistic Expectations

Expecting too little does not dignify our human spirit. And expecting too much steals the joy and excitement from our achievements. Knowing and altering expectations determines our peak of happiness and depth of disappointment. Being conscious of our expectations allows us to know how we enter situations, and how we are affected by our expectations.

3. Forgiving Ourselves

To forgive means to stop resenting. When we let go of resentment toward others and ourselves, we are able to live constructively in the present. Forgiving releases us from the burden of hostility that eats away at our energy and self-esteem. Accepting forgiveness from others likewise allows us to move on with our lives.

4. Taking Risks

The fulfillment of our potential requires risk. Unless we try new behavior, we may limit ourselves or get stuck in the familiar. Growth requires risk, and risk produces change. Successful risking produces self-confidence.

5. Trusting Ourselves and Others

Trusting others begins with trusting ourselves. Trusting ourselves, our judgment, and our competence inspires others to trust themselves. Trust usually involves risk, and frequently the risk is worth the growth from trusting others. Trusting others is related to our sense of vulnerability. The more vulnerable we are, the less trusting we are.

6. Expressing Our Feelings

Nothing is more important than sharing our state of being. We do this through the expression of our feelings. The expression of honest and real feelings creates the conditions for love and intimacy. Authentic expression of feelings allows others to know us, and we also come to know ourselves. Most problems of self-esteem which cannot be resolved are due to being stuck at the feeling level. We can only resolve human problems by resolving the conflict of feelings.

7. Appreciating Our Creativity

Our creativity is manifested in many different ways. We can be creative in how we handle our daily affairs and encounters. Creativity is usually an expression of our own unique style. Being creative means finding new ways to handle old problems. We can nurture and cultivate our creative impulses. Creativity involves new ways of thinking, feeling and acting.

8. Appreciating Our Spiritual Being

Cultivating a daily sense of the spiritual by recognizing the universal nature of man gives us a sense of belonging. Seeking the transcendent by developing multiple levels of consciousness is an activity which anyone may pursue, regardless of religious preference. By living in the "here and now," we may discover the spiritual foundation of life.

9. Appreciating Our Minds

The mind carries on an internal dialogue with itself. It seems that the mind has a mind of its own. The thoughts we think determine our experience of self. Negative thoughts create negative experiences, and positive thoughts create positive experiences. We can learn to monitor our self-talk and to encourage the thoughts that lead to positive self-esteem.

10. Appreciating Our Bodies

Most of us struggle with accepting our bodies. We are bombarded by the media with images of perfect bodies and told we can have the same result by using the right product. We need to develop a more realistic and a more human standard for our bodies. Perfectionism readily destroys an appreciation for our bodies and our worth.

11. Taking Responsibility for Our Decisions and Actions

Taking responsibility for ourselves means taking responsibility for our thoughts, decisions, feelings, reactions, and actions. When we take complete responsibility for our lives we do not blame others for our misery and unhappiness. We are highly conscious of our responsibility for our feelings. Ultimately, others do not determine how we feel. Through our actions, we decide the course our lives will take. We "own up" to our decisions and actions.

12. Being a Person of Integrity

Living with integrity is essential to valuing ourselves. One important aspect of integrity is being honest in our dealings with other people, which requires being honest with ourselves. Having integrity means being congruent in thoughts, feelings, and actions. We are what we seem to be. People of integrity are in touch with their humanity and the humanity of others.

13. Understanding and Affirming Our Values

Understanding our values comes from examining our values, knowing their source of origin and deciding whether we want to adhere to those values. Our values are not the best values, but they are "our" values. When we affirm our values, we do not impose them upon others. Being conscious of personal and cultural values and how they differ helps us know what we value. We need to understand, also, what our culture embraces as a value. Values give structure and form to our lives and help us achieve a meaningful existence.

14. Attending to Our Physical Health

Our self-esteem is significantly influenced by our degree of physical health. A sense of wellness promotes an enthusiasm about life and its challenges. We need to take responsibility for our physical health. Most of us need to consider a personal program which promotes and sustains our health. We need to be concerned about nutrition, exercise, and especially the adverse affects of stress.

15. Developing Basic Skills

The kinds of skills we possess and develop greatly affect our quality of life. Communication skills impact all aspects of our lives. Our ability to read, write, and speak is continuously shaping our experience.

16. Serving Humanity

Persons with healthy self-esteem choose to serve others out of their sense of personal fullness and their joy of being alive. In the process of serving, they deepen and reinforce their own self-esteem. By recognizing how inter-related and inter-connected we are with others, we begin to see the value in serving and committing ourselves to the care of others.

Self-Esteemometer

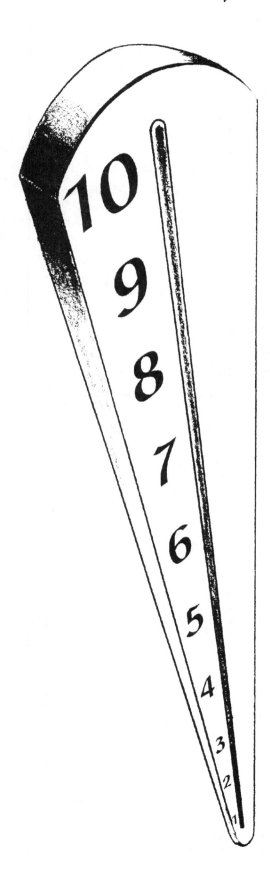

What are the daily changes on your self-esteemometer?

Have you observed that your self-esteem fluctuates daily?

Have you noticed that your self-esteem changes moment to moment?

Did you know that levels of self-esteem are related to levels of self-worth?

On a scale of 1 to 10 degrees, what is your level of self-esteem today?

Assessing Your Self-Esteem

Look at the self-esteemometer. What is your level of self-esteem?

You can assess your level of self-esteem by using the following method:

1. **Assess** your self-esteem for a period of two weeks.

2. **Rate** your self-esteem on a scale of 1 to 10, low to high. Rate your level 4 times a day: morning, midday, early evening, and night.

3. **Record** your estimates for the time period.

4. **Calculate** the average of each day in your 14 day monitoring period.

5. **Calculate** a total average for the 14 day assessment period.

Self-Esteem Chart

DAY	Date	MORNING	MIDDAY	EARLY EVENING	NIGHT	AVERAGE
1						
2						
3						
4						
5						
6						
7						
8						
9						
10						
11						
12						
13						
14						
					TOTAL AVERAGE	

Self-Esteem Chart Analysis

Review your self-esteemometer chart.

1. Do you recognize any patterns between the time of day and your self-esteem rating?

_____

_____

_____

2. When is your self-esteem lowest? _____

_____

_____

_____

3. When is it moderate? _____

_____

_____

_____

4. When is it high? _____

_____

_____

_____

5. Do you see a relationship between activities, time of day, and level of self-esteem?

_____

_____

_____

6. What activities are occurring when ratings are low, moderate, and high? _____

_____

_____

_____

Self-Esteem Results

For the purpose of this exercise, average estimates of 1 to 4 may be considered low self-esteem, 5 to 7 moderate self-esteem, and 8 to 10 high self-esteem. Remember that your moment to moment feelings can significantly affect your estimations of levels of self-esteem. You could be having a fantastic assessment period. You could be having a bad assessment period. This could be reflected on your total average estimation of your self-esteem. If you think that the fourteen days you used for your assessment period is truly representative of your state of being, you could consider this evaluation somewhat accurate in depicting your level of self-esteem.

1. If you scored in the high range of self-esteem, what do you think is contributing to your high level of self-esteem?

_____

_____

2. If you scored at the moderate range of self-esteem, what factors are sustaining this level?

_____

_____

3. If you scored at the low range of self-esteem, what factors are contributing to this level?

_____

_____

4. Do you think that the results of this exercise are an accurate indicator of your level of self-esteem? Why? Why not?

_____

_____

If you feel your level of self-esteem needs further evaluation, review the following:

1. The Triad of Self-Esteem
2. The Self-Esteem Pre-Chapter Inventory
3. How to Nurture Self-Esteem
4. The Strategy for Developing Self-Esteem

For further assistance in evaluating self-esteem, speak with a school counselor.

A Strategy for Developing Self-Esteem

1. Develop self-knowledge and self-awareness.
Increasing and expanding self-knowledge forms the basis for sustained positive levels of self-esteem.

2. Make a conscious decision to value yourself.
Actively deciding that you have self-worth will increase self-esteem.

3. Combat negative thinking.
Challenge negative ideas and assumptions about yourself. Do not allow negative self-thinking to go unchallenged.

4. Do what you want to do.
Doing what you want to do is the foundation for satisfaction and happiness in life.

5. Take responsibility for your life experience.
We are one hundred percent responsible for ourselves.

6. Cultivate self-acceptance.
Through self-acceptance, we establish our worth. Our sense of self-worth sustains self-esteem.

7. Act responsibly towards others.
How we regard others is inversely related to how we regard ourselves. A high regard for others supports a high regard for self.

8. Maintain positive relationships.
It is through relationships that we establish our worth. Others have a profound impact on how we regard ourselves.

9. Find a listener.
When others listen to us, we discover who we are and we find the resources to solve our own problems.

10. Pursue the transcendent.
The pursuit of that which transcends ordinary, everyday life experience is the foundation of many religious traditions. Search for that which is greater than you, whatever you choose to call it.

Chapter Conclusion:
Critical Analysis and Application

Select a concept from this chapter which has the greatest relevance and importance to you. Explain the nature of the concept and why it is relevant and important to you. Critically analyze the concept by discussing its essential features. Determine how this concept can be applied to everyday life.

Select: _____

_____

_____

_____

_____

Explain: _____

_____

_____

_____

_____

Analyze: _____

_____

_____

_____

_____

Apply: _____

_____

_____

_____

_____

Chapter 7

Self-Knowledge

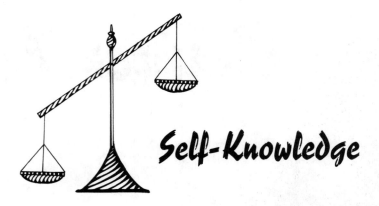

Self-Knowledge

Take this self-inventory by rating yourself with the following scale:

5 = This statement is true <u>all</u> of the time.
4 = This statement is true <u>most</u> of the time.
3 = This statement is true <u>much</u> of the time.
2 = This statement is true <u>some</u> of the time.
1 = This statement is true <u>almost</u> none of the time.
0 = This statement is true <u>none</u> of the time.

_____ 1. I know who I am.

_____ 2. I know where I come from.

_____ 3. I know where I'm going.

_____ 4. I know myself.

_____ 5. I know what I want.

_____ 6. I know my values.

_____ 7. I know my attitudes.

_____ 8. I am aware and in touch with my motivations.

_____ 9. I am conscious of my social and political attitudes.

_____ 10. I am aware of my behavior in most situations.

Knowing where you come from

Knowing where you are going

SELF-KNOWLEDGE

Knowing where you are

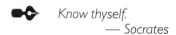 *Know thyself.*
— Socrates

The Self-Knowledge Triad

The Self-Knowledge Triad consists of Knowing where you are, Knowing where you come from and Knowing where you are going. Knowing where you are requires the greatest degree of introspection and self-analysis. It can be a difficult task to figure how you got to where you are. Clarity about where you are necessitates knowledge of where you come from. Knowing where you're going requires a clear knowledge of where you are and where you come from. The starting point in any personal journey is knowing where you are. It is very difficult to get to the other side of the river if you don't know what riverbank you're standing on. Self-knowledge requires a processing of knowledge and experiences about our past, our present, and our projections into the future. The development of self-knowledge is the principal task of life and without self-knowledge, our decisions may take us astray.

Factors of The Self-Knowledge Triad

Knowing Where You Are

Knowing where you are is the starting point towards self-knowledge. You clarify where you are by using The Self-Awareness Triad. You can get in touch, pay attention and reflect on yourself to increase awareness of where you are. You may want to get in touch, pay attention, and reflect on thoughts, feelings and reactions. Where you are reflects your drives, aspirations, hopes, attitudes, and many other factors which indicate where you are today in your life.

Knowing Where You Come From

Knowing where you come from includes personal, family, and group history. Family history plays a central role in understanding where we come from, and personal history occurs within a context of a family. The place, work, events, and personality characteristics of our families influence who we are and where we come from. The history of our racial and ethnic background defines where we come from and who we are. We learn that the past influences our present and may even determine the course of our lives.

Knowing Where You Are Going

Knowing where you are going is enhanced through awareness of the present. It is difficult to decide where to go when you do not know where you are and where you come from. Knowledge of these two factors helps us set our course. Planning for the future based on clarity of the past and present will greatly influence our direction and who we will become.

Self-Knowledge through Self-Discovery

SELF-KNOWLEDGE
Knowing where you are

 Men can starve from a lack of self-realization as much as they can from a lack of bread.
— *Richard Wright*

The magnitude and depth of the human mind is illustrated by the Hindu view of the mind as consisting of yet to be discovered continents.

> ***Hinduism sees the mind's hidden continents as stretching to infinity. Infinite in being, infinite in awareness, there is nothing beyond them that remains unknown.***
>
> **–Huston Smith**

These dimensions of the mind are depicted in the Freudian view which compares the mind to the form of an iceberg, most of which lies below the level of consciousness. The journey toward self-discovery involves the exploration of the deepest recesses of our minds. We take a mental journey into our past to recall experiences that have had an important effect on who we are and what we have become. We discover who we are when we uncover real desires, wants, and intentions that have been buried for a long time. We discover who we are in the present moment as we get in touch with our thoughts, feelings, and reactions. We invent ourselves daily through our interpretations of who we are and where we come from. Self-discovery is enhanced when we examine the history of our racial, ethnic, and social groups. By examining our sex roles and our families, we discover who we are. We create who we are by seeing ourselves engaged in a process of becoming. We create a new self by growing and changing. We realize that who we are is unfolding. We affirm our discoveries of who we are as others attempt to define us according to their designs. We are constantly defining ourselves, adding to our view of ourselves, and re-interpreting our experiences in determining who we are.

Self-discovery is a learning process which involves becoming more self-aware, getting in touch with feelings, changing old beliefs and values, trying new things, taking risks, setting goals, and changing the direction of our lives. Self-discovery is a present-centered process facilitated by a "here and now" focus. The route of self-discovery is usually arduous and frequently associated with pain.

The process of self-discovery allows us to seek new insights and greater understandings of how we have arrived at our place in life and to discover what possibilities are available to set new courses and directions.

The Journey toward Self-Knowledge and Success

The Journey toward Self-Knowledge and Success begins with **self-awareness.** Self-Knowledge is initiated and enhanced by increasing levels of awareness. We tend to function within the context of our present level of awareness. Self-awareness can be cultivated through a variety of methods. Awareness practice is the major technique advocated in this text. We are capable of becoming more self-aware. Self-awareness is the basis for the development of self-knowledge. We need to be aware of our thoughts, feelings, and reactions in order to increase self-knowledge.

Self-knowledge is a quest, a journey, an adventure. It involves taking risks in order to learn more about ourselves. When we risk, we choose to face fears and not simply to settle for safety. Self-knowledge is enhanced and developed by life experiences, relationships and interactions, maintaining an introspective attitude, the willingness to learn about ourselves, and a conscious effort to grow and change.

Self-understanding is the foundation of self-acceptance. If I do not understand myself, how can I accept myself? Similar to self-awareness, there are many methods that help us become more self-understanding. The learning process, as illustrated by The Self Knowledge Cycle, presents a major method for becoming more self-understanding.

The deeper our understanding of self, the more likely we are to accept ourselves. Self-awareness, self-knowledge, and self-understanding is the foundation for **self-acceptance.** When we do not accept ourselves, we need to look at the three preceding stages that lead to self-acceptance. When we lack self-awareness, self-knowledge, and self-understanding, we tend not to accept ourselves. The cultivation of each of these processes produces significant degrees of self-acceptance.

Self-acceptance is the basis for sustained positive levels of **self-esteem.** Self-esteem is variable when it is not anchored to high degrees of self-acceptance. Self-acceptance establishes our concept of our worth. Our worth is the basis of self-esteem.

Self-esteem is related to **performance.** When we feel good about ourselves, we tend to feel confident, competent, and capable of doing things well. A confident attitude significantly affects how we perform. A feeling of "I can do it" fills a person who has high self-esteem. Self-esteem and performance have a reciprocal affect. The better I perform, the more confident I feel, and the more confident I feel, the better I perform. Performance is the foundation of success.

High levels of performance result in **success.** What can you do, and how well can you do it? Our society is establishing higher and higher performance standards in all aspects of life.

Success is the culmination of all our efforts to be self-aware, self-knowing, self-understanding, self-accepting, self-esteeming, and performing at optimum levels. Success is a psychological state of being which results from self-knowledge.

The Self-Knowledge and Success Model

1. Self-Awareness

Self-awareness is the first step in any growth process. Increased self-awareness leads to increased self-knowledge. It is nearly impossible to increase self-knowledge without first increasing self-awareness.

2. Self-Knowledge

Self-knowledge is enhanced by the awareness process. The greater the scope of the awareness of self, the greater the degrees of self-knowledge. Self-knowledge is developed by applying The Self-Knowledge Cycle to one's life.

3. Self-Understanding

The more we know ourselves the more we understand ourselves. Self-awareness and self-knowledge are the foundations of self-understanding. Self-understanding is the precursor of self-acceptance.

4. Self-Acceptance

Self-understanding is the basis for self-acceptance. We need to understand the self we are to accept. The three preceding stages form the basis for self-acceptance. You need to be aware, know, and understand the self you are to accept.

5. Self-Esteem

Self-acceptance is the basis of self-esteem. Our self-worth is largely derived from self-acceptance, which results in high levels of self-esteem.

6. Performance

High performers know who they are. Self-esteem is directly related to performance. We need to have the confidence derived from high self-esteem to perform at high levels.

7. Success

Success is the result of the development of the preceding stages.

The Self-Knowledge Cycle

1. Self-Awareness

Self-knowledge begins with increasing self-awareness. Awareness of thoughts, feelings, and reactions facilitates the disclosure of these experiences. Access to our internal process through awareness allows the disclosure of that inner process.

2. Self-Disclosure

Revealing our internal reactions helps us in understanding our inner life more fully. When others know us through our self-disclosures, we begin to know ourselves more completely. Self-disclosure is the cornerstone of self-knowledge.

3. Interpersonal Feedback

When others give us feedback about the impact we have on them, they are giving us important information about our behavior. Feedback from various individuals helps define who we are.

4. Self-Exploration

Using feedback from others to explore our thoughts, feelings, and reactions facilitates our growth. Self-exploration is a means by which we come to know ourselves better. Self-exploration is important in promoting growth.

5. Experimentation

We can experiment with new behaviors resulting from increased knowledge derived from interpersonal feedback and self-exploration. Through experimentation we can determine what works for us and what does not work for us.

6. Behavioral Feedback

We not only receive feedback from others but from our behavior. We can determine what feels right for us.

7. Self-Awareness

We have come full circle. Now you can continue the process. Through increased self-awareness, we can determine if we have changed and whether we are growing. Increased self-awareness increases our level of functioning. Self-awareness is the foundation of self-knowledge.

Empowering Activity 5

Awareness is

pure
non-judgemental
deep
infinite
finite
blocked
limited
unlimited
choiceless
repressed
expanded
contracted
personal
transpersonal
individual
ordinary
non-ordinary
extraordinary
collective
verbal
non-verbal
sensory
inclusive of thought
exclusive of thought
freedom
universal

SELF-AWARENESS
Getting in Touch

The test of a civilized person is first self-awareness, and then depth after depth of sincerity in self-confrontation.
—Clarence Day

The Self-Awareness Triad

The Self-Awareness Triad consists of getting in touch, attention, and reflection. It is remarkable how we can get out of touch with ourselves.

Psychologically, we can make aspects of ourselves not exist. An example of this is the denial of feelings which exist, but which are removed from conscious awareness. Increasing the degree and level of self-awareness necessitates a greater degree of access to our experience. This means that we need to get in touch with a greater range and level of personal experience. In the process of getting in touch with ourselves, we also have to pay attention to ourselves. We pay attention to what we sense, feel, think, and do. As we pay greater attention to our experience, we also reflect on our experience. Through reflection, we are able to make sense of our experience, assess our experience, and see ourselves from a different viewpoint. Reflection is a type of contemplation—we think about our experience.

Increased self-awareness brings deeper meanings into our experience which we pay attention to and reflect upon. Greater self-awareness brings insight into the nature of who we are and what we are.

Factors of The Self-Awareness Triad

Getting in Touch

Getting in touch is the process of interacting with others, and becoming conscious and aware of what you feel. When you get in touch with your real feelings, self-awareness becomes enhanced.

The most immediate action we can take to increase self-awareness is to bring ourselves into the present. Awareness of the "here and now" increases self-awareness. The concrete and immediate reality of our experience is the present. The past and the future are abstractions. We expand our awareness when we notice where our attention is focused. We become conscious of our awareness.

Attention

Awareness of the "here and now" is the foundation of awareness. Our consciousness of the present moment greatly enhances our awareness of the "here and now." Awareness of the "here and now" requires our attention. Our attention in the "here and now" requires a focus which is concentrated.

Reflection

Reflection is a mental process of looking back into ourselves in order to derive new meanings, insights, and understandings about the significance of our experience. Reflective periods in our lives are usually quiet, solitary, and thoughtful. Reflection encourages growth, change, and coming to terms with conflicts which pull us in different directions. Reflection increases sensitivity to our internal process, and furthers an expansion of our awareness. Reflection is mental work on ourselves. Reflective moments are used to seek answers to perplexing problems and questions.

The Here and Now

SELF-AWARENESS
Getting in Touch

We only have the present, and it is essential that we live in the present. We live in the present by being fully aware of what is happening within us and around us at the moment in which we find ourselves. In actuality, we cannot live outside and apart from the present, but we can lose sight of the present by a narrowing of our attention and awareness. We can focus on the past by remembering the past through memory, but a memory of the past is not the past. The past is an experience of the present working through the abstracting process of the mind. The past is simply an abstraction and not a present reality.

The more concrete, non-abstract, "here and now", and the more in touch with immediate reality you are, the more you live in the real world. This is what being "here and now" means. You are not stuck in your imagination, fantasy, or memory. You are here. The immediate reality of your experience is missed when you are stuck in your mind. To be "here and now" means you are fully present.

When you are "here and now," you stop resisting experiences that are present with you. For example, when you stay in the "here and now," you may notice a deep sense of loneliness. If you are always abstracting, if you are in your head, if you are always planning, it is a way of keeping yourself from being in touch with your loneliness. Avoiding what we are never solves our problems. It only perpetuates them. You cannot work through painful experiences without being present with those experiences.

It is characteristic of high level functioning people that they live in the here and now. Being centered in the present allows us to focus, attend, and concentrate with greater acuity.

Self-Awareness

The development of self-awareness affects all levels of human functioning. Self-awareness is expanded by the learning process, and the learning process is enhanced by self-awareness. We need to be conscious of ourselves, of others, and of the world around us. We need to cultivate the capacity to attend to our physical, mental, and emotional life. Self-awareness is being in touch with your existence. Self-awareness implies that you are in touch with your thoughts, feelings and reactions. Self-awareness is the foundation of self-knowledge. You cannot know yourself if you are not aware of the self you are to know. Our level of self-awareness determines our level of functioning.

Focused Attention

Awareness is where I have my attention right now. Self-awareness is being in tune with myself and with other people's actions and reactions. Self-awareness means I fully recognize myself as I am. We defend ourselves by making ourselves less aware. A lack of self-awareness produces conflict and hampers human functioning.

Levels of Awareness

Self-awareness means that we are in touch with ourselves. Self-awareness is multi-dimensional and multi-leveled. We are not in touch with all levels of our experience. We exclude aspects of our experience from our awareness of ourselves. Usually we exclude experience from our consciousness without knowing we have done so, and these experiences are usually experiences of pain. We resist being more self-aware. Many thoughts and feelings are intolerable and unacceptable to us. Therefore, we may attempt to exclude them from conscious awareness. Whenever we exclude thoughts and feelings from our conscious awareness, we develop adverse effects, such as depression. We all tend to resist who and what we are. Resistance may prevent us from coming face to face with our world.

Self-awareness is the vehicle by which we come to know ourselves. Self-awareness means that you are conscious of your being. Self-awareness means that you are in contact, with your thoughts, feelings, reactions, surroundings, sensations, body, your immediate reality, and the totality of your experience.

Unknown Factors

Our behavior is always being influenced by unknown factors. We function more effectively the more we are capable of making unknown factors known. When you lack self-awareness, it can mean that you are unable to sort out how you feel about given situations, surroundings, and relationships. If you are not self-aware, it can thwart your ability to know what you want. If you lack self-awareness, it may mean that, at a gut level, you don't know where you stand with issues, problems, or people. When your awareness is constricted or limited, you may have a deep sense of being confused or lost.

Clarity and Focus

Increased self-awareness brings clarity and focus. It allows you to perceive issues, situations, surroundings and relationships more accurately. The more self-aware you are, the more mindful you are, the more conscious you are of what you perceive, feel, and do. The more self-aware you are, the more socially conscious you are.

The development of self-awareness is of far-reaching importance. You alone maintain a measure of control over your level of self-awareness. It is important to know that you will function according to your level of self-awareness. Therefore, if your level of self-awareness is limited, your ability to function is limited.

Using the Johari Window to Increase Self-Awareness

Unknown factors of human awareness have a powerful affect on our behavior. The Johari Window clearly illustrates the magnitude of these factors. To become more self-aware, it is imperative to address the unkown factors which influence awareness. Making the unknown known will increase awareness and will help us gain greater control over our behavior. We are frequently out of touch with our bodies, feelings, motives, and attitudes. Therefore, an increased awareness of our bodies, feelings, motives, and attitudes helps us function more fully. A lack of self-awareness is debilitating; an increase in self-awareness is liberating.

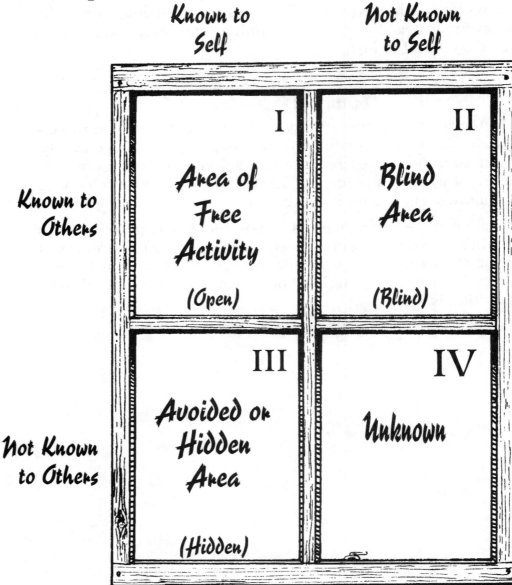

Known to Self / Not Known to Self

I — Known to Others — Area of Free Activity (Open)

II — Blind Area (Blind)

III — Not Known to Others — Avoided or Hidden Area (Hidden)

IV — Unknown

A Graphic Model of Personal and Interpersonal Awareness

Awareness Practice

Awareness practice is a method that increases your level of functioning by increasing your level of awareness. Self-awareness is a major part of how we function, and self-awareness can be cultivated and developed through awareness practice. Awareness practice can help you access more energy. Awareness practice is a way of looking inside and outside yourself.

Most methods of awareness practice are concerned with noticing where your attention is focused. Where is your attention now? As your attention drifts, bring it back to the concrete and immediate reality of your experience, bring it back to the here and now.

Awareness practice cultivates a type of mindfulness. This method emphasizes awareness of mind as opposed to figuring out your mind. Awareness practice often leads to valuable insights, which in turn lead to greater understanding. Increases in awareness, insight, and understanding all lead to an increased level of functioning.

Note: Awareness practice cannot be practiced every conscious moment of the day. The amount of practice you do will be determined by the degree and quality of your experience generated by awareness practice. You may want to intensify your practice during periods of intense conflict. Awareness practice can be done as you interact with others. Notice where your attention is focused.

The Method of
Awareness Practice

Step 1. **Stop** and become conscious of where your attention is focused. What is the object of your attention?

Step 2. **Watch** the activity of your mind. What are you thinking about? Are you in the here and now? Or, are you remembering past events?

Step 3. **Allow** the activity of your mind. Witness the activity of your mind.

Step 4. **Bring** your attention to the immediate concrete reality of your experience, the here and now.

Step 5. **Focus** attention on the here and now. When your attention drifts away from the here and now, allow it to drift for a few moments, and then gently but firmly bring it back to the here and now.

A Strategy for Developing Self-Awareness

1. Being Here and Now
We only have the present, but the mind tricks us into believing that we have the future and the past. A present centered awareness facilitates a consciousness of present reality. The only reality we have is the present.

2. Awareness of the Awareness Process
Awareness of the awareness process creates greater awareness because we derive greater insight into the functioning of the mind. Awareness is an ongoing process of the present.

3. Focusing Awareness
Focusing awareness on an object increases awareness. Commonly, individuals choose to focus on their breathing. Being conscious of inhaling and exhaling increases awareness. Expanded awareness is the product of such a mundane activity as being conscious of your breathing.

4. Attention
Without attention it is very difficult to increase levels of awareness. By being attentive, we become conscious. When we increase the attention to our awareness, we expand awareness.

5. Awareness of Feelings
The blunting of the awareness of feelings is a root cause of most emotional distress. The awareness of feelings greatly enhances the awareness of self. Feelings are a vital aspect of who we are.

6. Body Awareness
Awareness of body sensations, pain and discomfort increases self-awareness. Not to be aware of our bodies is to lose sight of ourselves. Giving attention to our bodies increases the level of our self-awareness.

7. Feedback From Others
The responses from others are important information about who we are. Others can see in us what we cannot see in ourselves. This information can help us become more self-aware.

8. Meditation
Meditation is a method for expanding awareness. There are innumerable techniques that fall within the category of meditation. There are many advocates of various techniques of meditation. You can choose one that feels right for you.

Chapter Conclusion:
Critical Analysis and Application

Select a concept from this chapter which has the greatest relevance and importance to you. Explain the nature of the concept and why it is relevant and important to you. Critically analyze the concept by discussing its essential features. Determine how this concept can be applied to everyday life.

Select: _____

_____

_____

_____

_____

Explain: _____

_____

_____

_____

_____

Analyze: _____

_____

_____

_____

_____

Apply: _____

_____

_____

_____

_____

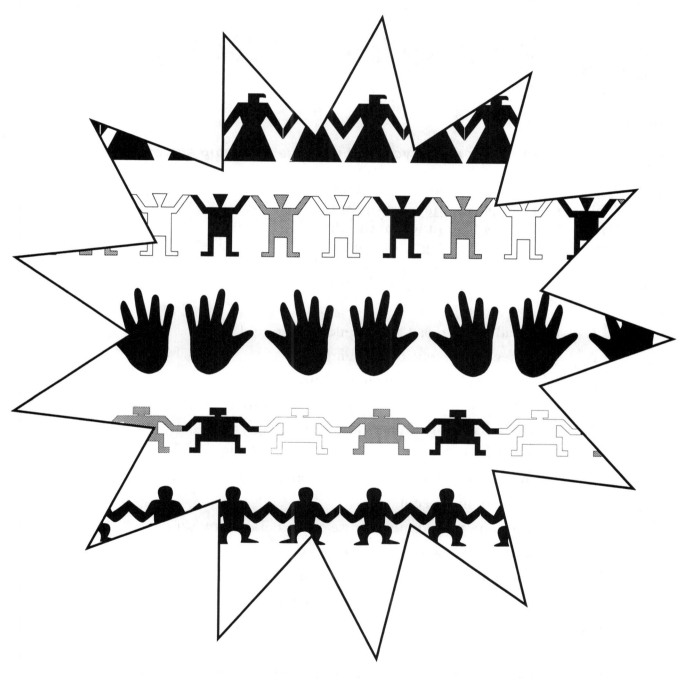

Chapter 8

Multiculturalism

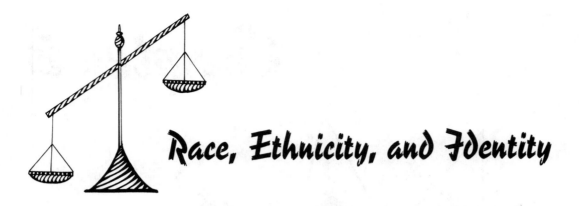

Race, Ethnicity, and Identity

Take this self-inventory by rating yourself with the following scale:

5 = This statement is true <u>all</u> of the time.
4 = This statement is true <u>most</u> of the time.
3 = This statement is true <u>much</u> of the time.
2 = This statement is true <u>some</u> of the time.
1 = This statement is true <u>almost</u> none of the time.
0 = This statement is true <u>none</u> of the time.

_____ 1. I am proud of my racial and ethnic background.

_____ 2. I do not feel racial tension on campus.

_____ 3. I believe the college reflects my culture.

_____ 4. There are very few people of my racial and ethnic group at the college.

_____ 5. I am excited about learning a foreign language.

_____ 6. My first language was a language other than English.

_____ 7. English is not the dominate language spoken in my home.

_____ 8. I am proud of my accent.

_____ 9. Students do not avoid me because of the color of my skin.

_____ 10. My friends do not have racist attitudes.

_____ 11. I worry about racial tension within our society.

_____ 12. I am American, and I really do not identify with any particular ethnic group.

_____ 13. We should all remember that we are Americans first and members of an ethnic group second.

_____ 14. I do not believe you have to forget where you come from to achieve academically.

_____ 15. I enjoy taking ethnic studies classes.

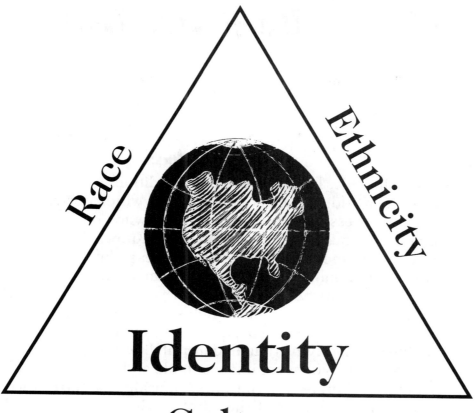

The Identity Triad

The Identity Triad includes the three factors, Culture, Race and Ethnicity. Knowledge of culture, race, and ethnicity contributes to our understanding of identity. Culture is how we think, act, and believe. It is the social context in which we were raised. We are defined by culture and our responses to culture. Race is determined by our physical background. It is the people from which we were born. In our society, race has played a major role in identity formation. The color on one's skin continues to influence the definition of group and individual identity. Our society continues to have a race consciousness. Ethnicity includes the customs, language, and social views of a group. Many individuals are defined by their ethnic background. Identity is what I think, feel, act, do, speak, wear, eat, celebrate, and practice. Identity is who I am and what I am.

Factors of The Identity Triad

Culture

Culture includes language, customs, traditions and different ways of adapting to the world. A social consciousness which derives from a knowledge of culture is essential in understanding who you are. Self-definition is a function of your social consciousness. Knowledge of the social and cultural environments allows you to increase knowledge of your relationship with the majority culture. You may or may not identify completely with the majority culture. Whatever your relationship with the majority culture, knowledge of culture helps you understand the world in which you live. In the recent past, our culture was described by many as a melting pot signifying that all cultural differences would "melt" together. Many found this concept unacceptable and see the metaphor of a mosaic as a more accurate description. A mosaic is a pattern with distinct elements which are part of the whole. The elements are distinguishable and essential to the overall pattern. These elements are inseparable from the whole. This change in metaphor allows for greater group and individual identification. You can be who you are.

Race

Race has played a significant role in the history of our country. Individuals have been categorized by skin color. We live in a society which is conscious of race and is struggling to accept racial differences. Since race is an essential element in defining who you are, it is important to understand the impact of race on the individual and society.

Ethnicity

Ethnicity is a concept which describes members of a group which share a common heredity and cultural traditions. Our society has many ethnic groups which contribute to the complex mosaic that represents our society. Ethnicity is another important defining element in identity. Many individuals are defined by their ethnicity. Knowledge of culture, race, and ethnicity helps you understand who you are.

Multiculturalism

●━◆ *Culture itself is neither education nor law-making: it is an atmosphere and a heritage.*
—H.L. Mencken

Multiculturalism means many cultures existing in one society. The composition of American society includes many racial, cultural, and ethnic groups.

Many Cultures in One

Multiculturalism is a perspective which addresses the diverse composition of American society. It is concerned with the issues and problems relevant to each of the major groups which comprise the American culture. Multiculturalism recognizes the strong presence and influences of African Americans, Latino Americans, Native Americans, European Americans, Pacific Islanders, and Asian Americans. Multiculturalism is concerned with how these groups come together to form an ever changing American society. The multi-cultural structure of American society produces forces which bind and separate the various groups making up our society. Multiculturalism is concerned with the common destiny shared by all Americans and the conflicts threatening the shared future.

Diversity

The diversity of American people represents a vast array of histories, experiences, attitudes, customs, traditions, languages, and adaptations to the American way of life. The members of the various racial, social, and ethnic groups display different attitudes regarding who they are, and from where they come. Many individuals want to retain their own culture by maintaining their customs, traditions, and language.

This chapter will help you appreciate the diversity of American culture by helping you evaluate your values in relationship to the dominant culture.

Identity

How do you identify? Who are you? What are you? Where do you come from? What is your racial, ethnic, and cultural identification? Are you bicultural or multicultural? Is identity important to you?

Identity is a psychosocial construction comprised of determinant and indeterminate factors. Race and gender are two of the more obvious determinant factors whereas many aspects of cultural identification are indeterminant. Where I choose to live, what I choose to eat, what I choose to wear, and the music I choose to listen to are all indeterminant factors. What I choose "to own" determines part of my identity. Identity is who you are. It is how you define yourself. Identity distinguishes you from others.

Becoming Your Own Person

Identity formation is the process of becoming your own person. It is the process of achieving personal autonomy. Identity is a central and important aspect of our everyday lives. It gives you a sense of belonging. Identity gives you a psychological home. Identity not only distinguishes you from others but also indicates what you share with others. Identity determines group membership. It provides the information by which others recognize you. Most importantly, identity may determine the course of your life.

Dimensions of Personal Identity

The dimensions of personal identity are very complex and may lead to confusion and conflict. We struggle to be ourselves and are sometimes confused about who we are since identity has both conceptual and affective aspects. The acquisition of identity is a struggle. In that struggle, we want to be real, authentic, and genuine. Frequently, we struggle against the expectations of others who want to define us according to their designs. Although, ultimately, we are engaged in a process of defining ourselves.

Living in a society which is comprised of diverse people who come from many cultural backgrounds requires an active process of deciding and defining ourselves. Identity is a creation of our social consciousness. We decide what is "I" and what is not "I". We can actively decide who we are or we can allow others to define us. In choosing our identities, we need to examine the experience and history of our family, group, and place. The social context in which we live causes many individuals to question and reflect on who they are. Those who are not part of the mainstream are frequently seen as outsiders. Many choose to emphasize differences which are accentuated by appearance, language, customs, and other factors.

Caught Between Cultures

Many in our society are caught between cultures and feel compelled to choose one over the other. Some individuals feel the need to relinquish their native language and adopt the language of the dominant culture. Many individuals discover a conflict between the values of their primary culture and those of the dominant culture. Many bicultural and bilingual individuals are caught between cultures, and standing between cultures is frequently difficult and painful. These individuals are inventing and choosing new social identities.

Identity Is Who You Are

Identity deserves attention, examination, exploration, and consideration. Identity is who you are. Identity issues are concerned with who you are and who you are not. They are concerned with the definition of your very existence. Identity may define possibilities for you, and you may need to re-define who you are. Your success in life is determined by your capacity to choose and define your identity. Identity is concerned with being true to ourselves. It is revealing to the world and to ourselves who we are.

Identity Clarification

Complete each of the following sentences to help clarify your identity.

1. I would describe my cultural identity as _____
_____
_____

2. The dominant features of my identity include_____
_____
_____

3. My primary language is _____
_____
_____

4. I question who I am because _____
_____
_____

5. Our society defines me as _____
_____
_____

6. I consider cultural identity important because _____
_____
_____

7. I enjoy my cultural identity because_____
_____
_____

Values Across Cultures

Values are expressions of who we are, where we come from, and how we relate to the world around us. Cultural values contribute to the way we are perceived by others, the way we perceive ourselves, and the way we perceive others. Values indicate what is important to us, and the experiences we prefer to embrace. Values distinguish us from other individuals and groups by giving our lives definition. Within American society, individuals who identify strongly with a particular racial or ethnic group frequently adhere to two sets of values: the values expressed by the majority culture and the values of their particular racial/ethnic group. These two sets of values frequently put individuals in conflict and force them to choose between values.

Values are transmitted through language, custom, and tradition. In recent times, there has been a strong advocacy to return to "traditional values." The plurality and complexity of American life precipitates an evolutionary process of our values. Our values change as our culture changes. Any individual may adhere to a broad range and scope of values.

This exercise is designed to help you clarify and understand your values in relationship to the values of the majority culture. Identify the values which have the greatest significance to you and the values you feel best represent the majority culture.

Your Values	Values of the Majority Culture	Your Values	Values of the Majority Culture
❏ Punctuality	❏	❏ Strong sense of the individual	❏
❏ Punctuality not important	❏	❏ Religious	❏
❏ Use of time highly important	❏	❏ Youth very important	❏
❏ Materialistic	❏	❏ Formalism in behavior	❏
❏ Honor and loyalty	❏	❏ Respect for hierarchy	❏
❏ Power and prestige	❏	❏ Patriarchal	❏
❏ Present-centered	❏	❏ Matriarchal	❏
❏ Cooperative	❏	❏ Extended family	❏
❏ Universal self	❏	❏ Emotional expression	❏
❏ Individual self	❏	❏ Education	❏
❏ Age-oriented	❏	❏ Money	❏
❏ Racial pride & reverence for lineage	❏	❏ Equality	❏
❏ Personal uniqueness and style	❏	❏ Democratic principles	❏
❏ Competitive	❏	❏ Submissive	❏
❏ Future oriented	❏	❏ Appearance	❏
❏ Intuitive approach to problems	❏	❏ Financial advancement	❏

	Your Values	Values of the Majority Culture		Your Values	Values of the Majority Culture
❑	Status	❑	❑	Harmony between man and nature	❑
❑	Independence	❑	❑	Blend past, present, and future	❑
❑	Touching	❑	❑	Self-control	❑
❑	Generations live together	❑	❑	Assertive	❑
❑	Strong kinship bonds	❑	❑	Rationality is highly prized	❑
❑	Godparents very important	❑	❑	Security	❑
❑	Family loyalty	❑	❑	Activity oriented	❑
❑	Individual identity subordinate to family	❑	❑	Ownership of home and land	❑
❑	Children reared collectively	❑	❑	Heroes and mentors	❑
❑	Children indulged & not punished	❑	❑	Anger not expressed	❑
❑	Males more valued	❑	❑	Individualistic	❑
❑	Parents sacrifice for children	❑	❑	Courteous behavior & good manners	❑
❑	Body contact decreased as child ages	❑	❑	Reverence for the dead	❑
❑	Verbal	❑	❑	Work oriented	❑
❑	Child is most important member of family	❑	❑	Spirituality	❑
❑	Anger (acceptable)	❑	❑	Business oriented	❑
❑	Self-reliant and independent	❑	❑	Individual achievement	❑
❑	Wife & mother are the most important female roles	❑	❑	Other_____	❑

Values

1. List 10 of your values which you believe conflict with the values of the majority culture.

1. _____

2. _____

3. _____

4. _____

5. _____

6. _____

7. _____

8. _____

9. _____

10. _____

2. How do you resolve the conflict between your values and those of the majority culture?

_____

_____

_____

_____

_____

_____

_____

_____

_____

_____

3. Do you associate your values with your social, racial, or ethnic group? If so, which values? Explain how these values are practiced in your daily life.

_____

_____

_____

_____

_____

_____

_____

_____

_____

4. Do you see your values changing, or have they more or less remained constant?

_____

_____

_____

_____

_____

_____

_____

_____

For further clarification of your values and how they may be culturally bound, you may want to share your responses to this inventory with someone from a different cultural background.

Racism and Victimization

The depth and the dimensions of racism are illustrated by Joel Kovel when he writes, "That racism, far from being the simple delusion of a bigoted and ignorant minority, is a set of beliefs whose structure arises from the deepest levels of our lives – from the fabric of assumptions we make about the world, ourselves, and others, and from the patterns of our fundamental social activities." Racism disempowers people. Racism dehumanizes people. Racism destroys the ability of people to manage their own affairs. It creates victims and victimizers. It is woven into the very social fabric of our society. Racism may be random or calculated, engineered and organized and directed against certain groups of people. Racism can be conscious or unconscious, intentional or non-intentional, overt or covert. It can be institutionalized. The goal of racism is domination. "Power over" others always has a corrupting effect, whether we are dealing with interpersonal situations, organizational operations, or institutional and societal structures.

Learned Helplessness

Since racism destroys the ability of individuals and groups to manage their affairs effectively, these people become powerless. People who are powerless are not respected or valued by society as a whole, nor do they respect or value themselves. People who are powerless develop the response of "learned helplessness." The chief characteristic of "learned helplessness" is hopelessness. People who exhibit "learned helplessness" make little effort to succeed even when given opportunities. People who have little value for themselves do not sustain efforts that result in achievement of significant goals. The efforts of the powerless are not rewarded by society and so result in self-devaluation and self-contempt. The powerless are caught in a vicious circle. Attempts at succeeding are not rewarded, causing self-contempt, and further attempts to succeed are not rewarded, causing more self-contempt.

The Environment and Victimization

Many individuals are victimized by situations, conditions, and circumstances. The environment has a powerful impact on the course of a person's life. These victims are rendered helpless and powerless and give up hope that they can ever live a productive and meaningful life. If one is a victim, one is faced with a decision of whether to remain a victim or to regain power and control over one's life. This may be extremely difficult to do in an environment which offers little opportunity and which is plagued with violence and hopelessness. The environment is capable of defeating people. Environments of neglect, distrust, and futility do not build positive motivation. Instead, they destroy self-esteem and do not teach the appropriate skills to succeed in our complex society.

Identity
Culture

Creating Hope

It has been demonstrated in laboratory experiments that animals can be taught "learned helplessness." These animals are subjected to repeated punishment with no opportunity to escape. The experimental situation is changed by later providing an opportunity for escape. These animals fail to find and take this opportunity because they have been defeated by the continuous punishment from the environment. There is a parallel that can be made with humans. If human beings are punished for long enough periods of time, they will give up, and they will not act on their best behalf even when positive opportunities are provided. To help people succeed in life, we must create hope. Hope is the foundation of positive levels of motivation.

Labeling

The labeling of individuals strips them of their individuality and frequently results in anger and resentment. Most of us feel that we are much more than a label. Many individuals resist being put into a category as the result of being labeled.

When the government puts people into categories without their consent, this causes much anger and loss of trust in the government. For example, many individuals of Latino background dislike the label "Hispanic." Mexicans, Mexican Americans, and Chicanos usually do not want to be called Hispanic. Persons of color in our society frequently dislike the label "minority" and most of its connotations.

Labeling is dehumanizing, yet the opposite attitude that we should not make distinctions between groups refuses to acknowledge real differences in race, culture, language, ethnicity and class. Many persons take pride in their differences. The attitude that "we are all Americans" reflects the resistance to make distinctions between individuals and groups. Individuals either choose to identify with a group or are put into a group by others. It is apparent that we all belong to groups.

Racial, Ethnic, and Social Awareness

Racial, ethnic, and social awareness is a consciousness which recognizes, understands, appreciates, adjusts to, and accommodates the diversity of people in our society. Racial, cultural, and ethnic awareness means that one recognizes and respects the differences between cultures. Racial, ethnic, and social awareness is dynamic and constantly changing.

Social Consciousness

A social consciousness derives from awareness of the social context in which we live. We share many similarities with others who are racially, ethnically, and culturally different. We live in a multicultural environment, which means we live with people who are both culturally similar and different from us. As one increases in social awareness, differences in language, food, music, customs, and traditions are not feared but respected and recognized. As we become more aware of the culture of other groups, we increase our awareness of our own group. A social consciousness is expanded through interaction and contact with groups that are culturally different. This interaction and contact helps us go beyond stereotypes and generalizations about people who are different.

Equality and Plurality

A social consciousness can be expanded if we believe in the equality of people and if we appreciate and respect others. The recognition of the contributions made by others to our society increases respect. The plurality of cultures within our country makes our society stronger. Other groups expand our view of the world, and we understand ourselves better by comparing ourselves to other people's cultures. If we learn to accept differences and look for the goodness in other people, we can become more aware of the humanity of others and see that at the most fundamental human level, we are the same.

Using the Johari Window to Understand Your Racial, Ethnic and Social Attitudes

The Johari Window illustrates that we are not aware of all of our racial, ethnic and social attitudes. Unknown racial, ethnic and social attitudes may operate in many situations, and we are not conscious of their presence or their affects. It is very difficult to free ourselves from negative racial, ethnic and social attitudes. We may defend and resist knowledge of these attitudes through denial of our true and honest feelings. We have racial, ethnic and social attitudes that are readily seen by others, and we have racial, ethnic and social attitudes which we hide from others. Some of our attitudes are seen by others and not by ourselves. Other attitudes are not seen by others and not seen by ourselves.

Open and honest communication about attitudes facilitates changing attitudes. We can express, explore and understand our attitudes with the help of others. Increasing the size of Quadrant I will facilitate this communication and increase the probability of changing attitudes.

We can begin to address our racial, ethnic and social attitudes by revealing to others some of the attitudes we keep hidden. We may address our attitudes by being open to others who are giving us feedback about our attitudes. We can seek to change our attitudes in a safe and secure environment. Only within this type of situation can we seek to uncover the deeply unknown attitudes that are hidden.

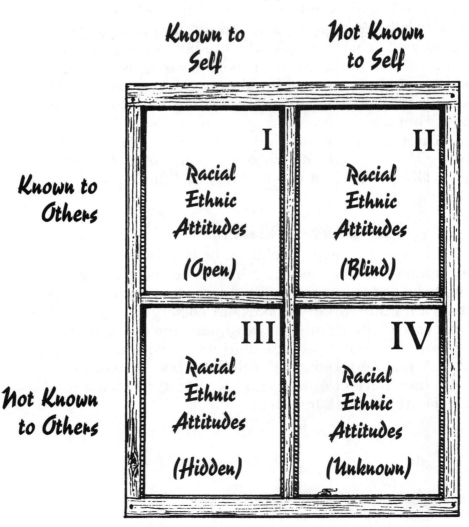

A Graphic Model of Racial/Ethnic Attitudes Awareness

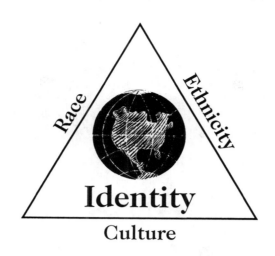

Race   Ethnicity

Identity

Culture

Racial, Ethnic, and Social Differences

Racial, ethnic, and social differences can be:

> appreciated
> feared
> envied
> hated
> prized
> denied
> recognized
> obliterated
> suppressed
> expressed
> subjugated
> incorporated
> assimilated
> celebrated

A Strategy for Communicating Across Cultures

Racial, ethnic, and social awareness is being aware of your own cultural experience and the influence it has on you when you interact with people who are culturally different. All of us behave from within the context of our socialization. Our socialization enhances and limits our ability to function and communicate effectively with individuals who are culturally different. Racial, cultural, and ethnic awareness is giving appropriate recognition to the importance of racial, cultural, social, and ethnic factors in human interaction. One of the most important factors in human interaction is cultural membership. There are profound, subtle, and complex factors operating when people of different cultural backgrounds interact.

1. **Increase awareness** of thoughts, feelings, and reactions regarding issues of race, ethnicity, and multiculturalism.

2. **Be honest** with yourself and acknowledge your thoughts, feelings, and reactions regarding issues of race, ethnicity, and multiculturalism.

3. **Explore** the root causes of your attitudes regarding race, ethnicity and multiculturalism.

4. **Acknowledge** the similarities and differences that exist between the different racial, ethnic and multicultural groups.

5. **Cultivate** a willingness to learn about other ethnic, racial, and multi–cultural groups.

6. **Respect** the customs, traditions, language, habits, food, religion, music, dance, and all other expressions of a culture.

7. **Initiate** a dialogue with individuals of other groups and focus on the things you have in common.

8. **Decide** whether you want to communicate attitudes and feelings regarding race, ethnicity and multiculturalism. What are the benefits? What are the consequences?

Chapter Conclusion:
Critical Analysis and Application

Select a concept from this chapter which has the greatest relevance and importance to you. Explain the nature of the concept and why it is relevant and important to you. Critically analyze the concept by discussing its essential features. Determine how this concept can be applied to everyday life.

Select: _____

_____

_____

_____

_____

Explain: _____

_____

_____

_____

_____

Analyze: _____

_____

_____

_____

_____

Apply: _____

_____

_____

_____

_____

Chapter 9

Relationships

Relationships

Take this self-inventory by rating yourself with the following scale:

5 = This statement is true <u>all</u> of the time.
4 = This statement is true <u>most</u> of the time.
3 = This statement is true <u>much</u> of the time.
2 = This statement is true <u>some</u> of the time.
1 = This statement is true <u>almost</u> none of the time.
0 = This statement is true <u>none</u> of the time.

_____ 1. Relationships are very important to me.

_____ 2. I have good interpersonal skills.

_____ 3. I have positive relationships.

_____ 4. I enter into loving relationships.

_____ 5. I have the ability to get close to people.

_____ 6. My relationships are enriching and fulfilling.

_____ 7. My relationships contribute to my growth.

_____ 8. My relationships do not interfere with the achievement of my goals.

_____ 9. I'm happy with my relationships.

_____ 10. I become dependent in a relationship.

_____ 11. I escape from loneliness through relationships.

_____ 12. I get lost in relationships.

_____ 13. I hide a lot in relationships.

_____ 14. My relationships create stress.

_____ 15. I handle relationship problems effectively.

_____ 16. My relationships are so demanding that they take me away from other important activities.

_____ 17. I avoid personal issues by concealing them in relationships.

_____ 18. I am not ready for a relationship that requires a major commitment.

_____ 19. I am easy to get to know.

_____ 20. I am open to relationships.

Man is a knot, a web, a mesh into which relationships are tied. Only those relationships matter.
—Antoine de Saint-Exupery

The Relationships Triad

The Relationships Triad consists of the following factors: Acceptance, Trust, and Love. Acceptance is one of the most important issues in relationships, and it is nearly impossible to build trust without acceptance. Acceptance and trust form the basis for love in a relationship. We usually love someone because we accept and trust them. We are usually loved by others because they accept and trust us. These three ingredients, when well established in a relationship, contribute to form a basis for a positive relationship. Positive relationships contribute to our level of self-esteem and our sense of belonging. Positive relationships also provide the support that we need in order to succeed in life.

Factors of The Relationships Triad

 Love is the active concern for the life and growth of that which we love.
—Erich Fromm

Love

Love is an expression of a deeply felt emotion of caring, empathy, and connection. It is through interpersonal communication that we allow others to know us, and through empathy that we learn to know others. "To love others you must first love yourself because you cannot give that which you do not possess, and you cannot give what you have not learned and experienced," according to Leo Buscaglia who sees love as a learned emotional reaction. Those who have been loved are capable of loving, and those who have not been loved are also capable of loving but may need to learn from valuable loving experiences. Loving and being loved is a fundamental human need. We can learn to love. We are capable of opening ourselves to others. We can take risks and allow ourselves to be vulnerable. We generate love through our awareness of the beauty and value of living.

Trust

Trust is a mental and emotional state characterized by confidence in another person to fulfill our expectations. Trust is usually assessed through feelings, actions, communication and past experience. Trusting others is an intuitive process. We rely heavily on internal sensory experience to make our decisions about trust. Based on sensory experience, we develop impressions about others and make decisions regarding their trustworthiness. We can assess trust on the basis of what people say and do. Consistency between behavior and verbal expressions are key elements of trust.

Acceptance

Acceptance is appreciating others the way they are without a desire that they be different. Acceptance is unconditional without approving of everything others do. We can make distinctions between accepting others and approving of their behavior. Taking others the way they are without critical judgements supports acceptance. Acceptance of others is an important aspect of maintaining positive relationships.

Relationships

There is no hope of joy except in human relations.
—Antoine de Saint-Exupery

Relationships provide us with the context for love, meaning, purpose, direction, identity, intimacy, and many other important human needs. We grow through relationships. We discover who we are in relationships. Our sense of reality remains intact because of relationships. Our very survival is dependent on a complex system of relationships. It is by working with others that we achieve important goals and make our lives productive. Relationships allow us to bridge our isolation and sense of loneliness. We are nurtured through our relationships. This chapter focuses on numerous dimensions and aspects of human relationships by addressing many issues which we all confront in our relationships.

Interaction

The complex network of our interactions with others forms the basis of who we are and what we are. These essential interactions occur within the context of relationships. A significant amount our time is spent appraising these situations. In relationships, much is given and much is taken. Our view of ourselves would be significantly different if it were not based on the interactions that we have with others.

Experience in Relationships

When we feel good or bad, we can attribute these feelings to what is happening in our relationships. Our feelings mirror the things that are happening in our relationships. Much of our emotional life is based on the life of our relationships. Our relationships are living processes. We struggle in our relationships, and we seek to find love and meaning in our relationships. When our relationships are vital and exuberant, we feel vital and exuberant. When our relationships are filled with painful experiences, we are filled with pain. Our experiences seem inseparable from our relationships.

Conflict

I hate and love. You ask, perhaps, how that can be? I know not, but I feel the agony.
—*Catullus*

Most relationships experience conflicts generated by disagreements and opposition to divergent interests, ideas, and persons. Conflicts exist at different levels for different relationships, and no relationship is conflict free. Conflicts may weaken or strengthen a relationship. They may lead to a deeper understanding of the other person and of ourselves. Conflicts help us learn about ourselves. Excessive conflicts may destroy a relationship, while manageable conflicts may keep a relationship interesting.

Many people believe that conflicts are a negative aspect of a relationship. This belief that conflicts are negative does much to suppress and contain them in relationships. Suppression and containment do not encourage the satisfactory solution of conflict.

Beneficial Consequences

Conflicts may have many beneficial or harmful consequences. One of the beneficial consequences of conflicts is that they accentuate our uniqueness and individuality by demonstrating our differences in regard to needs, desires, wants, and preferences. Conflicts also possess an intensity that reveals the depth of feeling that we have for one another. Conflicts frequently reveal the truth of where we are with ourselves and with our partners.

Harmful Consequences

Some of the harmful consequences of conflicts are the depletion of our energies, the encouragement of destructive behaviors, and the causation of deeply felt anger and resentment. Conflicts can divert people from important goals, resulting in wasted time and energy. Conflicts can also destroy enjoyment and love.

Assessing Your Relationship

Complete the following sentences to assess the relationship with your significant other.

1. Generally, I feel my relationship is _____

_____

_____

2. The most positive aspect of my relationship is _____

_____

_____

3. The most negative aspect of my relationship is _____

_____

_____

4. The things I want to change about my relationship are _____

_____

_____

5. I want to stay in this relationship because _____

_____

_____

6. Sometimes I feel like getting out because _____

_____

_____

7. If I get out, I will _____

_____

_____

8. I don't get out of this relationship because _____

_____

_____

Using the Johari Window to Improve Communication in Relationships

Communication in relationships is improved when free and open communication is encouraged and developed. Increasing the range of free activity in a relationship improves communication. Decreasing the covert aspects of relationships improves communication. This includes addressing the blind, hidden, and unknown aspects of the relationship. By increasing openness in a relationship, more is available to both individuals to acquire greater knowledge and understanding of the other. The hidden, avoided, and unknown areas in a relationship cause problems and issues to go unaddressed and unresolved. The Johari Window illustrates the extent to which covert factors influence awareness, communication, attitudes and knowledge of motives.

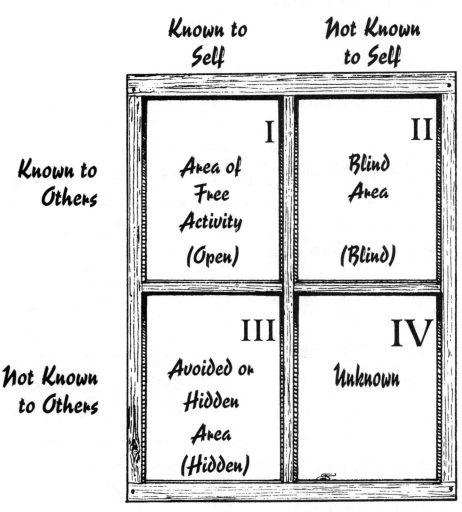

A Graphic Model of Human Communication

Feelings and Emotions

The emotions may be endless. The more we express them, the more we may have to express.
—E.M. Forster

Getting in Touch with Feelings

Feelings and emotions are an important part of who you are, and we are not always in touch with our feelings. Getting in touch with our feelings requires paying attention to our body and mind. Awareness of our internal reactions helps us get in touch with feelings. In order to express our feelings, we need to start by getting in touch with them.

Awareness of Feelings

Sometimes we are not even aware of what we feel. But if you are not aware of a feeling, how can you express it? Awareness of feelings is absolutely critical. Not to be aware of feelings is not to be aware of yourself. It takes practice to be aware of how you feel, because most of us habitually do not pay attention to our feelings. You need to change that habit and become accustomed to paying attention to your feelings. A learned pattern of "tuning in" to internal stimuli will heighten your self-awareness and thus increase your awareness of feelings.

Describing Feelings

Feelings may be difficult to express because of linguistic limitations. Just as awareness of feelings requires attention and practice, we also need to practice describing feelings. If I cannot describe how I feel, how can you possibly understand my feelings? It is through the description of feelings that we communicate feelings. It is through the labeling of feelings that we communicate feelings.

Labeling Feelings

It is important to be concise in our communication about feelings. We need to make concise statements about how we feel instead of giving elaborate explanations that may be confusing. For example, saying, "I feel sad" is clear and unambiguous, whereas a long explanation may be confusing and hard to follow. A concise statement which incorporates a feeling word facilitates feeling communication. Examples of feeling words are: angry, hurt, sad, lonely, depressed, lost, worried, happy, joyful, excited, and elated.

Expression of Feelings

We tend to be indirect when we communicate our feelings because it is often frightening to communicate feelings directly. I do not know how you are going to respond to my feelings; therefore, I avoid communicating feelings to you directly. Fear of expressing feelings is probably the greatest obstacle to the expression of feelings.

A five-step strategy may assist us in the communication of feelings. The steps include getting in touch with feelings, being aware of feelings, describing feelings, labeling feelings, and expressing feelings.

The Five-Step Strategy for Communicating Feelings

Step 1. *Get in touch with feelings.*
Pay attention to your internal responses in any given situation.

Step 2. *Be aware of feelings.*
Practice getting in touch with feelings. This produces awareness of feelings.

Step 3. *Describe feelings.*
Now that you are in touch and aware of your feelings, describe them to yourself.

Step 4. *Label feelings.*
Now that you have described your feelings, find accurate labels for them.

Step 5. *Express feelings.*
Now that you can describe and label your feelings, express them appropriately.

Chapter Conclusion:
Critical Analysis and Application

Select a concept from this chapter which has the greatest relevance and importance to you. Explain the nature of the concept and why it is relevant and important to you. Critically analyze the concept by discussing its essential features. Determine how this concept can be applied to everyday life.

Select:

Explain:

Analyze:

Apply:

Chapter 10

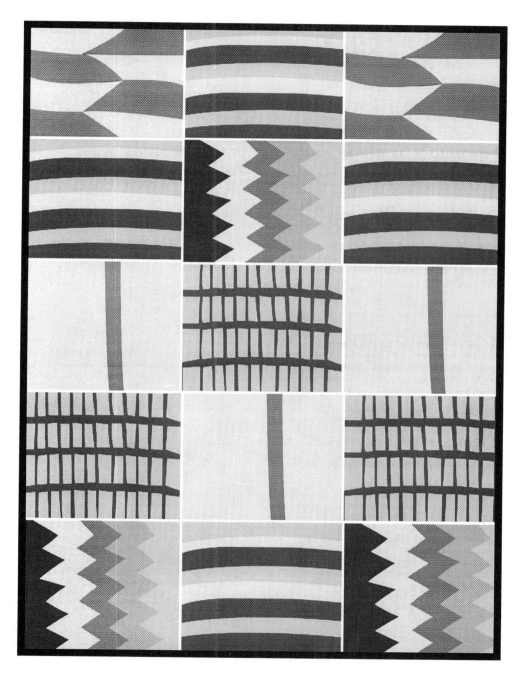

Life Skills

Life Skills

Take this self-inventory by rating yourself with the following scale:

5 = This statement is true <u>all</u> of the time.
4 = This statement is true <u>most</u> of the time.
3 = This statement is true <u>much</u> of the time.
2 = This statement is true <u>some</u> of the time.
1 = This statement is true <u>almost</u> none of the time.
0 = This statement is true <u>none</u> of the time.

_____ 1. I know how to set goals.

_____ 2. I know how to set priorities.

_____ 3. I manage my time effectively.

_____ 4. I have good social skills.

_____ 5. I'm a good communicator.

_____ 6. I'm an effective decision maker.

_____ 7. I'm a problem solver.

_____ 8. I have good coping skills.

_____ 9. I have good planning skills.

_____ 10. I am well organized.

_____ 11. I maintain a written time schedule.

_____ 12. I use a daily "to do" list.

_____ 13. I am task oriented.

_____ 14. I apply what I learn.

Life is a maze in which we take the wrong turning before we have learnt to walk.
—Cyril Connolly

The Skills Triad

Life skills significantly impact our life success. They include decision-making, problem solving, time management, interpersonal communication, language, work content, and many others. Life skills are applied for our entire lifespan. Skills allow us to perform a broad spectrum of activities with efficiency and competence. Skills increase our capacity "to do." Skills are related to our overall level of performance, and skills can increase our level of performance. The ability to apply what we learn increases our skill level. Beyond this, the future development of our society is based on high-tech skill development.

Communication

Good communication is stimulating as black coffee, and just as hard to sleep after.
— Anne Morrow Lindbergh

Communication consists of verbal and nonverbal messages which are expressed within the context of behavioral, emotional, and cognitive processes. Learning about communication involves learning how people exchange ideas in real life situations and learning how we communicate in addressing real life issues. Communication has many dimensions. We learn to communicate more effectively by examining how we communicate. Communication skills are vital since they are used in every aspect of our lives.

The Communication of Feelings

Effective communication includes the communication of feelings. Communication frequently breaks down at the feeling level, while the content level is usually understood. If you are to communicate well with others, it is imperative to be able to listen for the feeling basis of the communication. The feeling basis would include the total range of feelings about a given situation. We have feelings about content. The content of a situation might involve the fact that you have just ended a relationship. The content would include who, when, where and why of the ending. The feeling level would include the feelings you have about ending the relationship. Hurt, loss, loneliness, resentment and anger are some of the feelings an individual might experience. If our feelings are not received and validated by our partner in communication, we may be left feeling misunderstood, devalued and unrecognized. This could be considered a breakdown in communication.

Ways to Encourage Communication

You can use many approaches to encourage communication. Sharing something of yourself facilitates another person's communication. Questions directed at feelings frequently create opportunities for communication. Open-ended questions instead of closed questions will promote an individual to open up and communicate.

The following skills have been demonstrated to contribute to the effectiveness of communication. Taken in their entirety, they provide a comprehensive framework for communicating and relating to others.

Communication Skills

Precision of communication is important, more important than ever, in our era of hair-trigger balances, when a false, or misunderstood word may create as much disaster as a sudden thoughtless act.
— *James Thurber*

1. "Own" Your Communication and Perceptions, and Avoid Speaking for Others

When we "own" our communication, we make it clear that we speak for ourselves and no one else. Pronouns such as I, me, my, mine, show ownership of communication. This is sometimes called sending "I messages." By owning our communication and perceptions, we give others room to own their communication and perceptions. Owning communication creates clarity and allows for the acceptance of personal responsibility.

2. "Own" Your Problems and Resist Ownership of the Problems of Others

When I "own" my problems, I do not put my problems on you; nor do I expect you to resolve my problems. My problems can only be solved when I take responsibility for them. When I own your problems, I undermine your capacity to solve your problems. Therefore, I own my problems, and you own yours.

3. Take Responsibility for Your Thoughts, Feelings and Reactions

When I take responsibility for my thoughts, feelings, and reactions, I do not blame you for how I think, feel, and act. The quality of my experience is my responsibility. My happiness and satisfaction are my responsibility, and you are not responsible for creating these experiences for me.

4. Trust

Trust is essential for effective communication. Without trust, communication breaks down. Trust is difficult to define, and the dynamics of trust are complex. Trust is usually based on agreed-upon conditions and expectations about behavior. Violations of these agreements frequently destroy the trust and the relationship.

5. Be Open and Honest

By being open and honest, we develop authentic relationships. Openness and honesty form the basis for mutual understanding and the development of intimacy. Deception, hiding, and lying greatly interfere with the quality of communication.

6. Be "For Real" (Congruent)

When I am congruent, I say what I mean, and I mean what I say. Congruence means that there is a consistency between what I appear to be and what I actually am. Feelings and actions go together.

7. Take Risks

It is always risky to be open and honest with others. When we share our honest thoughts and feelings, there is always a potential for conflict. However, without risking conflict, we lose out on opportunities for intimacy and growth.

8. Avoid Asking Too Many Questions

Asking too many questions interferes with understanding the other person. Usually, the other person presents much of what we need to know to be understanding without needing to use questioning for more information. We tend to hide behind questions so that we do not have to be sensitive to the feelings of the other person. We frequently ask questions when we do not know what else to do. We may not know which information is important so we ask questions.

9. Be Cautious When Trying to Figure Others Out

Many people resent efforts to analyze and figure them out. This tends to result in a person feeling treated as a thing rather than as a person. Usually, people want to be cared for, supported and accepted, not "figured out." When we attempt to figure others out, we put ourselves in the position of being one up on the other person. We frequently assume that we know more about the other person than that person knows about him/herself. Figuring others out is best left to psychotherapists.

10. Get in Touch with Your Thoughts, Feelings, and Reactions

Many of us struggle with being in touch with our feelings. This creates significant barriers in communication. How we think greatly determines how we feel, and how we feel significantly affects how we act. By being in touch with our thoughts, feelings and reactions, we can better express and communicate to others our inner life.

11. Get in Touch with Your Needs

Our interactions with others are usually governed by our needs. By getting in touch with our needs, we may become more open and honest in our communication. Confusion about our needs causes us difficulties in our communication with others. We seek need-fulfillment through communication.

12. Clarify Messages and Meanings of Messages

We clarify the meanings of messages by asking others to repeat what they have said and by asking them what they mean by what they have said. We also clarify messages by communicating what we heard and what we think they mean. Thus, we clarify messages and the meanings of messages by talking about the messages. We try to reach agreement about what was said and what was meant by what was said to make communication effective.

13. Respond to Others' Feeling and Content Expressions

People usually communicate at two levels. One level is the content level, which is very similar to the story level, and the other is the feeling level. We frequently respond to the story level of an interaction but fail to respond to the feeling level of an interaction. Often it is more important to respond and understand the feeling level of communication as compared with the story level. Individuals have feelings, often strong, about their content (story) expression.

14. Attend to Verbal and Non-Verbal Cues

In communicating effectively we need to attend to both verbal and non-verbal cues presented by the other. The non-verbal communication is analogous to music which forms the background for the lyrics of a song. We need to listen to the music as others communicate to us. The non-verbal cues frequently contain the message. Ask yourself, "Am I getting the non-verbal message?" or "Have I listened to the music?"

15. Paraphrase Others' Communication

When we paraphrase, or restate, what others are saying, we demonstrate that we are paying attention, listening, and are concerned. Paraphrasing allows us to check on the messages that are being conveyed to us. Paraphrasing helps us understand the meaning of an expression. Paraphrasing demonstrates an intent to understand.

16. Be Cautious When Offering Solutions to the Problems of Others

It is usually best for people to come to their own solutions to problems. Offering solutions undermines the responsibility of others to direct their own lives. We frequently make the mistake of offering simple solutions to long term problems. Individuals are usually not committed to the solutions of problems that come from others. Solutions offered to others establish an unequal relationship. This frequently interferes with communication.

17. Maintain a Non-Judgmental Attitude

No one likes to feel judged by others. Nothing will cause a breakdown of communication more quickly than a person believing s/he is being judged. In many situations a non-judgmental attitude is required. We must be cautious of imposing our belief system on others which usually is the basis for judging others. Judgment of right and wrong greatly increases the defensiveness of others. Openness and flexibility through a non-judgmental attitude facilitates communication. Our moral system should not be imposed on others.

18. Accept Differences

We need to recognize the right of individuals to be different. Differences allow for diversity and make life more interesting. We can learn to accept differences by understanding the threat that the differences pose to us. The more clarity we have about who we are, the less threatening differences become to us.

19. Develop Empathic Responses

The cornerstone of effective communication is the ability to see the world through the eyes of others. Understanding the world from your viewpoint and being sensitive to that viewpoint greatly enhances communication. Being empathic requires careful listening, imagination, and the suspension of our own world view. We respond empathically when we accurately capture the nature of the experience of other people. Empathy forms the basis for love and compassion. Without empathy there is no compassion.

20. Don't Monopolize the Conversation to the Exclusion of Others

Many of us would rather speak than make an effort to listen. We become preoccupied with fulfilling our needs to the exclusion of others. Effective communication frequently requires that we suspend our judgments, beliefs, feelings, and needs. It is important to be for others and not only for ourselves.

Listening

Others inform us and tell us about their experiences, but are we listening? Listening requires that we stop, focus, and concentrate on what is being communicated to us. Whether we are in a classroom or visiting with friends, listening is a vital skill. We need to pay attention to our listening behavior.

Effective listening requires effort. Listening is much more than parroting back the words we have heard someone express. Listening involves being fully available and present for others. It is through listening that we come to know others. Knowing others is one of the ways we come to know ourselves. Listening governs the depth of our relationships because it is through listening that we come to understand the world of the other person. This type of listening allows us to empathize and fully appreciate the world of the other. When I understand your world, I become capable of caring about you. Listening sensitizes you to other people and their problems. I can only understand your experience through listening. Then I become sensitive to your experience.

Content and Process

When we listen to others, we listen to the content and process of their expressions. The content is the idea expressed, and the process is the associated feelings about the content. The President must carefully listen to the needs of the people. A cardiologist must carefully listen to the expressions of symptoms by a patient. A parent listens to the whimpering of a child, and the message it carries. The professor listens to the struggle a student has in incorporating new ideas. We can listen to the different levels of meanings being expressed and the problems being conveyed. We can listen for motives behind the expressions or the bias of the speaker. In the educational arena, we generally listen for information. When we listen, we may try to listen for the real message or messages. Verbal or nonverbal messages are always being expressed, and we need to be sensitive to the cues that alert us to the message. Frequently, messages are contradictory or mixed, and that results in camouflaging the message.

Listening as a Skill

Listening is a skill and is therefore something we can learn and develop. Listening is a communication skill, an interpersonal relationship skill, a job skill, an educational skill, a supervising skill, a parenting skill, a problem solving skill, a learning skill, and a therapeutic skill. To become an effective communicator, we must pause, stop, and listen.

Listening is also a problem solving skill that allows us to penetrate to the core of many problems. We fail to understand human problems because we fail to listen. When we listen to help, we need to listen non-judgmentally. When we listen for information, we need to listen receptively. When we listen to acquire knowledge, we need to listen critically.

Skills of Effective Listeners

1. Effective listeners make active, conscious decisions to listen.

2. Effective listeners know what to listen for.

3. Effective listeners go beyond the content of the discussion.

4. Effective listeners listen for meanings that are expressed at different levels.

5. Effective listeners have internal radar. They are able to sense the important communication.

6. Effective listeners attend to both verbal and nonverbal cues.

7. Effective listeners have the capacity to focus and concentrate exclusively on what is being said to them.

8. Effective listeners are good at using analytical skills.

9. Effective listeners are capable of suspending their own needs while they listen. (They reduce ego involvement.)

10. Effective listeners are non-judgmental.

11. Effective listeners want to solve problems.

12. Effective listeners can be empathic when the situation requires it.

13. Effective listeners are usually patient.

14. Effective listeners give others a sense of being heard.

15. Effective listeners listen because they care about people.

Listening and Responding

1. Stop! Pay attention! Notice!
Do you really listen? Are you a listener, or are you a talker?

2. Time yourself.
How much time do you spend listening to others? How much time do you spend talking to others?

3. Pay attention to the amount of time you listen and talk.
Others are encouraged to communicate when you listen to them.

4. Respond to feelings.
Others are encouraged to communicate when you respond to their feelings.

5. Ask for feedback.
You may want to ask others if you have listened to them.

Listening Check

As you listen to a conversation:

1. Pay attention to content and process.

2. Concentrate on verbal and nonverbal behavior.

3. Isolate major messages and the meanings of those messages.

4. Paraphrase the messages and their meanings, and convey those to the person sending the message to check out whether you are receiving messages as intended.

5. Speak minimally when you listen.

6. Stop, pause, concentrate and **listen**. Remember that listening requires effort.

Information

Decision-Making

✒ *It does not take much strength to do things, but it requires great strength to decide on what to do.*

— Elbert Hubbard

Decision-making is a vital part of personal growth and development. It involves taking control of one's life, nurturing self-esteem, and having a sense of empowerment. Decisions shape and form our lives. Choosing is life's defining factor. We are our decisions. By actively choosing, we take control of our lives. Making our own decisions solidifies our independence and autonomy. When we choose for ourselves, we are responsible for ourselves. By making our own decisions, we separate ourselves from others. Through decisions, we reveal who we are and for what we stand. Our decisions define the content of our character.

Students make many life decisions, such as which relationships to cultivate and maintain, which institutions to attend, and other career and lifestyle choices. These life decisions cause a great deal of stress because they have a long term impact on the life of the individual. Understanding the decision-making process eases the accompanying stress and conflict. Decision-making is a process of many discrete phases, stages, and events involving collecting information, defining problems, generating alternatives, selecting an alternative, and implementing the decision. Decision-making involves bringing about desirable situations, conditions, circumstances, events, and personal states of satisfaction.

The Complexity of Decision-Making

At times we recognize the need to make a decision when we are caught in a situation thrust upon us. All of a sudden we feel pressure from various sources. We feel ourselves pulled in different directions. We find ourselves caught in a quandary requiring a course of action in which we must decide to make difficult decisions regarding family, friends, employment, school, attitudes and circumstances we encounter in our daily lives.

The following example illustrates how students are caught in a situation requiring a decision about a major. The complexity of decision-making is also illustrated by this example.

The college setting pressures students to decide on a major. When you fill out an application, go through the registration process, see an academic advisor, you are asked, "What is your major?" This is usually a complex decision requiring a consideration of many factors. Deciding on a major involves assessing interests, abilities and aptitudes, values, and preparation for the major and investigation on how majors are related to various careers. Students want to know the occupational outlook of ca-

reers related to their major. Will jobs be available when they graduate? A decision on a major is a balancing act of all these factors. Adding to this complexity is the amount of uncertainty about ourselves and the changing world in which we live. So many factors impinge on a decision-making situation that we cannot possibly take into account the effects of every factor. Decisions are therefore frequently made on the basis of intuition or hunch.

The Fallacy of the "Right Decision"

Decision-making is hampered by an endless quest for information. We mistakenly believe that if we have all the information, we will make the right decision. Information is certainly a vital part of decision-making and determining when we have sufficient information is a factor in making a decision. But the point of making a decision requires a decision. You must decide to decide. The fallacy of the "right decision" serves to paralyze decision-making. At times we fail to make a decision because we believe that any given situation has a single "right" decision, and we must find it. Because we fear the consequences of our decisions, we are compelled to feel that there is a single right decision in a given situation. Most situations include a range of possible decisions. It is important to think of the consequences of our decisions and ways of bringing about desirable consequences rather than to mistakenly believe there is a single right decision.

Rational and Non-Rational Factors

The decision-making process incorporates both rational and non-rational factors. When we purchase a new automobile, we want to know its reliability, gas mileage, horsepower, safety features, and other characteristics. These factual characteristics contribute to a rational decision in purchasing an automobile, but the emotional appeal is a non-rational part of decision-making which cannot be underestimated in the decision to purchase an automobile.

The Methodical Nature of the Decision-Making Process

Using a methodical approach can enhance the effectiveness of decision-making. Decision-making may be viewed as consisting of the following stages: identifying, defining, and analyzing issues, problems, and concerns which require a decision, gathering information, generating decisions and alternatives, exploring feelings about decisions and alternatives, weighing decisions and alternatives, predicting outcomes and consequences, arriving at the decision, implementation of the decision, evaluation of the decision, and making new decisions.

Information

Example of Decision-Making

An example is useful to illustrate and help us understand the complexity and methodical nature of the decision-making process. A common student situation may serve as an example. A student discovers that s/he is unable to pay the coming semester's tuition. What is s/he to do? This is a problem, issue, and concern requiring a series of decisions. The identification of the problem might be as simple as seeing a balance on a savings account. The definition of this problem could be far more complex. Several definitions could readily be developed. The analysis of this problem tries to reveal how this situation developed, how it is sustained and what changes need to be made. Through the information gathering stage, this student could attempt to find additional sources of revenue. In addressing the immediate impact of not having money to pay for the coming semester's tuition, several decisions could be generated and considered. Some possible decisions could include finding employment, increasing working hours, borrowing money, pursuing financial aid, reducing expenses, and selling possessions.

The next stage involves exploring feelings about each of these decisions. Some students would feel very depressed at the thought of dropping out of school, while others would not borrow money no matter how crucial the situation. Students have feelings about each of their decisions. In weighing the decisions, the student will have to determine which decision will produce the most beneficial outcome and consequence. For many, the most beneficial outcome would be to continue with the educational plan.

After weighing decisions, predicting outcomes and consequences, a decision has to be made. The point of decision has been reached. Now that the decision has been made, it has to be implemented. This student might have decided to borrow money. At a later date, this decision will have to be evaluated. Did this decision bring about a desirable result? If not, new decisions will have to be made.

The Decision-Making Process

Step 1. **Identifying, defining, sorting, and analyzing** issues, problems, and concerns which require a decision

Step 2. **Gathering** information which sheds light on the issues, problems, and concerns which are being addressed

Step 3. **Generating** courses of action and alternatives

Step 4. **Exploring** feelings about actions and alternatives

Step 5. **Weighing** alternatives

Step 6. **Predicting** outcomes and consequences

Step 7. **Making** the decision

Step 8. **Implementing** the decision

Step 9. **Evaluating** the decision

Step 10. **Making** new decisions

Awareness
Alternatives
DECISION-MAKING
Information

The Decision-Making Process: Example

Step 1. Identify the problem

- Choosing a major

Step 2. Gather information

- Start self-assessment.
- Identify values, interests, aptitude.
- Find the availability of majors.
- Review academic backround.
- Find the relationship between majors and careers.

Step 3. Generate courses of action and alternatives

- Select an area such as science, math, humanities, social science.
- Identify majors within each area.
- Create a list of possible majors.

Step 4. Explore feelings

- Explore feelings about each major listed.
- Select majors with the strongest emotional appeal.

Step 5. Weigh alternatives

- Which major seems best to you and why?
- Which major is consistent with your values, interests, and aptitudes?
- Which major is consistent with your career direction?

Step 6. Predict outcomes and consequences

- Predict whether the major will meet your needs.
- Will you be satisfied with this major?
- What additional concerns will result from this decision?

Step 7. Make the decision

- Based on steps 1-5, make a decision.

Step 8. Implement the decision

- Begin taking courses in chosen major.

Step 9. Evaluate the decision

- You find that you do not like the courses in this major. Go back to Step 1.

Step 10. Make a new decision

- Repeat steps 1-8.

The Decision-Making Process

Step 1. Identify the problem

_____

_____

_____

Step 2. Gather information

_____

_____

_____

Step 3. Generate courses of action
and alternatives

_____

_____

_____

Step 4. Explore feelings

_____

_____

_____

Step 5. Weigh the decision

_____

_____

_____

Step 6. Predict outcomes and
consequences

_____

_____

_____

Step 7. Arrive at the decision

_____

_____

_____

Step 8. Implement the decision

_____

_____

_____

Step 9. Evaluate the decision

_____

_____

_____

Step 10. Make a new decision

_____

_____

_____

Empowerment Through Decision-Making

Freedom of Choice Is Fundamental to Decision-Making

When we view ourselves as decision-makers, we believe in our capacity to direct our own lives. A belief in the freedom to choose encourages decision-making. We cannot control all events in our lives, but we have a significant degree of control over our lives through decision-making. If we believe that everything is determined, we may feel that we have no ability to choose.

Decision-Making Skills Can Be Learned

Examining the decision-making process helps us understand how people decide. Skills such as collecting information, defining problems, generating alternatives, weighing alternatives, selecting an alternative, and implementing decisions are skills which can be learned. Decision-making involves bringing about desirable situations, conditions, circumstances, events, and personal states of satisfaction.

Our Behavior Results from Decisions

We make decisions about who we are and what we are. What we have decided about ourselves shapes our attitudes. Our attitudes determine how we think, feel, and act. We behave according to our decisions even in situations where we cannot remember making the decision. We decide what is right and wrong, what is desirable or undesirable, what is positive or negative, and what direction to pursue. We act in accordance with our decisions.

Look for Decisions Behind the Decision

Early life decisions form the basis of later life decisions. Our self-attitudes are a consequence of decisions we have made about ourselves. If we have decided that we have little worth, subsequent decisions will emanate from that decision. There is a decision behind the decision regarding our worth. For example, you might not date because of your prior decision that you are not worthy.

If You Don't Like Who You Are, Re-Decide Who You Are

Decision-making is a defining activity. We define who and what we are through decision-making. We can undo prior decisions we have made about ourselves. We can re-decide who we are. Consciously choosing ourselves is an enormously important process. Ultimately, we decide who we are. I define myself, and if I don't like my self-definition, I can re-decide who I am.

To Choose, You Must Know You Have a Choice

Many individuals do not acknowledge that choices have led them to where they are now in their lives. They did not realize that they had a choice. If you don't know you have a choice, you don't have a choice. Many individuals are so overwhelmed by their environments that they believe their lives are determined. Many of our personal problems are so confusing and frustrating that we do not realize that we have a choice. Awareness of choice is essential to the decision-making process.

We Are Often Unaware of the Decisions Which Govern Our Lives

Many vital decisions are made early in life. We forget what we have decided, and we act habitually without realizing our choices. We may not have been conscious of our choices when we made them and are now out of touch with our decisions. Awareness of our decisions is crucial to personal growth. A conscious awareness of decision-making increases our control over our lives.

It Is Important to Examine Feelings About Decisions

Decision-making is not a completely rational process. The last time you purchased a dress, suit, or car, did you decide on your purchase in a strictly rational manner? Of course not! Our decisions are greatly influenced by our feelings. Consequently, it is important to ask ourselves how we feel about alternatives available to us when we decide.

Awareness
Alternatives
DECISION-MAKING
Information

We Need to Examine How We Decide

By seeking to understand the decision-making process, we can gain insight into how we can make more effective decisions. This is particularly true when we are making decisions that are heavily weighed with emotion. Others may tell us how to decide, but we frequently resist this assistance. Acknowledging where you are with decision making allows you to make progress toward effective decision-making.

There Is No Single Right Decision

Many of us are paralyzed when confronted with a need to make a decision. The belief that there is only one right decision in any given situation is paralyzing. Many decisions involve moral judgements, but many others involve choosing between alternatives which do not create major moral dilemmas. We could spend a lifetime trying to resolve moral decisions without ever making a decision.

Every Decision Has Consequences, Results, and Effects

When we decide, we always attempt to mitigate negative consequences, results and effects. At times we can anticipate the consequences of our decisions, but at times we have no idea of the effects of our decisions. We need to get away from the idea of a single "right" decision, and to think in terms of consequences, results, and effects. We usually aspire to positive and beneficial consequences of our decisions.

Decisions Eliminate Options

When we decide, we gain something and we lose something. We can't have it all. If you love two people and want to marry, you can't marry both individuals. If you want to be a successful actor, as well as a physician, it is unlikely that you can do both. You have to choose one and possibly forsake the other. If you decide to be an actor, you may not be able to become a physician.

Decision-Making Is a Sorting Process

In deciding, we sort through information, alternatives, feelings, values, consequences, and many other factors that impinge on our decision-making. This sorting out of essential information affects the quality of our decisions. We must be prepared to sort out information vigorously when deciding.

By Actively and Consciously Choosing, We Direct the Course of Our Lives

Decision-making is the navigational tool by which we set the course of our lives. The more conscious we are of our decisions, the clearer the plotting of our course. When we get off course, we can decide to get back on course or to change direction completely. When you are not conscious of your decisions, you are not the navigator of your course.

Decision-Making Involves Hunches, Feelings and Intuitions

Decision-making is not a totally rational or scientific process. We frequently intuit our best alternative in a situation. Many of us need to trust our hunches, feelings, and intuitions. Some of our best decisions may not be based on rational thinking.

We Struggle with Decisions All the Time

Every day, we make many decisions, from deciding what to wear in the morning to what to eat for dinner in the evening. Depending on the importance of the decision, we experience varying degrees of dissonance. This dissonance is unsettling and causes discomfort and anxiety. We fear not making the right decision. We experience a paralysis when caught between alternatives. Decision-making is a painful process when we fear the consequences, results, and effects of our decisions.

Stress

Take this self-inventory by rating yourself with the following scale:

5 = This statement is true <u>all</u> of the time.
4 = This statement is true <u>most</u> of the time.
3 = This statement is true <u>much</u> of the time.
2 = This statement is true <u>some</u> of the time.
1 = This statement is true <u>almost</u> none of the time.
0 = This statement is true <u>none</u> of the time.

_____ 1. I feel like I have no control over my life.

_____ 2. I worry about the past.

_____ 3. I worry about my future.

_____ 4. I feel lonely and depressed.

_____ 5. I worry about dating.

_____ 6. I procrastinate when faced with difficult tasks.

_____ 7. I have a learning disability.

_____ 8. I find that I am lost and confused about my education.

_____ 9. I'm in college because I don't know what else to do.

_____ 10. I feel very isolated in college.

_____ 11. I don't have friends in college.

_____ 12. I feel lonely as a student.

_____ 13. I feel out of place in college because I am an older student.

_____ 14. At college, I feel like an outsider.

_____ 15. When I think about the extent of my class assignments, I get depressed.

_____ 16. I get anxious and panic when I take exams.

_____ 17. I have mental blocks when I take exams.

_____ 18. I usually have at least one professor that I don't like.

_____ 19. I worry about having enough money to pay for my expenses.

_____ 20. I am unable to postpone gratification.

Stress

➦ *To do great work a man must be very idle as well as very industrious.*
—*Samuel Butler*

It is vital that we learn to handle and manage our daily hassles and stresses. All of us experience daily stress; some of us may experience daily distress. Distress is more injurious than stress. Distress occurs when coping capacities are being taxed to the limit. The result is wear and tear on the body. Stress is a reaction to demands made on the body to adapt and change. Rapidity of change, daily hassles, and a hurried lifestyle all contribute to the stress and strain of living.

Appraisal of Stress

The impact of stress is largely determined by the interpretations of stressful events. The mental appraisal you make may be the single most important factor in determining the impact of stress.

Change and Stress

Life holds many changes which lead to stress. It is a good idea to decrease the rate of change. Researchers have determined that the more changes you have experienced in a year's time, the greater the likelihood you will get sick. The rapidity of change, frequency of change, and intensity of change are major sources of stress for people. A hurried lifestyle may be a sign of being under stress. This is another factor to consider in assessing your lifestyle.

Stress Reduction

Stress reduction begins with an assessment of lifestyle. Mechanisms to reduce stress need to be incorporated into our daily lives. Sleep, nutrition, and exercise form the foundation of a good stress reduction program. The quality of sleep, proper nutrition, and appropriate exercise contribute significantly to the quality of life. We need a place to remove ourselves from daily stresses. We need a place to rejuvenate and regenerate. We need a place to be alone and to be quiet.

Relaxation and Stress

One of the biggest problems in learning how to relax and relieve stress is that we do not know the difference between states of tension and relaxation. There are times we feel relaxed, but in reality we are not. We must learn to discriminate between states of tension and stress as opposed to states of deep relaxation.

Progressive Relaxation

A very simple technique used by many psychologists to help people relax is to tighten and contract muscles followed by relaxing those muscles, then feeling and sensing the difference. Make a tight fist for six seconds and pay attention to the way your muscles feel. Relax the tight fist and sense the difference between tight, tense muscles and relaxed muscles. You can do this with all muscle groups, including your facial muscles. Tense tightly, hold for six seconds, let go, and notice the difference. By inducing deep relaxation in the muscle groups, you are using the technique known as progressive relaxation.

There are many ways to alleviate and protect yourself from distress. An excellent option when you are confused about stress or distress is to pursue psychotherapy.

Stress

When you are under stress, how is it manifested?
Check the appropriate areas.

- ❏ health
- ❏ temper
- ❏ sleep
- ❏ rationality
- ❏ appetite
- ❏ concentration
- ❏ enjoyment

- ❏ sexual desire
- ❏ sense of humor
- ❏ school work
- ❏ class attendance
- ❏ motivation
- ❏ work
- ❏ relationships

- ❏ self-esteem
- ❏ self-confidence
- ❏ anger
- ❏ smoking
- ❏ drugs
- ❏ other _____

1. How many of these stress reactions do you manifest?

_____

_____

_____

2. How do you manage your stress reactions? Do you have a stress management plan? Explain.

_____

_____

_____

3. Where can you get help in order to manage stress?

_____

_____

_____

Quieting the Mind

Begin with 20 minutes daily.

Step 1. **Find** a quiet, peaceful place and sit quietly on a comfortable chair.

Step 2. **Assume** an upright position without rigidity. Hold your head up and try not to use a headrest.

Step 3. **Avoid** crossing your legs, feet and hands. Place hands in a comfortable position.

Step 4. **Breathe** normally and close your eyes.

Step 5. **Become** open and receptive while cultivating an attitude of non-resistance.

Step 6. **Be passive** and allow feelings, thoughts, and fantasies to occur.

Step 7. **Witness** yourself and watch the contents of your mind. Let experiences come and go.

Step 8. **Notice** your breath.

Step 9. **Cultivate** the attitudes of openness, receptivity, and passivity, allowing, witnessing, and non-resistance.

Support and Coping

Support

Support from others contributes to our sense of well-being, feelings of self-worth and our ability to cope with difficult situations. Support frequently takes the form of interpersonal communication. Relationships are an important part of our support system. The people we know and care about provide us with emotional support, which is especially important during a crisis. Most of us seek and need emotional support. We also want to know that others support our efforts, desires, and goals. At times we may also need love and acceptance, food, shelter, clothing, money, transportation, child-care, financial aid, and other types of support.

Gaining Support

Gaining support involves a broad range of skills. The ability to communicate effectively with others is a means of gaining support. We may need to learn to ask for help and need to learn where to get help. Others who are in a position to help may require that we fill out forms and meet other conditions for assistance. In gaining support, we may need to be persistent, assertive, and willing to question other people.

We can construct a support system which we can rely on by building a network of positive relationships. Other individuals usually behave supportively when we ourselves are supportive. Supportive people generally find it easier to gain support from others.

Coping with Life's Pressures

All of us are under demands to cope with life's pressures. For many, coping means handling the stresses and strains of living. We are constantly coping with problems, trying to find solutions to problems, and attempting to overcome obstacles to living.

Effective coping means developing skills and resources for effective problem solving. Coping skills are the skills we use to get through hard times. Coping is closely related to our interpersonal skills and our ability to communicate effectively with others. Problems of coping usually involve problems of coping with feelings such as love, loneliness, rejection, fear, and meaninglessness.

All of us cope with significant life demands and changes. Some of those

demands include divorce, joblessness, illness, financial problems, single parenthood, and even death. Our capacity to cope is occasionally activated by a crisis in living. The loss of a loved one and loss of employment create serious threats to our security and force us to cope with severe demands.

An effective coping system will help us learn to live with change, help us find strength and courage, and show that looking deep within ourselves we may find the peace and strength needed to manage the many demands of life.

A Strategy for Stress Reduction

1. **Maintain** proper nutrition, sleep, and exercise.

2. **Reduce** and manage daily hassles.

3. **Manage** frequency and intensity of change. Space changes to reduce accumulation of stress.

4. **Become** aware of your interpretation and appraisal of stressful events.

5. **Learn** and cultivate a relaxation response to stressful events.

6. **Increase** enjoyment in your life.

Chapter Conclusion:
Critical Analysis and Application

Select a concept from this chapter which has the greatest relevance and importance to you. Explain the nature of the concept and why it is relevant and important to you. Critically analyze the concept by discussing its essential features. Determine how this concept can be applied to everyday life.

Select: _____

_____

_____

_____

Explain: _____

_____

_____

_____

_____

Analyze: _____

_____

_____

_____

Apply: _____

_____

_____

_____

Chapter 11

Learning Skills

Learning Skills

Take this self-inventory by rating yourself with the following scale:

5 = This statement is true <u>all</u> of the time.
4 = This statement is true <u>most</u> of the time.
3 = This statement is true <u>much</u> of the time.
2 = This statement is true <u>some</u> of the time.
1 = This statement is true <u>almost</u> none of the time.
0 = This statement is true <u>none</u> of the time.

_____ 1. I know how to learn.

_____ 2. I know how I learn best

_____ 3. I know my learning style.

_____ 4. I am an auditory learner.

_____ 5. I am a visual learner.

_____ 6. I am a kinesthetic learner.

_____ 7. I use a combination of my sensory system to learn.

_____ 8. I recognize the value of practice when I learn.

_____ 9. I usually follow what I learn with a reward.

_____ 10. I have developed my own set of learning strategies.

Study Skills

College Survival Skills

Skills

Life & Learning Skills

Skills vary with the man. We must tread a straight path and strive by that which is born in us.

—Pindar

The Skills Triad

The Skills Triad consists of Life and Learning Skills, Study Skills, and College Survival Skills. Skills involve the development of aptitudes and abilities. It is through the application of skills that we optimize our performance. Learning skills enable us to learn more effectively and come to a deeper understanding of academic ideas. A learning skill is a method, principle, or procedure that facilitates the learning process. Learning skills are associated with learning principles. The conscious application of a learning principle which facilitates learning is a learning skill. Knowledge of how we learn allows us to consciously apply principles of effective learning. Study skills facilitate the learning process without the learner being conscious of the learning principle which underlies learning. For example, reviewing is a study skill, but there are several learning principles that underlie reviewing. The learning principles that underlie reviewing fall within the categories of cognitive learning and information processing. Knowledge and application of these learning principles result in a learning skill.

Learning Skills

Learning Skill 1

Practice

Few, if any, learning activities cannot be mastered through practice. Practice seems so obvious that we frequently fail to see its value. Through practice, we learn to solve algebraic equations, write research papers, and give effective speeches. Just as we learn to hit a powerful topspin backhand shot in tennis through practice, we master academic activities through practice. Repetition and review are techniques of practice.

Learning Skill 2

Knowledge of Results

The information that we gain regarding our performance on a learning task provides us with knowledge of effective and less effective responses. Knowledge of results shapes our responses. All the comments made on a research paper give us valuable information on how to write a more effective research paper. Knowledge of test results tells us what we can do to make more effective and correct responses. We need knowledge of where we go astray in order to get back on target.

Learning Skill 3

Use All Your Senses

Using all of your senses greatly enhances your ability to learn and remember material. When the senses are all used in combination, we strengthen our ability to remember. Each modality has its own memory sense. Many of us favor a particular sensory modality. But if you want to remember it, see it, hear it, say it, feel it, and act on it.

238

Learning Skill 4

Staying on Task

The ability to stay focused on a task for an extended period of time is difficult for many. Yet many learning tasks require patient and persistent effort. It is the completion of learning tasks that gets us through a course and eventually through college. Frequently, the more task oriented we are, the more we are able to succeed.

Learning Skill 5

Application of Effort

Effort is a conscious attempt to do our best at learning a task. Getting ready to learn isn't always automatic. Effort is easiest to apply when we are motivated to learn. Most learning tasks require a conscious decision to do it. At times effort means that we compel ourselves to act through internal pressure and demands. If you don't give it a try, you may not ever learn it. Trying is making the effort.

Learning Skill 6

Effortless Effort

The more we perform learning tasks, the more automatic and spontaneous our energy. You do it effectively without being conscious of how you do it. Although you have been trained and skilled in writing essays, through effortless effort, you write a great essay without being conscious of how you did it. Your level of functioning becomes more effective and spontaneous.

Learning Skill 7

Spaced Practice

Through spaced practice we learn more in the same amount of time than through time that has been massed together. Two one-half hour study sessions can be much more effective than a one-hour session. Studying a little seven days a week is more effective than extended study two days a week. Short study periods can be very effective.

Learning Skill 8

Trial and Error

We learn from our mistakes. We should expect to make mistakes and should not be discouraged by them. Our mistakes are a demonstration of knowledge of results. Mistakes tell us something about what we need to do and not do. Trials are further attempts at mastering a task. Sustaining trials requires motivation and effort.

Learning Skill 9

Modeling

We learn from the actions of others. Others learn from our actions. Modeling is a powerful form of learning. Mentors become valuable partners in learning because they become our models. We learn and teach through example. You can model the positive behavior you see in others, and you can also model the negative behavior you see in others. Be watchful and attentive of what is modeled around you.

Learning Skill 10

Reinforcement and Reward

Behavior that is reinforced or rewarded is strengthened. Behaviors that are strengthened tend to be repeated. Behavior is governed by its consequences. Study and learning behaviors must be reinforced in order to be sustained.

Learning Skill 11

Cognitive Learning

The learning activities of the brain are very complex. We learn and solve problems through complex mental operations. As human beings, we have a tremendous thinking capacity. We learn through our cognitive processes. The mental and intellectual activity of the mind appears to have no limit.

Learning Skills

Examine your learing skills by answering the following questions.

1. How do you approach a learning task such as reading a chapter?

_____

_____

_____

_____

_____

_____

2. Do you know the learning principle that underlies your study approaches?

_____

_____

_____

_____

_____

3. Are you able to determine what works for you and what doesn't work for you? Explain.

_____

_____

_____

_____

_____

Learning Styles

Do you pay attention to the way you learn? Do you know how you learn best? Do you know what type of cues from the environment help or hinder your learning? When you are in a classroom, what type of instruction do you prefer?

Individuals generally can be classified into three categories of learning styles: visual, auditory, and kinesthetic-tactile. Which best fits you? Of course, most of us use all of our senses in learning and in responding to the environment, but we probably have definite preferences.

Visual Learners

Visual learners are prompted to learn more effectively when presented with a series of visual cues. They learn best by seeing and reading. Visual learners frequently prefer to work alone, enjoy conducting research, and like writing about their findings.

Auditory Learners

The auditory learner learns best by listening and hearing. Auditory learners enjoy discussion and interaction and do not enjoy assignments involving substantial reading. Auditory learners like to interact with others and participate in group discussion.

Kinesthetic-Tactile Learners

Kinesthetic-Tactile learners learn best using motor activities. Kinesthetic-Tactile learners enjoy manipulating objects and using various digital movements while learning. Kinesthetic-Tactile learners feel compelled to get up and move about while engaged in learning activities. They enjoy sports and are mechanically inclined.

Knowing, understanding, and using your learning style will help increase your learning effectiveness. The following activities are designed to help you determine your preferred learning style, evaluate your learning style, maximize your learning style, and match your learning style with study techniques.

Learning Styles Survey

Check the visual, auditory or kinesthetic-tactile activities which are <u>most</u> characteristic of you.

Visual

- ❏ I like reading.
- ❏ I use pictures, charts and graphs to study.
- ❏ I prefer written directions.
- ❏ I remember by taking notes and making lists.
- ❏ I am good at using maps.
- ❏ I enjoy reading books, magazines, and newspapers.
- ❏ I enjoy research and writing.
- ❏ I enjoy drawing, designing and sketching.
- ❏ I use mental pictures to remember.
- ❏ I spell difficult words by writing them down.

Auditory

- ❏ I remember oral directions.
- ❏ I read aloud to understand new concepts.
- ❏ I enjoy listening to music.
- ❏ I enjoy listening to a lecture or play.
- ❏ I understand academics better when listening to a lecture or tape.
- ❏ I like discussion and exchange of ideas.
- ❏ I remember things people say.
- ❏ I enjoy hearing foreign languages.
- ❏ I spell difficult words by sounding them out.
- ❏ I enjoy listening to books on tape.

Kinesthetic-Tactile

- ❏ I enjoy working with computers.
- ❏ I doodle during lectures.
- ❏ I enjoy sightseeing.
- ❏ I enjoy contact with others such as hugging and handshaking.
- ❏ I enjoy dance and movement.
- ❏ I participate in sports.
- ❏ I prefer to create and build projects.
- ❏ I snack, smoke, or chew gum while studying.
- ❏ I fidget with objects while studying.
- ❏ I enjoy using machines.

Evaluating Your Learning Style

Evaluate your learning style by answering the following questions.

1. What is your dominant learning style?

_____

_____

_____

_____

2. Describe key characteristics of your learning style.

_____

_____

_____

_____

3. Describe strengths and weaknesses of your learning style.

_____

_____

_____

_____

4. How can you use this information to improve your learning effectiveness?

_____

_____

_____

_____

Maximizing Your Learning Style

Maximize your learning style by emphasizing your strengths.
Use the following techniques to increase learning efficiency.

Visual

Read silently.

Write directions.

Use visual study notes and cards.

Underline or highlight in your textbook.

Visualize meanings.

Auditory

Explain material to others.

Use recitation.

Use tape recordings.

Focus on verbal directions and instructions.

Use study pairs and groups.

Kinesthetic-Tactile

Write outlines.

Make lists and graphs.

Take notes.

Underline or highlight in your textbooks.

Stand or walk while studying.

Learning Styles and Study Techniques

The following study techniques are from the Study Skills chapter. Increase your learning effectiveness by matching the technique to your learning style.

Visual	Auditory	Kinesthetic-Tactile
Quick Survey	Quick Survey (out loud)	Questioning
In-Depth Preview	In-Depth Preview (out loud)	Underlining
Skimming	Read, Stop, Recite	Outlining
Scanning	Questioning	Terminology
Read, Stop Recite	Recitation	Awareness Practice
Questioning	Review	Observe Results Without Judgement
Underlining	Terminology	Techniques for Reading Comprehension
Review	Word Attack Skills	Recorders
Don't Read Past A Word You Are Not Able To Define.	Recorders	
Terminology	Awareness Practice	
Word Attack Skills	Techniques for Reading Comprehension	
Awareness Practice		
Observe Results Without Judgement		
Techniques for Reading Comprehension		

Memory

 Memory is the library of the mind.
— Francis Fauvel-Gourand

Human beings are very complex information processors. We are bombarded with vast quantities of information of which only a fraction is processed. We pay attention to and recognize only a small amount of information which comes from the environment. Memory, like all other psychological processes, cannot be directly observed. Therefore, models have been developed which are attempts to explain the complex functions of memory. Information processing theorists who study how humans encode, store, process and retrieve information use flow charts to describe and represent these complex functions of human memory. Flow charts are graphic representations used to illustrate the complex functions of memory.

Memory Stores

Many memory theorists assume that we have three memory stores, each of which holds different amounts of information and for different periods of time. These memory stores are called sensory register (SR), short-term memory (STM), and long-term memory (LTM).

Sensory register is considered to be very brief and registers information from the environment in its original form. Sensory register lasts about four seconds. Short-term memory holds a limited amount of information for a short period of time. Short-term memory holds about seven bits of information for about fifteen seconds. Unlike sensory register and short-term memory, long-term memory can hold vast quantities of information for a lifetime.

Many memory theorists believe that information stored in long-term memory is permanent. Not only is this information permanent, but we seem to have an unlimited capacity to store information. Information that reaches long-term memory has been encoded by mechanisms which have facilitated the storage of that information.

Encoding and Retrieval

Of special concern to college students is how to encode information so that it will be permanently stored. Not only must it be stored, it also must be retrieved. Encoding strategies and retrieval strategies assist in the processing of information and the retrieval of information from long-term memory. Information which has not been processed into long-term memory cannot be retrieved.

Control Processes

Processes which govern the flow of information between memory stores are called control processes. Some control processes maintain information in memory stores for further processing, while others encode the information into permanent storage.

Attention and recognition are examples of control processes which maintain information in memory stores for further precessing. Attention and recognition allow for the registration of information by the sensory register and its processing into short-term memory. The mechanisms of special concern facilitate the flow of information from short-term memory into long-term memory.

Rehearsal

A major encoding mechanism which is also a control process is repetition. Repetition is a major information processing mechanism. There are at least two types of repetition; maintenance rehearsal and elaborative rehearsal. Maintenance rehearsal is the type of repetition that helps keep a phone number in mind for immediate use. Elaborative rehearsal is the type of repetition used to learn a complicated famous speech. In this type of repetition, we compare the speech we are learning to previously learned famous speeches, to famous speech givers, and to our own experience. In elaborative rehearsal, information being remembered is compared and associated with information already in long-term storage. Elaborative rehearsal is a powerful mechanism for storing information permanently.

Encoding Strategies

Others mechanisms which help with the storage of information include organization, meaningfulness, mnemonic devices, and activity. By organizing information into meaningful clumps, we can greatly facilitate remembering. These clumps may provide cues for the remembering of other organized clumps. Organization reduces the number of clumps we need to remember. Meaningful information is one of the most easily remembered. Information which is related or associated with previously learned information is more readily remembered because it is usually meaningful.

Mnemonic Devices

Mnemonic devices are important because they help with the encoding of information which makes it easier to retrieve. Mnemonic devices are mechanisms used to make information more meaningful thus more memorable. A common mnemonic device is the acronym. Acronyms use a first letter system of a series of items to make up a word. For example, SCUBA is an acronym for Self-Contained Underwater Breathing Apparatus. Acronyms need not be real words. The first letter technique to form real or nonsense words can provide important cues to aid in the retrieval of information. Similar to the acronym is the acrostic which is a sentence mnemonic using the first letter of each word in a sentence. Verbal and physical activity helps in the encoding of information. The memorization of foreign language vocabulary is facilitated by activity. For example, when learning the word stand, you stand, when learning bend, you bend.

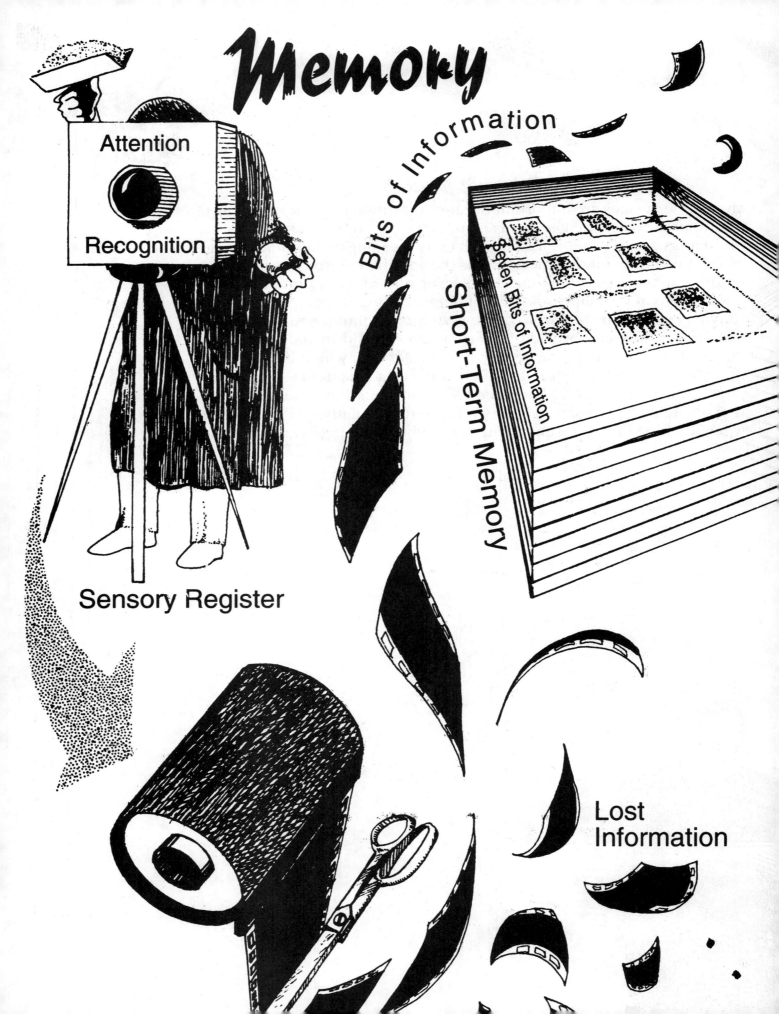

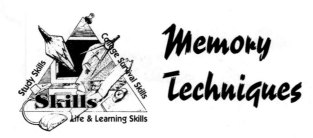

Memory Techniques

1. Repetition

Repetition is immediate and easy to use. We can rely on repetition to hold information in short-term memory by simply repeating information verbally and mentally. We can hold on to it for a longer period of time through repetition which allows for the maintenance of information in short-term memory and creates the possibility for further processing. Repetition may create different patterns and sensory impressions, which may add additional meaning and therefore allow for further processing of information.

2. Association

Associating a new idea with an old idea may be one of the easiest ways to remember the new idea. Associations make connections of new information with stored information creating possibilities for deeper processing of information. Associations create patterns which may introduce meaning and therefore facilitate further processing of information.

3. Meaningfulness

Meaningfulness may be one of the most powerful encoding mechanisms for processing new information into long-term memory. Meaningfulness relates new information to stored information in long-term memory and allows us to encode information.

4. Organization

Organizing information into meaningful patterns helps us process and remember the information. Chunks of information which contain little meaning can be organized into clumps of information which do have meaning. New clumps can reduce the number of chunks to remember, and the new clumps may give us cues to remember other clumps.

5. Vividness

Chunks of information that are vividly encoded are more memorable than chunks that do not get our attention. Attention is captured by size, color, intensity, novelty and unexpectedness.

6. Distinctiveness

By concentrating on distinctive features of information, we can remember it with greater ease. For example, when studying a foreign language noticing the distinctive features of words can help you remember the vocabulary. Some foreign language words offer very few cues that help us remember them. By noticing the distinctive features, you can begin to notice patterns which will further assist in learning vocabulary.

7. Rehearsal

Rehearsal is a type of repetition. There are two types of rehearsal; maintenance and elaborative rehearsal. Maintenance rehearsal is used to hold bits of information in short-term memory. Holding a phone number in short-term memory until it is used is a type of maintenance rehearsal. The repetition used to remember a complicated speech is an example of elaborative rehearsal. In this type of rehearsal, you use stored information to help remember your speech. You relate the new speech to previously learned speeches, famous speakers, and memories triggered by the new speech.

8. Interference

Learning new information is interfered with by previously learned information. Learning new information also interferes with the remembering of old information. Learning situations produce both types of interferences. These interferences obstruct the acquisition of new information, and the retrieval of old information.

9. Using Your Senses

Using various combinations of your sensory system, hearing, seeing, touching, smelling, and tasting facilitate remembering information. Each sense possesses its own memory system. We can remember the sound of an old song, the smell of flowers, the taste of an old favorite dish, and the touch and sight of an old friend.

10. Acronyms

Acronyms are usually formed by taking the first letter of a series of items to be remembered and forming a word. Acronyms need not always form a recognizable word. Acronyms help in both the storage and retrieval of information. Acronyms are very useful in organizing random bits of information into meaningful clumps of information. For example, the acronym HOMES is very useful in remembering the Great Lakes: Huron, Ontario, Michigan, Erie, and Superior.

11. Acrostics

Acrostics are similar to acronyms in that they both use letters and position of letters to provide cues to remember more complicated information. Acrostics use the first letter of words in a phrase or sentence to act as cues for the retrieval of information.

12. Use

Use contributes to the remembering of information. Using information helps with the retrieval of information.

13. Visualization

Forming mental images of information we want to remember helps in the processing, storage, and retrieval of the information. Visualizations which catch our attention by size, inappropriateness, exaggeration, and ridiculousness help us remember information. Visualization allows for the use of right-brain hemispheric functions. Visualization allows us to use more of our brain.

14. Recitation

When you study, it is a good idea to recite everything you need to remember. Say it aloud in your own words. Reciting information through verbal expression helps in processing information. When you recite information, you pay attention to it. Attending to information helps process information.

15. Activity

Actively discussing information helps in making it memorable. Walking slowly as you read may emhance remembering material. Standing as you study can help in the retention of information.

16. Use Several Strategies

By combining memory techniques, you can process information in a variety of ways which helps in the retrieval of information.

Critical Thinking

When I am working on a problem, I never think about beauty. I think only how to solve the problem. But when I have finished, if the solution is not beautiful, I know it is wrong.
—Buckminster Fuller

"The student who asks probing questions, who seeks to figure out the logic of things, who examines assumptions, analyzes concepts, scrutinizes evidence, tests implications and consequences has always had an enormous advantage over the learner who memorizes bits and pieces of information as if they were so many BB's in a bag." -Richard Paul

Asking Questions

The key elements of critical thinking are found in the statement above. Asking probing questions is an important step toward thinking critically. Many students are hesitant to ask questions in a classroom environment. Many students fail to ask questions because they fear how they may appear to others. Other students may have difficulty formulating questions. The ability to question what you are learning is an important step in learning and thinking more critically.

Open-Mindedness

An obstacle to critical thinking is the tendency to protect and defend what we already believe to be true. Previous learning and conditioning easily interferes with the acquisition of new information and knowledge. It is essential to think for ourselves, but we need to maintain open-mindedness which allows for the acquisition of new information and knowledge. Questioning your assumptions is an important way to examine previous learning and beliefs.

Scientific Method

The major framework for learning to think more critically in the academic setting is the scientific method. The major method based on the scientific method is the experimental method. By learning to conduct well-controlled experiments, we learn to think critically. Through the scientific method, we conduct systmmatic observations, generate theories, formulate and test hypotheses, generate and collect data, analyze data, and report results. If the hypotheses are re-tested under controlled conditions and yield the same results, we gain a higher degree of confidence in our conclusions because of the replication.

Conversation and Participation

Asking questions is one way we can engage in the learning process. An additional way is to engage the instructor and other students in conversations about issues which are thought-provoking and require critical thinking. Learning to think critically through conversation and participation is the substance of learning. Many students fail to participate in the conversation because they feel that what they have to say is not important or relevant. Others think they are not capable of being intellectual or do not desire to be so. Anyone who enjoys ideas is an intellectual. Many students need to be encouraged to use their abilities to think and participate with others.

Critical Thinking

Intellectual standards that apply to thinking in every subject:

Clear	Unclear
Precise	Imprecise
Accurate	Inaccurate
Relevant	Irrelevant
Consistent	Inconsistent
Logical	Illogical
Deep	Superficial
Complete	Incomplete
Significant	Trivial
Adequate	Inadequate
Fair	Prejudicial

Reference: 12th International Conference on Critical Thinking

A Strategy for Memorization

Step 1. **Organize** it.

Step 2. **Repeat** it, say it, explain it.

Step 3. **Relate** and connect old ideas to new ideas.

Step 4. **Make** it meaningful.

Step 5. **Use** acronyms, chunks, and codes.

Step 6. **Use** it or lose it.

Step 7. **Repeat** again.

Chapter Conclusion:
Critical Analysis and Application

Select a concept from this chapter which has the greatest relevance and importance to you. Explain the nature of the concept and why it is relevant and important to you. Critically analyze the concept by discussing its essential features. Determine how this concept can be applied to everyday life.

Select:_____

_____

_____

_____

_____

Explain:_____

_____

_____

_____

_____

Analyze:_____

_____

_____

_____

_____

Apply: _____

_____

_____

_____

_____

Chapter 12

Study Skills

Study Skills

Take this self-inventory by rating yourself with the following scale:

5 = This statement is true <u>all</u> of the time.
4 = This statement is true <u>most</u> of the time.
3 = This statement is true <u>much</u> of the time.
2 = This statement is true <u>some</u> of the time.
1 = This statement is true <u>almost</u> none of the time.
0 = This statement is true <u>none</u> of the time.

_____ 1. I am adequately prepared for college.

_____ 2. I have a study plan.

_____ 3. I study at the same time and place each day.

_____ 4. I can study for long periods of time.

_____ 5. I stop, pause, and think about what I'm reading.

_____ 6. I use recitation when I study.

_____ 7. I use the review technique to remember what I study.

_____ 8. I participate in study groups.

_____ 9. I like to study in the college library.

_____ 10. I use numerous memory techniques to help me remember class material.

_____ 11. I'm a good listener.

_____ 12. I take good notes.

_____ 13. I carry a dictionary.

_____ 14. I concentrate in academic situations.

_____ 15. I am motivated in academic situations.

_____ 16. I relate what I am learning to what I already know.

_____ 17. I use learning strategies.

_____ 18. I know how to learn.

_____ 19. I enjoy studying.

_____ 20. I use the latest technologies for effective study.

The Skills Triad

The Skills Triad consists of Life and Learning Skills, Study Skills, and College Survival Skills. Skills involve the development of aptitudes and abilities. It is through the application of skills that we optimize our performance. Study skills give us power to learn and increase our confidence in learning situations. Study skills are specific methods, procedures, and techniques used in learning. They influence our ability to learn and succeed in college. The greater the range and development of study skills, the more effective we can be as students. Study skills are tools which can be applied to learning situations and combined give us strategies when approaching learning tasks. Study skills help us learn to learn and to increase the efficiency, expediency, and depth of our learning. When we are able to use study skills effectively, we feel encouraged, and our motivation increases.

Guidelines for Effective Study and Learning

1. Assess Motivation to Study

Motivation is an essential factor in performance but is not easy to assess. You may want to ask yourself the following questions: Am I ready to undertake the demands of an academic program which requires substantial study? How will I get myself ready? How can I motivate myself to study? What are the benefits of study?

2. Make Studying a Priority

When studying becomes a priority, other activities are less likely to interfere with the process of studying. This will make it easier for you to make a firm commitment to studying. Where does studying fall on your list of priorities? Are your actions consistent with the activities you consider priorities?

3. Make a Study Schedule

A study schedule is a product of effective time management. Do you have sufficient time to study? If not, which activities interfere with studying? Remember, time management obstacles are major interferences with effective study.

4. Select a Place to Study

A consistent place to study helps make study habitual. A place to study makes it easier to get started on study assignments and prevents wasting time deciding where to study. Quick and easy access to your place of study is essential to support your study commitment. Many students use the college library to study because they find it difficult to study at home with the family or in an apartment with roommates. You may have to negotiate with others to help you create a conducive study environment.

5. Gather Materials and Resources for Study

After you have selected a place for study, it is important to have all the materials and supplies at your disposal. Proper lighting, desk, chair, pens, pencils, paper, dictionary, thesaurus, calculator, erasers, notebooks, pads, binders, recorders, computers, and other reference materials are all essential supplies for the study environment.

6. Attend Class

Class attendance is essential in order to perform well in college. If you are not in class, you can acquire the information you need only through secondary sources. You have to be in class in order to get the most out of your learning experience.

7. Take Notes

Notes are a transcript of material covered in a class lecture. Notes should include the fundamental material of the course being taken. It is essential to be committed to effective note-taking. The quality of note-taking can easily determine the level of performance on exams. Note-taking techniques can improve your ability to take notes.

8. Develop Concentration and Avoid Distraction

By increasing your motivation, you can increase your ability to concentrate on a learning task. Concentration cannot be forced. Increasing levels of interest will increase levels of concentration. It is almost impossible to avoid distraction; we must be careful not to allow distractions to derail our efforts. Learn techniques to develop concentration and techniques that mitigate the effects of distraction.

9. Use Study Techniques, Skills, Strategies, and Procedures

Effective study skills can significantly increase your level of academic performance. It is important that you learn how to learn. Look for ways to increase your study effectiveness. Learn study techniques, strategies, skills, and procedures.

10. Use Learning Strategies

Learning strategies combine knowledge of how we learn with strategies for effective learning. Underlying a learning strategy is a learning principle. Learning a task can be accomplished through practice, by how that practice is to be applied is a matter of a learning strategy.

11. Identify Study and Learning Difficulties

Study and learning difficulties are any obstacles that interfere with study and learning. Difficulties in comprehending reading material may be an example of a study or learning difficulty. Learn to identify and describe study and learning difficulties. Examples of study and learning difficulties may fall into the areas of memory, attention, and interest.

12. Seek Help for Study and Learning Difficulties

Most colleges have individuals with expertise in the areas of study and learning problems. Seek help in diagnosing any study or learning problem you think impedes your effectiveness as a student. Many students have study and learning difficulties which are not necessarily considered disabilities.

13. Consider a Tutor

Having a tutor helps you stay on task and understand the material. Some tutors are trained in specific areas, while others may have a broad range of expertise. An important function of the tutor is to be supportive and help you do the work.

14. Find a Mentor

Many colleges and universities have mentoring programs. Frequently mentors are individuals who are already working in your chosen field. They can offer you valuable guidance and support. Mentors are valuable models who demonstrate that it is possible for us to achieve our goals.

15. Form Study Pairs and Study Groups

Finding just one other person to share your classroom experience may be very helpful. If your study partner helps you to focus on the course tasks, the combined effort may be beneficial. Being completely alone and

isolated in a difficult course may readily result in poor performance in that course. A study partner or group helps you bridge the isolation of being a solitary student. Find an individual with whom you can share the pressure that you experience in difficult courses. You and your study partner or study group need to keep in mind that addressing the assignments of a course is the primary function of the study group. Study groups can perform tasks in many different ways. Some groups emphasize the division of the workload which is later brought back to share with the rest of the group. Most study groups emphasize the discussion of the material to be learned. Others emphasize where individuals go wrong in the solution of problems. This is especially true of math and science study groups. The formation of study pairs and study groups is a college survival skill which can make the difference between poor and optimum performance in any course.

16. Know Exactly What Is Expected From You In Each Course

Be sure you have the syllabus for each course you take. Carefully read the requirements of the course. Ask your instructor any questions you have about those requirements. If you find you do not know what is expected, make an appointment with your professor or teaching assistant. Know what is expected early in a course. Do not wait until the midterm exam to find out what is expected.

17. Start Early on Assignments

There are many advantages to starting assignments early. The first is to give yourself sufficient time to do the best job. Second, you will alleviate the pressure that accumulates from doing assignments late. And you can get help early if you run into any difficulties.

18. Develop a Strategy for Each Assignment

Formulate a plan to complete each assignment. Break the assignment into different steps, stages, and phases. This enables you to know where to start, continue and end the assignment. If you don't formulate a strategy, you may be lost and unable to effectively complete the assignment. Without a strategy, you may lack organization and waste valuable time.

19. Make an Effort

Anything worth doing requires a conscious effort. Making an effort implies that the mere application of your will power contributes to whether important undertakings are completed. Making an effort means that you try to do your best when given an assignment. In short making an effort means that you're willing to work.

20. Have a Positive Attitude

A positive attitude is the natural evolution of believing in yourself and knowing that you can accomplish your goals. A positive attitude is a product of having a hopeful attitude about the future. If you cannot maintain a positive attitude, you may need to address some self-esteem issues.

21. Look For The Value, Relevance, Meaning, and Purpose of Learning

At times it is difficult to recognize the value, relevance, meaning, and purpose of our coursework. Just as you cannot see the beauty of a house when a foundation is being put in, neither can you see the value, relevance, meaning and purpose of your education as you are acquiring it. Learning carries its own purpose, and it is through constant learning that life derives much of its meaning. All learning is relevant if you see the relationship between what you learn and other aspects of living.

22. Look for Application

For many of us, it is difficult to see the relationship between theory and practice. The application of learning is a vital leap from theory. Look for ways to apply your learning. Ask yourself, "How can I apply this to my daily life?" Application makes learning relevant and gives us the ability to do. Through application, we change our world.

23. Make Connections

Recognizing that life is a complex pattern of relationships allows us to construct innumerable meanings. Seeing the connection in our learning gives us great insight and understanding. Seeing how different things are related makes the discovery of learning very exciting.

24. Be Prepared

Preparation before and after class will greatly enhance your performance. Taking the time to do a brief review before a class is useful in understanding course content. It is important to be mentally prepared for your courses much like an athlete mentally prepares for competition. The preparation after class is the follow-through of the learning and mastery of the material. Preparation includes reviewing notes, completing reading assignments, other course assignments, attitude, and developing strategies for the completion of coursework.

25. What Kind of Learner Are You?

Discover your learning style. Look at your sensory system. Which sense do you favor when you learn? Do you like using your eyes? Ears? Your sense of touch and movement? Your sense of smell? Which of these senses do you combine when you learn best?

26. Keep It Quiet!

A quiet environment is most conducive for study. In all probability any kind of noise, including music, interferes with learning. The more consistently you keep a quiet study environment, the more likely you are to learn to enjoy the quietude.

27. Maintain Moderate Levels of Anxiety

Too little or too much anxiety interferes with performance. Excessive anxiety interferes with focusing on a task. Low levels of anxiety do not energize you to take on a task. Moderate levels of anxiety keep you alert and focused on the task.

28. Follow Study Sessions with a Reward

Behavior that is rewarded or reinforced is sustained. Study behavior is a type of behavior that students want to maintain and

develop. Rewards are pleasant activities, objects, and experiences which we enjoy and give us pleasure. There are many types of rewards, and you must discover what is rewarding for you.

29. Cultivate a Strong Belief in Yourself and in Your Abilities

A belief in oneself and one's abilities creates a reservoir of strength that is helpful when any demands are made upon you. Believing in your capacity to do well in specific activities greatly enhances performance and a sense of self-competence. A strong belief in oneself comes from real accomplishments and a strong sense of self-worth.

30. Evaluate Study and Learning Effectiveness

Periodically take the time to evaluate how well you are learning and how you are doing in your classes to determine what can be improved. Your grades are one indicator of study and learning effectiveness. You might even consider establishing your own criteria in regard to your academic performance. Examine the things you do well and the things you do not do well. How can you make yourself more efficient and more effective in the things you don't do well?

31. Learn Actively

Learning is a participatory process which requires your involvement. An active engagement in the learning situation significantly promotes learning. Learning is a dialogue, a conversation between you, your professors and other students. Find ways to express yourself meaningfully in the classroom setting.

Introduction to Study Techniques

Study techniques are useful in understanding, remembering, and learning material. Here are some proven techniques. **Quick Survey** will help you acquire an overview of the material to be studied and learned when you glance through the required reading material. **In-Depth Preview** will help you develop a comprehensive overview of the material when you read the first and last sentence of each paragraph. **Skimming** is used to identify and find main ideas by quickly searching for them. **Scanning** is a technique used for understanding main ideas by finding and then learning the main ideas. **Read, Stop, and Recite** is an important study technique designed to help the student learn, understand, and remember the material. **Questioning** enables the student to focus attention and learn the reading material by formulating probing questions about that material. **Recitation** is a powerful study and learning technique requiring the recall of important information which is stated in the student's own words. **Underlining** and **Highlighting** are important study techniques because they force the student to be selective and decide what information should be underlined or highlighted. Review consolidates learning by giving the student the necessary practice to learn, remember, and master the material. **Don't Read Past A Word You Are Unable To Define** is a technique which prevents the collapse of understanding material because the student defines all unknown words. **Outlining** is a study and learning technique which allows the student to organize material by using the traditional outline structure. **Terminology** brings attention to the importance of knowing the terms of a particular discipline when the student learns the vocabulary in that discipline. **Word Attack Skills** increase your comprehension of material when you use important word attack clues. **Recorders** provide an exact transcript of a lecture which allows you additional learning opportunities by repeatedly listening to the recording. **Awareness Practice** is a major technique for increasing your concentration by noticing where your attention is focused. **Observe Results Without Judgement** creates trust in your capacity to be self-correcting when you withhold judgement of performance.

Combining these techniques will greatly increase your learning efficiency by discovering through trial and error which combination of techniques work best for you. In order for these techniques to be helpful, a sufficient amount of application and practice is necessary. **Read** the steps of each technique, **apply** the technique, and **determine** whether it works for you.

Study Techniques

1 ▶ Quick Survey

Quick Survey gives you an overview of the material to be read. Quick Survey may be your first step in approaching a reading assignment. Quick Survey takes only a few minutes.

Step 1. - Survey
Quickly survey material to be read.

Step 2. - Read
Table of Contents • Chapter Titles • Subheadings
Illustrations • Graphs • Charts
Chapter Summaries

2 ▶ In-Depth Preview

In–Depth Preview gives you a comprehensive overview of the material to be read. This technique will take substantially longer than Quick Survey.

Step 1. - Read
All Headings • Chapter Summaries • Captions

Step 2. - Observe
Photos • Illustrations • Maps • Graphics

Step 3. - Read
Read first and last sentences of every paragraph.

Study Techniques

3 ▶ Skimming

Skimming introduces you to the main ideas of a chapter or a book. Skimming lets you search for main ideas; it is not reading word-for-word. Skimming is useful when locating main ideas in the process of reviewing. Skimming is more in-depth than Quick Survey and more selective than In-Depth Preview.

Step 1. - Glance
Glance over material to be read.

Step 2. - Search
Search for the main ideas of the material.

Step 3. - Identify
Identify main ideas as quickly as possible.
Do not focus on one main idea to the exclusion
of other important ideas.

---

4 ▶ Scanning

Scanning is a search for a main idea. Once that idea is encountered, you stop and read about the main idea in-depth. The objective of scanning is to identify a specific idea you have set out to find.

Step 1. - Find
Find the idea.

Step 2. - Focus
Focus on the idea.

Step 3. - Learn
Learn the idea.

Study Techniques

5 ▶ Read, Stop, Recite

Read, Stop, and Recite is a study technique requiring you to recall and put into your own words what you have just read. Many educators consider Read, Stop and Recite to be the most important study technique available.

Step 1. - Read
Read a small amount of material.

Step 2. - Stop
Stop and think about the material you have just read.

Step 3. - Recite
Recite or write in your own words what you have just read.

Study Techniques

6 ▶ Questioning

Questioning allows you to focus your attention on specific information you are looking for while reading. The questioning process starts by reading the chapter title. As you read through a chapter you will be questioning the material. Questioning the material facilitates understanding and remembering the material.

Step 1. - Turn
Turn chapter title and all subheadings into questions.

Step 2. - Focus
Focus your attention on looking for the answers to the questions you have formulated.

Step 3. - Write
Write the answer to the questions you have formulated.

Step 4. - Go back
Go back and find the answers if you cannot answer the questions formulated.

Study Techniques

7 ▶ Recitation

Recitation is a technique emphasizing the verbalization of material to be learned. Recitation facilitates memorization and learning and is a form of self-testing. Recitation is a powerful study and learning technique requiring the recall of important information stated in your own words. Rather than go back and read a chapter a second or third time, go back and use recitation. Increase the percentage of time reciting the material compared to reading the material.

> ### Step 1. - Recite
> Recite answers to questions, definitions and facts.
> Recite everything to be remembered.
>
> ### Step 2. - Explain
> Explain out loud important ideas and theories to be learned from material studied.

8 ▶ Underlining or Highlighting

Underlining or highlighting are study techniques requiring you to identify and decide on the most important ideas and underline or highlight them. Most students underline or highlight too much indicating a lack of selectivity. Effective underlining or highlighting reduces the size of your memorization task.

> ### Step 1. - Identify
> Identify the most important ideas in the
> material you are studying.
>
> ### Step 2. - Decide
> Decide what is the most important idea on a page,
> and <u>underline</u> or highlight it.

Study Techniques

9 ▸ Review

Review is the use of additional attempts to learn, remember, and master the material. The purpose of review is to consolidate, check and test, learn and re–learn, and process previously studied material into long term memory. Without review you may quickly forget the material you are trying to remember. Review is an extremely important technique enabling you to learn and commit material to memory. Study schedules should include specific sessions for review. Brief review periods can be very effective.

Step 1. - Go Back

Go back to previously studied material and identify gaps in your understanding and memory of the material.

Step 2. - Use Memory Techniques

Use memory techniques to help you recall and learn the material.

Step 3. - Re-Read Lecture Notes

Determine if they are complete and accurate. Identify gaps in learning, understanding, and remembering.

Step 4. - Re-Read Required Reading Material Notes

Determine what is essential for you to learn and remember. Use cues provided in lecture as to essential material to be learned and remembered.

Continued Next Page

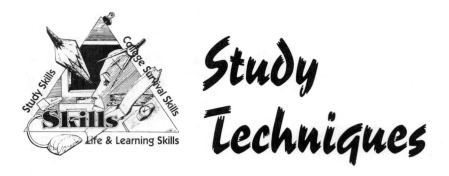

9 ▶ Review *(continued)*

Step 5. - Recite

Recite again the essential material to be learned and remembered.

Step 6. - Re-Organize

Re-organize material to be learned and remembered.

Step 7. - Use New Perspective

As you review study material, attempt to see different patterns, relationships, details, and new connections between the parts to the whole, or anything that gives you a new perspective on the material.

Step 8. - Self-Test

Test your knowledge and recall of the material by using the question and answer study format. This will help you determine whether information has been processed into long-term memory.

Study
Techniques

10 ▶ Don't Read Past A Word You Are Not Able To Define!

Don't read past a word you are unable to define; look it up in the dictionary! When you read past a word you cannot define, your understanding of the material begins to collapse. The greater the number of words you read past that you cannot define, the greater the number of holes in your understanding. Some educators believe this is the most significant study breakdown.

Step 1. - **Stop**
Don't read past a word you cannot define.

Step 2. - **Pause**
Try to determine the meanings of words by using context clues.

Step 3. - **Use the dictionary!**

Study Techniques

11 ▶ Outlining

Outlining is a versatile study technique. You can outline a chapter, term paper, speech, lecture notes, and even a book. Outlining is also an organizing technique. Outlining gives order and structure to ideas. Outlining illustrates the relationship between parts to the whole and shows how ideas are interrelated.

Step 1. - Identify Major Topics

Use Roman numerals to place each major topic into sequential order.

Step 2. - Identify Sub-topics

Place sub-topics under appropriate major topics. Sub-topics are usually assigned capital letters.

Step 3. - Identify Supporting Details

Place supporting details under sub-topics. Supporting details are given as number symbols

Step 4. - Identify Details of Supporting Details

Place details under appropriate supporting details. Use a lower case letter to identify the detail.

Study Techniques

12 ▶ Terminology

Step 1. - Organization of Terminology

Determine how the terminology is organized in your textbook. Some texts may incorporate a glossary. Many texts define the terms as they appear in the text.

Step 2. - Listen to Instructor

Listen to the instructor for correct pronunciation of subject terms.

Step 3. - Subject Dictionary

Look for a dictionary on your particular subject. Not all subjects may have this available.

Step 4. - Learn the Terms

Use study, learning, and memory techniques to learn the terminology.

Step 5. - Index Cards

Consider using index cards to collect and define terms.

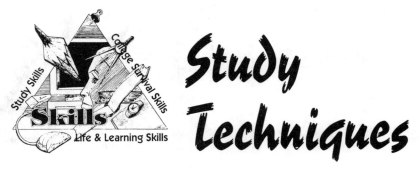

Study Techniques

13 ▶ Word Attack Skills

Word attack skills help you read fluently and comprehend material you are studying. Word attack skills include a knowledge of sound (phonics), knowing the structure of words (prefixes, suffixes, roots) and determining word meanings from syntax and context clues.

14 ▶ Recorders

Recording lectures can be very beneficial because you are able to listen to the lecture repeatedly. Listening to recorded lectures is a valuable way to use commuting time. Recording lectures gives you the opportunity to re-take notes and evaluate previously written notes. When you hear something the second or third time, you learn from a new perspective. You recognize things that didn't previously register. The cassette recorder and use of cassettes is valuable and especially useful with foreign language learning. **Please note:** Be sure you know the policy of your college and instructor regarding the use of recorders in the classroom.

15 ▶ Awareness Practice To Develop Concentration

You probably have noticed that the times you have greatest difficulty concentrating are the times you are preoccupied with conflicts which demand your attention. It is difficult to concentrate when you are burdened by financial problems, relationship problems, transportation problems and a myriad of other conflicts. If your life is one crisis after another, you may have to attend to the pressing demands of situations in order to be released to apply your energy to concentrate on learning tasks. It is sometimes easier to give attention to that which presses the greatest for attention in order to move on to other important activities. Coping with, managing, and resolving conflicts affects our ability to concentrate. Refer to Chapter 6 and review The Method of Awareness Practice.

Study Techniques

16 ▶ Observe Results Without Judgment

Almost all tasks, projects, exams, and assignments result in the evaluation of performance. The grade assigned to the task ranges from fail to excellent. Performance is judged on a grading continuum. Most of us would not consider average performance or below a desirable level of performance. Usually we judge this as bad performance. Most students internalize their judgments and become attached to them. They feel intense pressure from what is considered substandard performance. It seems nearly impossible to observe and be aware of results without judgment. Severe judgment of results readily diminishes levels of performance. Is it possible to be aware of performance results without getting attached? Observe, increase awareness and don't get attached. Trust in your capacity to be self-correcting when you're off the mark. Awareness releases the spontaneous resources of your mind and body. Trust the natural learner in you.

Step 1. - **Observe Results**

Step 2. - **Increase Awareness of Results**

Step 3. - **Don't Get Attached**

Step 4. - **Trust the Natural Learner in You**

Techniques for Developing Reading Comprehension

1. **Use** word attack skills.

2. **Develop** vocabulary.

3. **Use** context clues.

4. **Practice** reading.

5. **Stop!** What did I read?

6. **Carry** a dictionary and look up words.

7. **Develop** and focus concentration.

8. **Put** into your own words what you read.

9. **Paraphrase** and write what you have read.

10. **Read** out loud.

11. **Read** along.

12. **Tell** someone what you have read.

13. **Re-read.**

14. **Use** speed reading techniques.

15. **Use** self-testing.

16. **Make** reading fun.

17. **Use** a reading strategy.

A Strategy for Effective Study and Learning

1. **Develop** a positive attitude towards study and learning.

2. **Make** studying a habit by having a schedule and selecting a time and place.

3. **Use** study, learning, and memory techniques.

4. **Improve** reading skills.

5. **Develop** attention and concentration.

6. **Evaluate** learning to determine how you learn best and how you can improve.

7. **Increase** motivation, build self-confidence, and expand skills for study and learning.

8. **Incorporate** rewards for effective study and learning.

Chapter Conclusion:
Critical Analysis and Application

Select a concept from this chapter which has the greatest relevance and importance to you. Explain the nature of the concept and why it is relevant and important to you. Critically analyze the concept by discussing its essential features. Determine how this concept can be applied to everyday life.

Select: _____

_____

_____

_____

_____

Explain: _____

_____

_____

_____

_____

Analyze: _____

_____

_____

_____

_____

Apply: _____

_____

_____

_____

_____

Chapter 13

College Survival Skills

College Survival Skills

Take this self-inventory by rating yourself with the following scale:

5 = This statement is true <u>all</u> of the time.
4 = This statement is true <u>most</u> of the time.
3 = This statement is true <u>much</u> of the time.
2 = This statement is true <u>some</u> of the time.
1 = This statement is true <u>almost</u> none of the time.
0 = This statement is true <u>none</u> of the time.

_____ 1. I like college.

_____ 2. I feel comfortable in the college environment.

_____ 3. I am motivated to learn.

_____ 4. I am involved in student activities.

_____ 5. I have a mentor.

_____ 6. I seek a tutor when I need academic assistance.

_____ 7. I seek a college counselor for advisement.

_____ 8. I use the college health services.

_____ 9. I use college support services when I need assistance.

_____ 10. I use the college library.

_____ 11. I know how to take effective notes.

_____ 12. I have good language skills.

_____ 13. I have good math skills.

_____ 14. I have effective test taking skills.

_____ 15. I experience test anxiety.

_____ 16. I understand the writing process.

_____ 17. I have financial support.

_____ 18. I know where to go for help if I have problems.

_____ 19. I have several individuals who support my educational efforts.

_____ 20. I think what I study is relevant to my life.

➤ *Skill and confidence are an unconquered army.*
—George Hubert

The Skills Triad

The Skills Triad consists of Life and Learning Skills, Study Skills, and College Survival Skills. Skills involve the development of aptitudes and abilities. It is through the application of skills that we optimize our performance. College survival skills are needed to survive the college environment. The skills include understanding the college system, overcoming alienation on campus, joining and participating in college clubs, and getting along with professors. College survival skills are a broad category of skills which overlap with study skills and life skills.

College Survival Skills

College survival skills require that you perform actions leading to the conditions which enhance college survival. Our effectiveness is determined by the behavior we exhibit and the skills we possess. Identifying the behavioral skills which constitute knowing **the system** helps us understand what we have to do to be effective. Knowing and functioning within the system requires a broad range of skills.

Knowing how to access and use **services** will enhance our success in college. Making friends on campus will increase our sense of belonging. **Belonging** is not a skill but a state of mind brought about by the use of effective social skills. **Involvement** in all aspects of academic affairs will influence survival in college. Involvement in college **clubs** produces many benefits such as lifelong friendships, support, leadership skills, project development, and future employment opportunities. **Study Partners** can make the difference between success and failure in a college course.

Using the college **library** is indispensable to academic success for many reasons. It is a place of study, a place to research, and a place to go for assistance. Pursuing **counseling and advisement** will help prevent wasted time and energy. A clearly understood educational plan will further your success. Counselors help you address personal, life, and career issues. Knowing the **policies and procedures** of your college will provide you with the framework to resolve a wide range of academic issues. Knowing your **professors** could be the most important avenue to college success. Their excitement and commitment to the subject matter may influence your attitude about the subject. A **course load** which is not consistent with your interests, abilities, and desires can derail your academic success. The size and mix of your course load will influence your performance.

The **location** of your college may be an important consideration because it will influence your life as a student. Become familiar with the **resources** on your campus. Accessing resources skillfully is essential in fulfilling your academic needs. Doing the **work** required in your courses is essential in order to succeed. **Asking questions** is an important learning activity. By asking questions your needs are addressed, and you may acquire the information you need. Knowing your **school calendar** will help you be aware of important events, holidays, exam periods, and other significant dates. Be aware that your **attitude** will influence the people around you as well as influencing your success.

The "System"

Knowing the system and how to use it is a skill. Knowing the organization and structure of the institution you attend can help you function more effectively. Knowing polices, procedures, and your rights as a student will help you understand the system. In institutional settings, many individuals feel alienated with associated feelings of not belonging. The more you know about the system, the more comfortable and effective you will become.

Services

Learning about and using the services available to you as a student can help determine whether you will succeed or limit your success in school. Most colleges offer a broad range of services including financial aid, opportunity programs and services, tutoring, health services, counseling, mentoring and many others. It is up to you to seek out and take advantage of the services available to you. Using services effectively is a fundamental college survival skill.

Belonging

If you feel you do not belong in college or at your particular institution, your success can be limited. Involvement in college life and affairs can help you feel like part of the college. Consider seeking out individuals who share your experiences. Social skills are an important part of creating a feeling of belonging.

Involvement

Involvement in your studies will help generate interest and commitment to those studies. Get involved in and out of class. Seek out activities sponsored by the departments of classes which you attend. Alienation and being a loner may limit your success in college.

Clubs

Belonging to a school club contributes to a feeling of being part of something important. You can meet peers and develop friendships through school clubs. Clubs will encourage involvement in student affairs. Participation in college life will enhance your success.

Study Partners

A study partner is a valuable asset in surviving a course of study. Mutual support can do much to alleviate the pressure of the requirements of a demanding course. Many study techniques can be used with a partner in order to understand and remember material. Building bridges with others will help you succeed.

Library

The library is your most important academic resource. The library provides you with a place for study and tremendous access to information. Most libraries provide sessions to familiarize the student with the organization of the library. Ask your librarian about opportunities to learn your library system and how to access information.

Counseling and Advisement

Through counseling and advisement, you will learn the system and learn what will be required of you in an academic course of study. Counseling is a vital part of college survival. Counselors can help you with setting goals, study problems, relationship issues, educational and career planning, personal problems, time management and many other obstacles you may encounter.

Policies and Procedures

As you encounter academic problems in school, make it a habit to learn the school policies and procedures which apply to your situation. Make certain that you know your rights as a student and how you are to address legitimate grievances. Grading policies are an important part of college survival information. Refer to the college catalogue and student handbook for this type of information. It is your contact with the institution.

Professors and Instructors

Your choice of instructors is an important college survival decision. It is important to know something about the teaching style and requirements of professors you are going to take. Positive relationships with instructors and professors will make it easier for you to succeed. Defiance, rebellion, and anger directed at professors will do little to enhance your academic success. Remember that the professor has the last word with grade assignment.

Course Load

Carefully balancing your course load can do much to insure your academic success. Taking too many courses in a semester may limit your success. You need to be especially careful when combining math and science courses. You may need to carefully evaluate the requirements of each course you take.

Location

Careful consideration of where you live in relation to school is an important factor. Extreme commuter time can consume valuable study time. However, commuter time also may be an excellent opportunity to use audio cassettes for study.

Resources

Resources may be monetary or may take the form of a service. Most colleges offer an array of services to their students. Knowing what services are available and how to use them can help you succeed in college.

Work

Doing the work required of academic programs is essential for academic success. You need to be on top of all assignments, readings, projects, and papers in order to succeed.

Questioning

Questioning is an important aspect of the learning process. You may need to overcome fears which prevent you from asking questions.

School Calendar

Familiarization with the academic calendar will make you aware of important dates including periods for adding and dropping classes, financial aid deadlines, application dates, holidays, exam periods, and many other important dates.

Attitude

Your attitude will significantly affect your success. A positive attitude will enhance your ability to get along with others by encouraging positive responses from them.

Note-Taking

 All our knowledge has its origins in our perceptions.
— Leonardo da Vinci

Note-taking gives us a written transcript of facts, opinions, ideas, theories, and information presented in an academic course of study enabling the student to learn the material. This transcript is used for organizing, processing and remembering, and reviewing material at a later date.

Observation initiates the note-taking process. Many learning situations start with observation. Observation is the conscious and unconscious use if our sensory system to acquire and process information. Observation allows you to access verbal and non-verbal information from the learning situation. Observation allows you to understand important concepts which are presented through demonstration. Observation is one of the primary methods by which we accumulate vast amounts of information and draw conclusions.

Listening actively to class lectures provides the basis for effective note-taking. Listening means paying careful attention to the content of the class lecture. Knowing what to listen for is central to the note-taking process. There are many signals and cues that alert the note-taker to the importance, order, and structure of ideas presented. Frequently, instuctors will give a topic to their lecture, identify issues and problems to be presented, identify a time span to be covered, present a formula, and introduce problem solving methods and procedures. By listening actively, you will be able to determine the content, structure, and importance of ideas presented in class lecture.

Processing and sorting material as presented in lecture is an important part of learning. Students are not merely recording what is being presented but actively, thinking, analyzing, reflecting, and processing information while it is being presented. When great quantities of material are presented, the student needs to sort out what is important. By carefully processing and sorting information, students are able to reduce the amount of information necessary to record in note-taking.

Writing quickly and legibly increases the usability of your notes. Writing quickly allows you to keep up with the lecture. Selecting appropriate and comfortable tools will help you with quick writing.

Formats for note-taking help organize ideas to help you understand the structure of ideas presented in lecture. Some note-taking formats include:

- Outlining
- Short Phrase
- Short Paragraphs
- Mapping
- Key Word
- Margin and Page Formatting

Examine and revise your notes the same day. Are your notes usable and legible? If not, this is the time to examine your notes and determine if they need to be revised. If you find gaps and incomplete ideas, you may have to first revise, then re-write your notes. By examining and revising the same day, it will be easier to remember what was presented in class lecture. Examining, revising, and re-writing all contribute to the understanding of class lecture. These procedures provide valuable repetition and the means to remember important material.

Compare and discuss your notes with another member of the class. This becomes an additional method for learning class material, and it allows you to find gaps in your transcript of the lecture. Comparing and discussing your notes with another member of the class provides another valuable step in the learning process.

Introduction to Essentials of Note-Taking

The ingredients of effective note-taking include: ***attention, concentration, interest, skill*** and ***effort.*** Your ability to attend to and stay focused on a class lecture will determine the quality of your notes. ***Attention*** is the foundation of ***concentration,*** and concentration is focused attention. Boredom is a big obstacle to paying attention. Boredom may be seen as one of many distractions. Try to resist distraction and notice where your attention is focused. The mind drifting away from the note-taking situation is one of the greatest obstacles to effective attention and concentration. By noticing where your mind goes when it drifts, you can cultivate attention and concentration. Notice where your mind drifts and gently bring it back to the note-taking situation. ***Interest*** is an antidote for mind drifting.

Interest is the product of many diverse experiences. Interest is related to the pleasure derived from learning. Interest is related to how you feel and how you are attracted to ideas. Learning new ideas is central to the lives of many individuals. Exploring your attitudes and interests promotes involvement in subject matter. Keep in mind that involvement precedes interest. Interest is not something automatic, but something that must be cultivated.

Note-taking consists of a series of skills that can be learned. A conscious decision to make an effort to take quality notes will facilitate the note-taking process. You can easily "give in" to boredom and distraction taking you away from the task of note-taking, an essential element of high academic performance. If you can maintain ***attention, concentration, and interest,*** your effectiveness will be assured with appropriate ***skills*** and ***effort.***

Essentials of Note-Taking

Attention

If your attention is directed to the lecture, your ability to observe and listen will be enhanced. Therefore, you will be able to take better notes.

Concentration

The ability to focus your attention and concentration on what is being presented in class lecture is basic to note-taking.

Interest

If you are interested in the material being presented, it is easier to stay focused on lecture.

Skills

The development of appropriate skills will enhance your ability to take good notes.

Effort

Note-taking requires that you make an effort to initiate, maintain, and complete the tasks associated with note-taking. Effort means that you make a conscious decision to do the task of note-taking.

Guidelines for Note-Taking

1. Assess Motivation

Taking effective notes requires both motivation and skill. Are you motivated to take notes and learn the skills of note-taking?

2. Assess Note-Taking Needs of Each Course

Most courses are structured around a combination of lectures and readings. Some courses are structured around the required readings, others are structured around lectures. Courses which rely heavily on lecture require more note-taking. Your notes then will be an important source of test preparation.

3. Preparation

Make sure you come to class with necessary supplies such as paper, pencils, pens, erasers, notebooks, required readings and books, calculators, and any other supplies specified by the instructor.

4. Note-Taking Format

There are several note-taking formats such as short paragraphing, outlining, mapping, short phrasing, margin and page formatting, and key word method. Choose the format that works best for you and your classes.

5. Notes Verbatim

Avoid trying to take word-for-word notes. You will soon tire and not be able to keep up with the lecture.

6. Selection

Make yourself decide what is important, and write it down.

7. Develop Your Own Shorthand

Develop your own shorthand, and maintain a key to your abbreviations. For example, environment may be abbreviated "evt." and psychology, "psy."

8. Usability of Notes

It is very important to have notes you can read. Your notes are useless if you are unable to read them. If notes are incomplete and ineffective, re-assess your motivation to take notes.

9. Learn It Now

Learn material when it is presented.

10. Boredom

Boredom is a significant obstacle to note-taking. Increased involvement in your courses is the best antidote for boredom.

11. Attention, Concentration, Interest, Skill, and Effort

Attention, concentration, interest, skill, and effort are some major keys to effective note-taking. Your ability to attend and concentrate for extended periods will enhance your note-taking. Interest increases your ability to attend and concentrate. Skills facilitate the note-taking process. Finally, note-taking requires that you make an effort.

12. Distraction

Actively combat distractions. Increased involvement in your courses may help mitigate the effects of distractions.

13. Tape Recording Lectures

Consider tape recording lectures which contain vast amounts of data and details that need to be remembered. Never record a lecture without informing the instructor that you will be tape recording. Check the policy of your school regarding tape recording.

14. Listening and Observing

Listening and observing form the foundation for effective note-taking.

A Strategy for
Listening to a Class Lecture

1. **Use** all your senses.

2. **Use** listening skills.

3. **Maintain** a non-judgmental attitude.

4. **Notice** when you resist.

5. **Process** information actively and sort out the essentials.

6. **Notice** your feeling response.

7. **Take** responsibility for your boredom.

8. **Generate** interest.

Cues and Signals

Knowing what to listen for is central to the note-taking process. There are many signals and cues that alert the note-taker as to the importance, order, and structure of ideas presented. Cues and signals can alert you to the following: main ideas, concluding ideas, supporting ideas, linking ideas, and transitions. Here are some words and phrases which signal important material. Pay attention to what follows these cues and signals and be ready to write.

The main idea

In conclusion

The relationship is

However

Moreover

Therefore

Furthermore

The data support

The results indicate

The proof of the matter

The evidence indicates

Consequently

In addition to

Henceforth

More importantly

It was believed

It clearly states

The implications are

To summarize

Let me remind you

Don't forget

As previously stated

It is not known

It is supposed

The causes are

We can assume

But

Exception to the rule

Going back to the original idea

I must emphasize

It has been said

The following

Let's compare and contrast

Let's examine

It's really not important

Developing Your Own Shorthand

The following method may help your develop your own shorthand for taking notes. It involves three simple steps:

1. Use the first letter of the word.

2. Decide the distinguishing feature of the root of the word. This is a personal determination.

3. Use the last letter of the word.

Here are some examples:

Word	Abbreviation
1. Environment	evt
2. Committee	ctte
3. Communication	cmmn
4. Behavior	bhr
5. Extrapolation	expn

Use these rules flexibly and don't forget to keep a key for commonly used words in each course.

Note-Taking Formats

Outlining

Outlining is a very useful note-taking format because it provides an organization of major ideas along with subordinate and supporting ideas. Outlining notes allows you to see the relationship between the parts to the whole. Outlining your notes encourages detailed note-taking.

Short Phrase

The short phrase method allows you to capture the essence of a lecture by writing down short phrases of the key ideas presented in lecture. The short phrasing may contain both the major and supporting ideas. Short phrasing allows you to abbreviate and use concise wording to capture the meaning of main ideas.

Short Paragraph Technique

The short paragraph technique allows for the stringing together a series of ideas. A continuity of ideas has advantages over a series of ideas which may seem disconnected in some of the other formats.

Mapping

Mapping is a diagrammatic method which illustrates the branching of subordinate ideas to a main idea. Branches are used to illustrate a descending support of details to main ideas. Mapping is a method which illustrates the integration of ideas in support of a main idea.

Key Word Method

The key word method focuses on terminology and concepts presented in lecture. The key word method alone usually does not provide all the information needed to be recorded. The main purpose of this method is to formulate lead-ins to more involved ideas. Key words function as cues to something important.

Margin and Page Formatting

You can decide how best to use an 8 1/2" x 11" sheet of paper. It may be helpful to use a wide left margin. You can divide the page up in any manner which helps you organize your ideas. Do not be tied down to accustomed structures for using a sheet of paper. You may want to make a distinction between how you use the upper and lower halves of your paper.

Note-Taking Formats

Examples:

Outlining

I.   The Success Triad
    A.   Motivation
          1. Success Factor
          2. Triad of Motivation
              a. Self-Knowledge
              b. Knowing what you want
              c. Goals
          3. Types of Motivation
              a. Growth
              b. Efficiency
    B.   Self-Esteem
          1. Success Factor
          2. Triad of Self Esteem
              a. Self-knowledge
              b. Self-responsibility
              c. Self-acceptance
          3. Aspects of Self-Esteem
              a. Self-worth
              b. Self-confidence
              c. Believing in ourself
    C.   Skills
          1. Success Factor
          2. Triad of Skills
              a. Life and Training Skills
              b. Study Skills
              c. College survival skills

Short Phrase

- The Success Triad
- A model for Success
- Motivation considered primary success factor
- Triad of Motivation consists of three factors: self-knowledge, knowing what you want, and goals
- Two types of motivation, growth and deficiency

Short Paragraph Technique

The Success Triad is a model for success. Self-esteem is a primary success factor. The Triad of Self-Esteem consists of three elements: self-knowledge, self-responsibility, and self-acceptance. Important aspects of self-esteem include: self-worth, self-confidence, and believing in oneself.

Key Word Method

Success Triad
Motivation
Self-Esteem
Skills
Success Factor
Triads
Self-Knowledge
Knowing what you want
Goals
Self-Responsibility
Self-Acceptance
Life and Learning Skills
Study Skills
College Survival Skills

Mapping

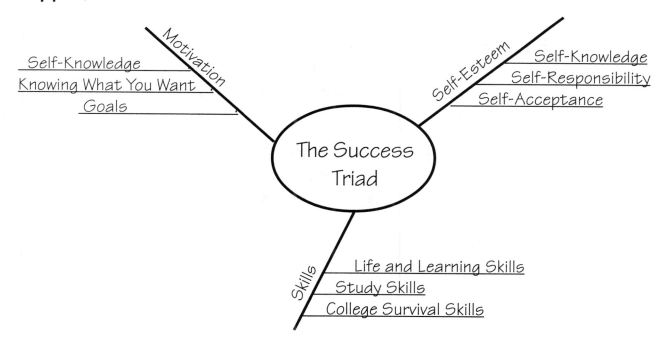

Margin and Page Formatting

The Success Triad

The Success Triad is a conceptual model for student success. It is a triad illustrating the success factor of motivation, self-esteem, and skills.

Motivation

Motivation is one of the success factors. The Motivation Triad is comprised of self-knowledge, knowing what you want, and goals.

Self-Esteem

Self-esteem is one of the success factors. The Self-Esteem Triad is composed of self-knowledge, self-responsibility, and self-acceptance.

Skills

Skills is one of the success factors. The Skills Triad is comprised of life and learning skills, study skills, and college survival skills.

A Strategy for Note-Taking

1. Observe
   a. Sit in a place where you can easily observe what the instructor is doing.
   b. Observe the teaching style of the instructor.
   c. Use all your senses while observing.
   d. Develop a sense of the classroom environment including the students and the room.
   e. Observe the verbal and nonverbal behavior of the instructor.

2. Listen
   a. Actively listen to the instructor's lecture.
   b. Listen for cues that indicate what is important.
   c. Listen to other students as they participate in class.

3. Process and Sort
   a. Think about the ideas that are being presented by the instructor.
   b. How are the ideas organized?
   c. What do you think you are expected to know?
   d. Reflect on the ideas, analyze them, and write them down.
   e. Actively sort out important material.
   f. Actively learn important material in class lecture while being presented.

4. Write
   a. Select an appropriate note-taking format.
   b. Write down the important ideas expressed in class lecture.
   c. Pay attention to the details, they may be important to write.
   d. Write down anything written on the chalkboard.

5. Examine and Revise
   a. Read your notes. Are they usable and legible?
   b. Did you get all the main ideas?
   c. Did you capture the structure of the lecture?

6. Rewrite
   a. If your notes are not legible, rewrite them the same or the following day.

7. Compare
   a. Compare your notes with another student in class.
   b. Make sure important material has not been omitted.

The Brief Note-Taking Strategy

Observe
Take in as much as you can as fast as you can.

Listen
Listen for the essentials.

Think
Think about the main ideas.

Write
Write quickly and get down the supporting details.

The Crash Note-Taking Strategy

Write

Write as fast as you can. Get everything down that you possibly can.
Don't worry about organization at this time.

Organize

Later the same day, organize your notes.
Use a format that will make your organization clear.

Test-Taking

Test-taking is an integral part of academic life. It is through effective test-taking that we achieve academic success. Since grades are seen as important in society, we are pressured into competing and pursuing high marks. We need to recognize the importance of grades because they are used as criteria for completion of academic programs, entrance into graduate and professional schools, scholarships, employment opportunities, and the grades you receive on tests are frequently seen as measures of competence and ability.

Test Performance

Students frequently use grades as measures of self-worth and intelligence. Consequently, there doesn't seem to be any college event more threatening to a student's self-worth than test-taking. Poor performance on tests can be devastating to students for many reasons and can easily lead to catastrophic thinking: "If I do poorly on tests, I am worthless. If I do poorly on tests, I am dumb. If I do poorly on tests, I will never succeed." This type of thinking contributes to a poor sense of self-worth, fear and test anxiety. When we are doing poorly, this is the time to persist and give our best effort. Persistence in the face of adversity is what will most further our success. Poor test performance is a message that we need to work harder, study more, set priorities, and learn skills which will improve our test performance. Tests give valuable feedback about what we are doing right and what we are doing wrong. Many students view test-taking as a challenge rather than a threat and have the experience of completing items on examinations with feelings of complete confidence. Good test performance builds confidence and helps initiate and establish a pattern of academic success.

Improving Test Performance

Since grades are important and are largely products of test-taking, it is important to perform well on tests. There are many ways to improve performance on tests: preparation, practice, prediction, memory techniques, relaxation techniques, self-testing, study pairs and groups, time management, and using available resources. The most obvious and immediate method for improving test performance is practice. Through practice, you will become a better test-taker. The application of practice in taking tests and mastering material for tests will increase your test performance. Practice is an essential part of preparation, and there is no substitute for preparation in order to improve test performance. If we expect to do well on exams, we must do the necessary preparation.

Memory Techniques

Good test performance relies heavily on the ability to retrieve information from long-term memory. Have you learned the material so that you can remember the information during the test? Using various strategies to encode information into long-term memory should aid with retrieving the information during the test. Effective use of memory techniques will improve test performance. With reviews, you are more likely to remember important material that will appear on tests. Frequent reviews will help you deep-process information needed for exams. Self-testing is an excellent test preparation technique. Creating and taking your own exam will help you when you take the course exam. Self-testing provides valuable review and practice. Using study pairs and groups can be helpful for exam preparation. Explaining to others course material and being questioned by others regarding course material provides important recitation and practice which aids learning and memory.

Prediction

A major technique used in preparing for exams is prediction. Predicting what will be on an exam will help with your preparation. With practice you will be able to predict a high percentage of the material that will be on exams. Determining the main concepts and ideas covered in a course should aid in your prediction and preparation for exams. Occasionally, professors will indicate what will be on a test, and you need to learn that specified material well. "Knowing that you know" the content material of a course should do much to alleviate anxiety and ensure good test performance. You can increase your sense of "knowing that you know" through review, practice, and overlearning.

Test-Taking Perspective

If you find that you are having significant test-taking difficulties, you may need to take advantage of services offered by your school. You may need to obtain a tutor, learn relaxation techniques, test-taking strategies and memory techniques. Keep a proper perspective on tests. Remember that tests are not a measure of your worth. Tests of course content do not measure intelligence, frequently do not test what they are supposed to test, and can be culturally biased. Guard against catastrophic thinking and learn to relax when it comes to test-taking.

Exam Preparation Techniques

1. **Develop** a sense of urgency.

2. **Do** daily reviews.

3. **Keep** track of preparation days before an exam.

4. **Rearrange** calendar, prioritize, allow more study time.

5. **Organize** notes.

6. **Form** study groups.

7. **Engage** in self-testing.

8. **Use** memory techniques.

9. **Rest** and don't get sick.

10. **Talk** to your instructor if you're having problems.

11. **Find** out if the exam is cumulative.

12. **Post** and date a reminder that you have to get organized for exams.

13. **Give** yourself a reward for each of the things you do to get prepared for exams.

14. **Use** all the study techniques learned in text.

15. **Review** all the test-taking information in the text.

16. **Make** sure you know the terminology used in courses.

Tests
and Grades

Agree	Disagree	Indicate whether you agree or disagree with these statements regarding tests and grades.
		1. I like taking tests.
		2. Tests are a measure of our worth.
		3. Tests allow us to set standards which are very important.
		4. Society overemphasizes the value of tests.
		5. Tests are very important because they let us know what we need to learn.
		6. Valid tests are difficult to construct.
		7. Tests can be culturally biased.
		8. We need tests in order to force students to study.
		9. Tests have great value.
		10. College tests indicate level of intelligence.
		11. Tests usually engage a particular type of memory.
		12. Tests let us know how much we have learned.
		13. Grades are a measure of our worth.
		14. Grades are very important to the system.
		15. Grades are important because they allow us to select the best qualified people for academic programs.

Tests and Grades

1. Which of the statements about tests on the previous page has the greatest relevance to you? Explain your thoughts and reactions.

_____

_____

_____

_____

_____

_____

_____

2. Which of the statements about grades has the greatest relevance to you? Explain your thoughts and reactions.

_____

_____

_____

_____

_____

_____

3. Survey the questionnaire. What conclusions do you derive about tests and grades from your responses on the questionnaire?

_____

_____

_____

_____

_____

A Strategy for Test-Taking

Step 1. **Read** test instructions. Pay close attention to what you are being asked to do.

Step 2. **Review** the entire test and determine the assigned value of each item.

Step 3. **Time** yourself. Decide how much time you are going to devote to each test item.

Step 4. **Do** easy items first and go back to difficult items later.

Step 5. **Complete** all items. Do not leave any items blank.

Step 6. **Guess** when you don't know.

Step 7. **Check** your response for each test item.

A Strategy for Taking Multiple Choice Tests

Step 1   **Read** the question carefully. What are you being asked to do?

Step 2   **Be alert** to "all of the above" and "none of the above" response alternatives.

Step 3   **Be prepared** to make fine discriminations. The more precise the discrimination between responses, the more difficult it is to make the correct response.

Step 4   **Read** each of the given answers and initiate a process of elimination. If you don't know the correct response, increase your odds of making the correct response through the process of elimination.

Step 5   **Select** study strategies. The careful selection of study strategies can increase your ability to recognize correct responses on a multiple choice exam.

A Strategy for Taking Essay Exams

Step 1. **Read** the instructions. Pay attention to key words which describe what you are being asked to do.

Step 2. **Organize** your thoughts. Before you begin to write your answer to an essay question think through your answer.

Step 3. **Write** ideas and structure them before you begin writing the essay.

Step 4. **Respond** to the question and keep focused.

Step 5. **Include** main points instructor may be looking for.

Step 6. **Proofread** your essay response.

A Strategy for Reducing Test Anxiety

1. Prepare

Go into the test situation well prepared. The more confident you feel about having mastered the material for the test, the less likely you are to become anxious.

2. Overlearn

Once you have mastered the material, continue learning the material beyond your previous level of mastery.

3. Relax

Use the relaxation techniques outlined in this book. Attempt to cultivate an alert and relaxed response to testing situations. You want to replace anxiety with an alert, relaxed response.

4. Don't Catastrophize

Catastrophic thinking follows this pattern: "If I fail this exam, I will fail this course. If I fail this course, my grade point average will go down. If my grade point average goes down, then I will not be able to get into graduate school. If I can't get into graduate school, I will not become a professional. If I don't become a professional, then others will think that I'm not worthy. If others think I'm not worthy, then I will be unlovable. If I'm not loved, then I will be miserable for the rest of my life." Avoid falling into this trap.

5. Use Imagery of Success

Imagine yourself in the testing situation feeling alert and relaxed. You are completing each test item with a high degree of confidence. You feel excited but not anxious. You see yourself making correct responses on the exam and ultimately receiving back the exam with an A+ at the top of your paper.

6. Use Awareness Practice

Notice where your attention is focused. Awareness of anxiety frequently reduces anxiety. Awareness of your responses frequently helps you control your responses.

7. Learn Test-Taking Techniques

The more test-taking techniques you know, the less anxious you may feel when confronted with a test-taking situation. Knowing how to take a test helps alleviate anxiety. Test-taking techniques tend to increase self-confidence and reduce anxiety.

8. Tests Do Not Measure Your Worth

A test is not a measure of your worth. Always combat feeling inadequate when you perform poorly on an exam. A test is not the measure of a person. A test result is usually a particular score on a specific day for a specific test.

The Writing Process

For me, the big chore is always the same: how to begin a sentence, how to continue it, and how to complete it.

— Claude Simon

Introduction

Writing is having a voice. We write in order to commuunciate our experiences and ideas to others. Writing is powerful. Writers are capable of transforming their world and the world of others. Writers have tremendous influence. Writers inform, persuade, challenge, transform, articulate, interpret, analyze, and change the ideas and issues of our time. There are a few who become the voice for the many because of their ability to write. Those few can have a powerful social impact.

Nothing specific qualifies an individual to write; anyone can write. If you have something to say, you can write. The primary purpose of writing is to communicate. Everything else in the process is subordinate to that purpose.

Writing consists of several different activities, stages, phases, or steps. The stages consist of pre-writing, organizing, writing a rough draft, revising and editing and proof-reading. These activities are repeatable and through practice you increase your skill in doing these activities. The various stages of writing can help you concentrate on one activity at a time. Knowing the specific tasks of each stage helps you identify where you are in the writing process.

Writing is a different name for conversation.
—Laurence Sterne

Pre-Writing

The greatest obstacle to writing is not understanding the writing process. We fail to write because we feel that everything we put on paper should immediately come out accurate and correct. Your attitude as you approach a writing assignment will influence the starting, sustaining, and completing of your writing project. In the initial stage of writing, it is helpful to abandon perfectionistic demands and pressures of needing to be correct and accurate in your writing. Let go of the censor in your head. Most of us have this censor which makes excessive demands to perform perfectly on writing projects.

One of the most effective techniques for letting go of the "censor," or "critical parent," as you write is free writing. Free writing consists of allowing a free flow of ideas without censorship and recording them as they emerge. Free writing is a powerful technique for getting started and working through writer's block. Free writing is similar to brainstorming, another writing technique which can help you get started on a writing project.

This technique also allows you to quiet the censor. The brainstorming activity consists of writing everything down that occurs to you regarding a subject matter. Brainstorming may involve the listing of ideas, feelings, reactions, and impressions regarding a particular topic. Free writing allows for loosely written paragraphs, whereas brainstorming involves writing ideas spontaneously without regard to structure.

An additional technique for getting started on a writing project is to talk with people who have expertise in your subject. Before you begin to write, gather information, ideas, and impressions from others. Talking about your subject and topic is very helpful in generating a broad range of options for writing.

Another pre-writing technique is to talk directly into a recorder about your subject. As you think about your subject and come up with ideas, stop and record them before you lose them. Depending on the type of writing assignment you have been given, you may have to do some preliminary research. Many college writing assignments involve the use of a limited number of references. You may want to identify the leading works and authorities on your topic. For comprehensive research papers, a computer search on your topic may be very helpful. The reading techniques of surveying and skimming may be extremely useful in quickly reviewing many references for important ideas.

The pre-writing activities help you get organized. Generating freely written sentences and paragraphs by using free-writing, listing ideas from brainstorming, talking with others, talking into a recorder, and preliminary research usually give you enough information to get started and organized. Pre-writing activities should help you select and limit your topic. These activities should also help in the formulation of your thesis.

Organizing

Organizing the products of your pre-writing activities should help yield a limited and focused topic, a thesis statement and a rough outline of your writing project. The thesis statement allows the reader to know what the paper is about. A thesis statement is sometimes controversial and gives some indication of what you want your audience to understand, and reveals your opinion and position on a topic. It is the central organizing idea of your paper.

Writing a Rough Draft

You can begin writing your rough draft by using free writing. After you have written several paragraphs, you can compare the contents of these paragraphs with your outline. If you get stuck and your free writing does not yield additional material you can look at your brainstorming list for main ideas that you may want to develop. You may be able to develop your rough draft by adhering to your outline. Some find this difficult. As long as you can sustain your writing, you will have something to work on. A blank sheet of paper gives you nothing to work with. As you write your rough draft you can repeatedly ask yourself if you are writing to your outline and thesis. It is possible to write a paper without a rough outline. You can generate many paragraphs through free-writing and later examine the content of those paragraphs, and then write an outline.

Revising

After completing your rough draft, you can start with the revision process. Most writers believe that revision is the most critical stage of writing. Many writers spend more time on revision that any other writing activity. When you revise, you re-think, re-examine, re-interpret, re-analyze, and re-construct arguments, presuppositions, logic, conclusions, and implications incorporated in your first draft. Some writers will revise a paper several times. Revision frequently includes major changes to a paper.

Editing

Editing is the phase in the writing process where the primary focus is the accuracy of your writing. In the editing phase, you examine your grammar and sentence structure. The other major function of editing is to examine your writing style. Is your style appropriate for your audience?

When you examine the correctness of your sentences, your first concern should be whether you have written complete sentences. When you edit you should be concerned about the following: complete sentences, subject-verb agreement, pronoun antecedent agreement, and avoid fragments, run-ons and dangling phrases. Editing initiates closure to the writing process of the first draft, it does not involve major revisions. If you are dissatisfied with your first draft, you may need to go back rewrite, revise, and develop a second draft, and initiate the editing process again.

Proofreading

Proofreading is the last function of the writing process. In this phase you are no longer concerned with making major changes to your work. The focus of proofreading is to insure correct punctuation, capitalization, and spelling. Proofreading is not an additional examination of the content of your work.

Summary

As described previously, the writing process consists of several definable activities: pre-writing, organizing, writing a first draft, revision, editing, and proofreading. All writers seem to employ these major activities of the writing process, but not all writers strictly adhere to any proper reference of writing. Several of the writing activities can be done simultaneously. Some writers edit and proof immediately after writing or while writing. It is your task to discover how you best engage in the various activities of writing. There is no set formula for writing, although writing seems to consist of several definable activities.

A Strategy for Writing

Step 1. **Pre-Writing**

Pre-writing may include brainstorming and free writing to initiate the writing process.

Step 2. **Organizing**

Organize your pre-writing products to define a limited and focused topic or thesis statement.

Step 3. **Writing**

Write your first draft from your organized pre-writing products such as an outline.

Step 4. **Revising**

Revise your first draft by re-examining the ideas, organization, conclusions and logic of your first draft.

Step 5. **Editing**

Edit your draft by examining grammar, sentence structure and writing style.

Step 6. **Proofreading**

Proofread for correct punctuation, capitalization, and spelling.

Chapter Conclusion:
Critical Analysis and Application

Select a concept from this chapter which has the greatest relevance and importance to you. Explain the nature of the concept and why it is relevant and important to you. Critically analyze the concept by discussing its essential features. Determine how this concept can be applied to everyday life.

Select: _____

_____

_____

_____

_____

Explain: _____

_____

_____

_____

_____

Analyze: _____

_____

_____

_____

_____

Apply: _____

_____

_____

_____

_____

Chapter 14

Careering

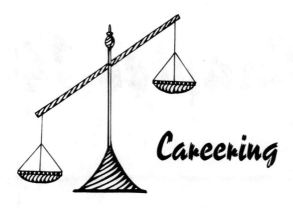

Careering

Take this self-inventory by rating yourself with the following scale:

5 = This statement is true <u>all</u> of the time.
4 = This statement is true <u>most</u> of the time.
3 = This statement is true <u>much</u> of the time.
2 = This statement is true <u>some</u> of the time.
1 = This statement is true <u>almost</u> none of the time.
0 = This statement is true <u>none</u> of the time.

_____ 1. I have career goals.

_____ 2. I have a vision for my life.

_____ 3. I have discovered my passion.

_____ 4. I know my interests.

_____ 5. I have identified my strengths.

_____ 6. I know my values.

_____ 7. I have special talents.

_____ 8. I have a range of skills.

_____ 9. I have had several jobs.

_____ 10. I know my abilities.

_____ 11. I have matched my personality type with a career.

_____ 12. I know who I am and what I want.

_____ 13. I have made contacts that can help me in my career.

_____ 14. I know how careers are organized.

_____ 15. I use the college career center.

Career Search

Job Hunt

CAREERING

Self-Assessment

With ordinary talent and extraordinary perserverance, all things are attainable.

—Thomas F. Buxton

The Careering Triad

The Careering Triad consists of Self-Assessment, Career Search, and Job Hunt. Self-assessment is the foundation of the careering process. Most self-assessment methods and procedures rely on testing and subjective techniques. Self-assessment procedures usually involve examining interests, values, abilities, personality traits and styles, and other factors which assist in career planning. A career search involves a series of activities designed to help you identify specific careers which are consistent with your values, interests, abilities, wants, needs, and preferences, and a job hunt consists of a series of activities leading to the acquisition of a job.

Factors of The Careering Triad

Self-Assessment

A comprehensive process of self-exploration, self discovery, self-examination, and self-evaluation comprises the self-assessment process. We explore needs, wants, preferences, and past experience including both work and school. We may discover additional assets and find new sources of strength. We examine values, interests, skills, and discover our purpose. Our purpose forms a framework for our life's vision and reflects our passion. We use journals, interest and value inventories, personality type indicators, and computerized career planning systems to augment our self-assessment. We synthesize and evaluate the results of this process in order to make career decisions.

Career Search

A career search leads us to the college library and career center. We use the results of our self-assessment to narrow our search. We look for careers that match our values, needs, wants, preferences, and vision for our lives. We use standard publications such as *The Dictionary of Occupational Titles* and *The Occupational Outlook Handbook* to conduct our search. Our career search may include networking with others to find career opportunities.

Job Hunt

A job hunt leads us to a job or series of jobs which ultimately lead us to a career. A job hunt includes traditional and non-traditional strategies for obtaining a job. We usually find a job through people we know. Making contact with others is essential to effective job hunting. A job hunt frequently involves finding the person with the power to hire within the organization in which you are seeking employment. The ability to market yourself is essential to effective job hunting and job attainment.

Starting Where You Are

"What do I want to do with my life?" The careering process begins when you ask yourself this question. A good starting point is to start where you are. However, examining the past can help clarify the present. A look at your past in order to examine your educational background, work experience, and personal history will produce a picture of what you have been and what you are now.

High School Experience

Evaluate your high school experience. What was your favorite subject? What were your favorite activities? Were you a college prep student? Do you have good language skills? What was the last math class you took in high school?

College Background

What is your college background? What courses have you completed? As you think through these questions, try to make some conclusions about the kind of person you are and where you want to go.

Evaluation

After making a preliminary evaluation, consider scheduling an appointment with a college counselor. Be prepared to discuss your educational background and your work experience. The counselor may advise you to take various testing instruments that will yield additional results.

Career Center

Go to your college career center to determine what services they offer. Talk with others and see what information they can provide you with in order to answer the question, "Where do I go from here?" Get started in your career planning.

Vision

A vision stirs us into action. It provides a framework for our existence. A vision consists of mental pictures about our past, present, and future. It is our mental plan for our life's direction. We can describe and articulate our vision to ourselves and to others. It contains the range of possibilities available to us to actualize our potentialities.

Power of Vision

A vision is both a conscious and unconscious construction. A vision is what you want it to be. It's what you see for yourself. A vision gives strength, meaning, purpose, and personal power. A vision directs and focuses our energies. A vision is an expression of our values, purpose, and goals. A vision frequently contains a self-transcending aspect, a belief in something greater than ourselves. For many, a vision involves the pursuit of religious experience. A vision is an anchor which holds us steady through life's turmoil and disappointments. A vision provides hope in times of despair.

Vision-Makers

We are vision-makers and can create a positive vision for our lives. A positive vision creates hope and many possibilities for the future. Have you actively created your vision? Have you created your vision by default? If you need to recreate your vision, you may want to start by examining your values and dreams and determine what gives your life purpose and meaning.

Importance of Vision

A vision is important because it gives us a sense of where we have been, where we are now, and where we are going. A vision can help us overcome a profound sense of emptiness and loneliness. A vision gives us a sense of safety and security. A vision gives our lives purpose. A vision gives us a reason to live.

Trends

Most of us would like to be able to predict the future in order to know how best to prepare ourselves. Studying trends is one way to predict the direction of our society and the world. John Naisbitt the author of *Megatrends* and *Megatrends 2000* has devoted himself to studying and predicting trends. The books reveal where we have been and where we are going. Selected from many trends presented by Naisbitt the following trends will have a profound effect on career planners.

Industrial to Information Society

The first major trend is the restructuring of America from an industrial to an information society. The 1990s have seen an explosion of communication and computer technology along with other high technology industries. Career planners are no longer preparing for an industrial society but an information society.

Specialist to Generalist

The second major trend is a shift from the specialist who is soon obsolete to the generalist who can adapt. The information society will create rapid change and this will preclude individuals from staying in the same occupations for a lifetime. The result may be several careers and jobs requiring an ability to adapt to the changing work environment.

Melting Pot to Cultural Diversity

The third major trend is a move from the myth of the melting pot to a celebration of cultural diversity. With the increase in immigration, the United States can no longer be characterized as a melting pot because many of the new immigrants are retaining much of their cultural heritage. Many continue to speak their native language. This diversity has created enormous economic opportunities through the development of ethnic products and international trade.

Values and Careers

The following values are associated with work. Identify and check the values which you desire in a career.

_____ 1. Money

_____ 2. Survival

_____ 3. Meaning

_____ 4. Control

_____ 5. Certainty

_____ 6. Problem-Solving

_____ 7. Creativity

_____ 8. Leadership

_____ 9. Power

_____ 10. Excitement

_____ 11. Prestige

_____ 12. Respect

_____ 13. Possessions

_____ 14. Identity

_____ 15. Satisfaction

_____ 16. Security

_____ 17. Accomplishment

_____ 18. Association with others

_____ 19. Service to others

_____ 20. Benefits

_____ 21. Work environment

_____ 22. Independence

_____ 23. Adventure

_____ 24. Travel

_____ 25. Working for causes

Values and Careers

Empowering Exercise 20

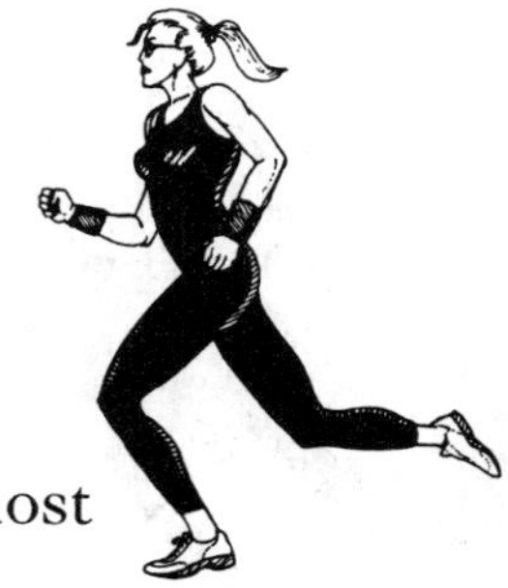

Select and write ten values from the list which you consider the most important. Describe the importance of each value in a sentence.

Value	Importance of Value
1. ____________	1. ____________
2. ____________	2. ____________
3. ____________	3. ____________
4. ____________	4. ____________
5. ____________	5. ____________
6. ____________	6. ____________
7. ____________	7. ____________
8. ____________	8. ____________
9. ____________	9. ____________
10. ____________	10. ____________

Describe a career that incorporates some of these values, and explain how they are incorporated in the career.

Identifying Your Interests

What are the things that concern and move you? These things indicate your interests.

Respond to the following questions to identify your interests.

1. What do you enjoy doing?_____

_____

_____

_____

2. What do you do in your free time?_____

_____

_____

_____

3. List your favorite activities.

_____   _____

_____   _____

_____   _____

4. How do your interests relate to a career?_____

_____

_____

_____

5. Are you developing new interests that will relate to a career?_____

_____

_____

_____

Identifying Your Strengths

It is important to identify and build on your strengths. Your strengths may hold the key to your success.

1. What do you do well?_____

_____

_____

2. What are your recognized accomplishments? _____

_____

_____

3. What are your special talents? _____

_____

_____

4. What personal characteristics are your strengths?_____

_____

_____

5. How is your family, cultural, and personal background a strength?_____

_____

_____

6. How can you apply your strengths to a career?_____

_____

_____

_____

Career Environments and Personality Types

Thousands of careers and jobs have been identified and placed into career and occupational categories. This categorical approach makes choosing a career significantly more manageable. One aspect of career planning involves matching your personality type to an occupational environment.

According to John Holland in *Making Vocational Choices: A Theory of Careers*, people can be divided into six personality and occupational environment types. They include Realistic, Investigative, Artistic, Social, Enterprising, and Conventional. These six personality types and occupational environments are organized into a hexagon.

Realistic people are robust, practical, and strong. They work in skilled trades or technical jobs.

Investigative people are scientific, task oriented, shy, and introspective. They work in scientific and laboratory jobs.

Artistic people are creative, and expressive. They work in jobs that involve words, music, or art.

Social people are humanistic, responsible, and sociable. They work with people in healing , teaching, and helping.

Enterprising people are driven, dominating, and enjoy leading others. They work in sales, merchandising, and politics.

Conventional people are conforming, systematic, and well structured. They work in office jobs and organizations.

This personality-occupational system is designed to help you match your personality type with a career category.

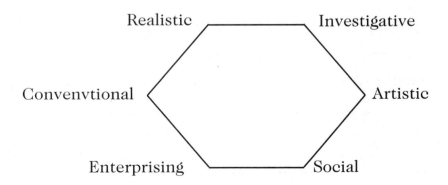

Introduction to A Strategy for Career Development

Self-Knowledge is the foundation of career development. People who know themselves know what they want. Exploring and clarifying what we need, want, and prefer will further self-knowledge. Discovering what we want facilitates setting career goals. The development of self-knowledge is the first step in the career planning process. A **journal** is a powerful tool for keeping a record of our life experiences. A close examination of your life experiences helps further self-knowledge and identifies interests, talents, skills, values, and passions which are all integral to the career planning process. **Interests** and **strengths** reveal your preferences, sources of motivation, and the things you do well. All of us have strengths; be sure not to overlook your obvious strengths and consider building on those strengths. **Values** are central to career planning. They indicate the ideas, beliefs, experiences, and activities which are most important to you. It is important to find a career that is consistent with your values. **Information** provides a framework for understanding the complex world of work. It allows you to identify what careers are available and in demand. Information tells you about the global economy, trade, employment, new technologies, trends, and other factors which affect career planning. Making **contact with others** or networking helps identify individuals who can assist in the career development process. Others may play a central role in your success. These individuals may be family, friends, acquaintances and other contacts you try to establish. A Strategy for Career Development will help you think systematically and plan effectively for your career.

A Strategy for Career Development

1. **Develop** self-knowledge.

2. **Maintain** a journal.

3. **Identify** interests.

4. **Identify** strengths.

5. **Clarify** values.

6. **Gather** information.

7. **Make** decisions.

8. **Make** contact with others.

Chapter Conclusion:
Critical Analysis and Application

Select a concept from this chapter which has the greatest relevance and importance to you. Explain the nature of the concept and why it is relevant and important to you. Critically analyze the concept by discussing its essential features. Determine how this concept can be applied to everyday life.

Select: _____

_____

_____

_____

_____

Explain: _____

_____

_____

_____

_____

Analyze: _____

_____

_____

_____

_____

Apply: _____

_____

_____

_____

_____

Conclusion

You have taken a major step toward self-empowerment by completing **The Empowered Student**. The Triadic System of Success is plugged into your life, and you may need to review it periodically for maximum performance. The path to success requires a powerful storehouse of motivation, high levels of self-esteem and diversified skills. These success factors are powerful guides to self-empowerment. You have initiated a process of self-discovery through **The Goal Setting Journal** and have set your course. Through hard work and perseverance, you have determined how you learn best, learned how to learn, increased reading comprehension, and remember material with greater ease. You are a more effective learner. Even though you have finished **The Empowered Student**, you may want to re-visit key concepts in the future.

The knowledge of what it takes to succeed will remain with you the rest of your life. You have learned conceptual systems which will guide you through effective action. You have the knowledge and the framework to evaluate performance and progress. You have learned the key factors associated with success. You have learned to apply several personal growth models. You have learned the importance of decision-making, believing in yourself, examining important attitudes, and addressing issues of identity. You have identified and examined the driving forces in your life. You have learned to understand your motivation as one aspect of expanding self-awareness. You have learned and applied processes that nurture self-knowledge. You have identified the barriers that interfere with academic performance. You have learned models, problem solving skills, and strategies to overcome these barriers. You have learned specific strategies for behavior change.

You have increased your knowledge of the multicultural nature of our society. You have identified the key elements of positive relationships. You have set goals for education, family, career, and personal. You have initiated the process of self-empowerment. You will no longer wait to be empowered because you now have the knowledge and confidence to empower yourself.

Bibliography

Anthony, Dr. Robert. *Total Self-Confidence.*
New York: Berkeley Books, 1984.

Barrett, Susan. *It's All in Your Head.*
Minneapolis, MN: Free Spirit Publishing Co., 1985.

Benson, Herbert, M.D. *The Relaxation Response.*
New York: Avon Books, 1971.

Blanchard, Ken. *The 3 Keys to Empowerment.*
San Francisco, CA: Berrett-Koehler Publishers, Inc., 1999.

Bliss, Edwin C. *Doing It Now.*
New York: Bantam Books, 1984.

Block, Peter. *The Empowered Manager.*
San Francisco, CA: Jossey-Bass Publishers, 1987.

Branden, Nathaniel. *The Psychology of Self-Esteem.*
New York: Bantam Books, 1971.

Buscaglia, Leo. *Love.*
Thorofare, NJ: Charles B. Slack, Inc., 1972.

Campbell, David. *If you don't know where you're going you'll probably end up somewhere else.*
Allen, TX: Argus Communications, 1974.

Carkhuff, Rubert, Anthony, William. *The Skills of Helping.*
Amherst, MA: Human Resource Development Press, 1979.

Corsini, Raymond J. *Current Psychotherapies.*
Itasca, IL: F.E. Peacock Publisher, Inc. 1984.

Frankl, Viktor. *Man's Search for Meaning.*
New York: Washington Square Press, 1971.

Freud, Sigmund. *The Interpretation of Dreams.*
New York: Avon Books, 1965.

Greely, Andrew M. *Why Can't They Be Like Us?*
New York: Institute of Human Relations Press, 1969.

Herrigel, Eugen. *Zen in the Art of Archery.*
New York: Vintage Books, 1971.

Jourard, Sidney M. *The Transparent Self.*
New York: Litton Educational Publishing, Inc., 1964.

Kilpatrick, William, Ph.D. *Identity and Intimacy.*
New York: Dell Publishing Co., Inc., 1975.

Koberg, Don, Bagnall, Jim. *The All New Universal Traveler.*
Los Altos, CA: William Kaufmann, Inc., 1981.

Krishnamurti, J. *The Network of Thought.*
San Francisco, CA: Harper & Row, 1982.

Lakein, Alan. *How to Get Control of Your Time and Your Life.*
New York: New American Library, 1973.

Le Shan, Lawrence. *How to Meditate.*
New York: Bantam Books, 1975.

Luft, Joseph. *Of Human Interaction.*
Palo Alto, CA: National Press Books, 1969.

Lynd, Helen Merrell. *On Shame and the Search for Identity.*
New York: Harcourt, Brace & World, Inc., 1958.

Maslow, Abraham H. *Motivation and Personality.*
New York: Harper & Row, 1970.

May, Rollo, Editor. *Existence.*
New York: Simon and "Schuster, 1958.

Naisbitt, John. *Megatrends.*
New York: Warner Books, Inc., 1984.

Naisbitt, John. *Megatrends 2000.*
New York: William Morrow and Company, Inc., 1990.

NTL Institute for Applied Behavioral Science.
Human Relations Training News, 1961, 5(1), 6-7.

NTL Institute for Applied Behavioral Science.
The Reading Book. National Education Association, 1972.

Powell, John. *Fully Human Fully Alive.*
Niles, IL: Argus Communications, 1976.

Progoff, Ira. *At A Journal Workshop.*
New York: Dialogue House Library, 1975.

Queen, Stuart A, Haberstein, Robert W. *The Family in Various Cultures.*
New York: J.B. Lippincott Company, 1974.

Rogers, Carl R. *On Becoming a Person.*
Boston, MA: Houghton Mifflin Company, 1961.

Rubin, Theodore Isaac, M.D. *Compassion and Self-Hate.*
New York: Collier Macmillian Publishers, 1986.

Selye, Hans. *Stress Without Distress.*
New York: New American Library, 1974.

Sherman, James R. *Get Set Go.*
Golden Valley, MN: Pathway Books, 1983.

Smith, Huston. *The World's Religions.*
San Francisco, CA: Harper & Row, 1991.

Stipek, Deborah J. *Motivation to Learn.*
Englewood Cliffs, NJ: Prentice-Hall, 1988.

Task Force Report on Self Esteem. *Toward a State of Esteem.*
Sacramento, CA: California State Department of Education, 1990.

Townsend, Richard F. *The Ancient Americas.*
Chicago, IL: The Art Institute of Chicago, 1992.

U.S. Department of Labor, *Dictionary of Occupational Titles.*
Landham, MD: Bernan Press, 1991.

U.S. Department of Labor, *Occupational Outlook Handbook.*
Washington D.C.: U.S. Government Printing Office, 1999.

Vander Zanden, James W. *American Minority Relations.*
New York: Alfred A. Knopf, 1983.

Watts, Alan. *The Wisdom of Insecurity.*
New York: Vintage Books, 1951.

Williams, Robert, Long, James. *Toward a Self Managed Life Style.*
Palo, Alto, CA: Houghton Mifflin Company, 1979.

Notes

Notes

Notes

Notes

Notes

Notes

Notes

Notes

Notes

Notes

Notes